FINDING JESUS ON THE MAT

YOUR YOGA DAILY DEVOTIONAL

Ask and it will be given to you; seek and you will find;
knock and the door will be opened to you. (Matthew 7:7)

Bethany B. Connelly

ISBN: 1468127209
ISBN-13: 978-1468127201

THE INVOCATION

This book offers you the opportunity to combine your yoga practice with a love for Jesus. Whether your practice or faith tends to waver, use the words written here to quietly commune with Jesus and explore any grace, light or love that may appear through it. Breathing sweetly, hear Acts 1:8, *and you will receive power when the Holy Spirit comes on you*. Feeling these words come to life in you, prepare for your body to be blessed, your mind renewed and your soul nourished on the mat. Shalom. Selah. Amen.

Day 1
THE MEANING OF YOGA

The word yoga means to yoke or to form union. It is the union with the Holy One. The practice connects your breath, intention and action. Have you experienced uniting in movement and spirit on the yoga mat? Close your eyes and visualize being yoked to Jesus, experiencing God-breathed verses igniting you from the inside out. Explore how this feels in your mind and heart. How may you further experience a connectedness through your practice? Take a moment to commune with Jesus.

SCRIPTURE:

Come to me, all you who are weary and burdened, and I will give you rest. Take my yoke upon you and learn from me, for I am gentle and humble in heart, and you will find rest for your souls. For my yoke is easy and my burden is light. (Matthew 11:28-30)

PRAYER:

Jesus, I come to my mat to take your yoke upon me and learn from you. Heavenly Father, may your prefect love drive out any fears I have of engaging on this journey. I hear *Psalm 51:6: Surely you desire truth in the inner parts; you teach me wisdom in the inmost place.* Please help me discover your holy purpose and plan for my life. I remember *1 Corinthians 3:17: God's temple is sacred and you are that temple.* Here I am, oh Lord, your temple. Please equip me with the foresight needed to treat my body as your holy vessel. Draw me into experiencing an intimate and wondrous spirit of connectedness with you in body, mind and heart. In love and light, I say Amen.

෬

Day 2
THE ENORMITY OF YOGA – PART 1

Yoga is a practice that is vast in philosophies, postures and practices. Sometimes it seems as though it has endless offerings. That is how it is with God; His works

1

are vast, powerful and illuminating. Hear *Isaiah 40:13:Who can fathom the Spirit of the LORD, or instruct the LORD as his counselor?* What aspects of God are hard for you to grasp? Likewise, what aspects of your practice are hard to grasp? What are the big questions in your mind and heart right now? Take a moment to share them with Jesus.

SCRIPTURE:

Then Manoah inquired of the angel of the LORD, "What is your name, so that we may honor you when your word comes true?" He replied, "Why do you ask my name? It is beyond understanding." (Judges 13:17-18)

PRAYER:

Lord, how majestic is your name over all the earth; *the heavens declare the glory of God; the skies proclaim the work of his hands (Psalm 19:1).* In awe of the array of your splendor, Father, thank you for the ways you continue to teach me and expand my vision. I remember *Isaiah 40:28: Do you not know? Have you not heard? The LORD is the everlasting God, the Creator of the ends of the earth. He will not grow tired or weary, and his understanding no one can fathom.* Wondrous Lord, please help me to learn more of you through the practice of yoga. Amen.

☙

Day 3
THE ENORMITY OF YOGA – PART 2

Yoga was not designed or intended to be confined to the mat; it is a practice for life. The daily practice of yoga helps you experience life to the full! The postures are simply a vehicle to prepare your body for deeper states of mediation, restoration and rejuvenation, thus essentially drawing you closer to God. The practice is about feeling the Lord's presence within you, experiencing ultimate unity and letting that radiance flow out of you to others. Have you taken the benefits you have received on the mat and extended them to all the facets of your life? Close your eyes and invite Jesus to commune with you about the places and people you might attend to and bless now.

SCRIPTURE:

Go therefore and make disciples of all nations, baptizing them in the name of the Father and of the Son and of the Holy Spirit, teaching them to observe all that I have commanded you. And behold, I am with you always, to the end of the age. (Matthew 28:19-20 EVS)

PRAYER:

Lord, here I am to do your will and be a witness of light for you. Reveal to me the places you are calling me to and the people to whom you want me to extend your love. Father, I marvel at your words in *Genesis 1:28 (EVS): Then God said, "Let us make man in our own image, after our likeness."* What a glorious gift you gave us when you made us in your image! Thank you, Lord, for creating me in your likeness and choosing me to be your disciple. Help me to move and breathe boldly in spirit and truth both on and off the mat. Amen.

∽

Day 4
REVELATION

Moments of revelation come through practicing yoga, such as the moment you get into a challenging posture for the first time or you feel your breath synchronized with your movement. Yoga provides space where you may attune to God's kingdom within you in a newly profound and physical way. What moments of revelation have you had on the mat? What have been some of your biggest moments of revelation in life? In what ways might you invite the Lord to provide you with a fresh spirit of revelation? Share your responses with Jesus.

SCRIPTURE:

Now Mary stood outside the tomb crying. As she wept, she bent over to look into the tomb and saw two angels in white, seated where Jesus' body had been, one at the head and the other at the foot. They asked her, "Woman, why are you crying?" "They have taken my Lord away," she said, "and I don't know where they have put him." At this, she turned around and saw Jesus standing there, but she did not realize that it was Jesus. He asked her, "Woman,

why are you crying? Who is it you are looking for?" Thinking he was the gardener, she said,
"Sir, if you have carried him away, tell me where you have put him, and I will get him." Jesus
said to her, "Mary." She turned toward him and cried out in Aramaic, "Rabboni!" [which
means "Teacher"]. (John 20:11-16)

PRAYER:

Lord, thank you for calling me by name and illuminating me with your light. Let
each moment here on the mat further awaken me to your truth. Help me to recognize each revelation that comes through the practice. I remember John 20:27:
Then he said to Thomas, "Put your finger here; see my hands. Reach out your hand and put
it into my side. Stop doubting and believe." Holy One, you transform moments of
doubt and moments of tears into overwhelming light. May I stop doubting and
believe, for all is possible with you. Father, let that revelation move me and shape
me here on the mat. Amen.

∽

Day 5
THE THREE GUNAS

According to yoga philosophy, the three gunas, which can be likened to life
strands or forces, are thought to reside in all physical objects and matter.
The gunas include sattva, raja, and tamas. Sattva is thought of as purity, consciousness, spiritual essence and goodness. Raja is thought of as fiery light,
raw energy, passion or activity. Tamas is considered motionless, steadiness,
inertia or darkness. People and things have them in different amounts, and
these portions can fluctuate. Practitioners of yoga theory aim to cultivate
mindfulness around these elements. Think of how these affect your life: at
times you might feel light, clear-minded and connected in your heart with
the Lord; essentially, sattva. At other times you might feel heavy, burdened
or lethargic; essentially, tamas. Take note of your disposition now—how you
feel in your body, your mind and your heart. Commune with Jesus about the
three gunas—sattva, raja and tamas—and how they apply to your current
state of being.

SCRIPTURE:

It was I who taught Ephraim to walk, taking them by the arms; but they did not realize it was I who healed them. I led them with cords of human kindness, with ties of love. I lifted the yoke from their neck, and I bent down to feed them. (Hosea 11:3)

PRAYER:

Father, I come to you, seeking to be aligned in your truth. I acknowledge your holy presence and thank you for your healing touch. Please forgive me for my inattentiveness to your voice. Forgive me for the times I have displayed fiery energy when I should have been steady and still, and for the times I have rested when I should have been passionately engaged. Draw me into alignment with your purifying light, for I come to refocus on your indwelling love and grace. I thank you for lifting the oppressive yoke of sin from my neck and for clothing me in your heavenly fabric of compassion. I remember *Leviticus 26:13: I am the LORD your God, who brought you out of Egypt so that you would no longer be slaves to the Egyptians; I broke the bars of your yoke and enabled you to walk with heads held high.* Thank you for breaking the bars of sin, tying me back together with love, wrapping me with your cords of kindness and shepherding me on the path of freedom. My confidence is in your saving grace. Amen.

∽

Day 6
YOGA SUTRAS

There is a famous ancient yoga text called the *Yoga Sutras*. It is attributed to Patañjali, and traditional yoga philosophy stems from this text. It dates from around the second century BCE. According to the sutras, there is an eightfold path in yoga. These include:

1. *Yamas*—representing universal morality or outward observances
2. *Niyamas*—personal/inner observances
3. *Asana*—seat or physical position
4. *Pranayama*—control of prana (breath)

5. *Pratyahara*—control of the senses
6. *Dharana*—concentration and cultivating inner perceptual awareness
7. *Dhyana*—devotion, meditation on the divine
8. *Samadhi*—union with the divine

All these steps may help draw you into God's presence. When pondering these eight sutras, reflect on the activities and daily practices you do that connect you with the Lord. Also note certain practices you may want to cultivate. Commune your responses to Jesus.

SCRIPTURE:
Jesus answered, "I am the way and the truth and the life. No one comes to the Father except through me." (John 14:6)

PRAYER:
Jesus, illuminating the way, embodying the truth and radiating the fullness of life, your glorious nature is ineffable. Thinking of the man in *Mark 9:24*, I also say, *"I believe; help me overcome my unbelief."* Please increase my faith for I trust your holy way. Here to follow in Truth and Life, I say Amen.

૭૦

Day 7
FIRST LIMB OF THE EIGHT LIMB PATH: YAMAS

The yamas are outward observances that have to do with willpower and/or restraint. There are five yamas:

1. *Ahimsa*—non-violence
2. *Satya*—truthfulness
3. *Asteya*—non-stealing
4. *Brachmacharya*—moderation
5. *Aparigraha*—non-hoarding

Ponder these acts and consider how you may (or may not) act in alignment with them. In what ways do you act justly, express mercy and walk humbly with the Lord? Which of these areas may you need to recommit to doing? Commune with Jesus.

SCRIPTURE:

He has shown you, O man, what is good. And what does the LORD require of you? To act justly and to love mercy and to walk humbly with your God. (Micah 6:8)

PRAYER:

Father, you have shown me what is good. I sing *Psalm 8:1: O LORD, our Lord, how majestic is your name in all the earth!* Help me to observe the world as you see it, and where there is a need for justice and mercy, use me! Awaken my heart to those needs during my time here on the mat. As I bow down in this practice, let it express humility, reverence, and gratitude to your holiness, and as I lift my heart, may it express my willingness to pour out your love. Each motion an act of reverence to you, oh Lord. Amen.

∽

Day 8
FIRST LIMB: FIRST MORAL RESTRAINT – AHIMSA

Ahimsa means nonviolence. Essentially, ahimsa is about restraining from acting in a harmful way. Yogis around the world demonstrate this principle by engaging in practices such as using gentle, kind, considerate language. Non-harm can also be demonstrated by not killing bugs or any other creature, for that matter. When you find yourself confronted by violence or fear, what do you do? How can you be present enough in your daily life to end any cycle of violence you might encounter? Commune with Jesus about this principle.

SCRIPTURE:

If someone strikes you on one cheek, turn to him the other also. If someone takes your cloak, do not stop him from taking your tunic. (Luke 6:29)

PRAYER:

Lord, I come in peace and I come to bless. I remember *Proverbs 1:33: But whoever listens to me will live in safety and be at ease, without fear of harm.* Listening to your voice, I take heart in your protection. Let me be a peacemaker, an extender of your love to all—even the little creatures like spiders that from time to time cross my path. Forgive me for any harm I have caused others knowingly or unknowingly. Guide me in offering grace and turning my cheek when confronted with violence. Help me to give grace to those who have been harmful or acted negatively towards me, and help me apply to my own life what Paul cries out in *Acts 7:60: Do not hold this sin against them.* May your peace, grace and provision span this space as I open my heart, stretch my body and enliven my spirit here on the mat. Amen.

❧

Day 9
FIRST LIMB: SECOND MORAL RESTRAINT – SATYA

Satya means truthfulness and is about being open and honest. How do you share what you believe and feel even when you know it is not what another person or group will want to hear? How do you feel when you think one thing but say something else? How can you be more honest with yourself, with others and with God? Share your responses with Jesus.

SCRIPTURE:

I do not understand what I do. For what I want to do, I do not do, but what I hate I do, I do. And if I do what I do not want to do, I agree that the law is good. As it is, it is no longer I myself who do it, but it is sin living in me. (Romans 7:15-17)

PRAYER:

Lord, I come humbly to you today, for like Paul, *'I desire to do what is good, but I cannot carry it out' (Romans 7:18).* Forgive me, Lord, for all the ways I have failed to be truthful to you, to those around me and to myself. Holy One, teach me here on the mat to express your truth with openness and honesty. Let me move and speak at the impulse of your Spirit as I follow the teaching in *Matthew 5:37: Simply let your 'Yes' be 'Yes' and 'No', 'No'*. Yes, let me speak and act with that sort of clarity. Amen.

೧৩

Day 10
FIRST LIMB: THIRD MORAL RESTRAINT – ASTEYA

Asteya means non-stealing or non-hoarding. This does not just refer to physical things but also time, speech and energy. If you are a student, one way you can demonstrate this through your practice is to be on time for your classes as a sign of respect to the teacher and other students. Reflect on this principle: that showing up punctually and honoring ending times demonstrates *not* stealing other people's time. Think of this in terms of speech, as well. Do you balance your time talking and listening in conversations? What are some ways you balance giving and receiving? As it relates to non-stealing, what are some ways you can grow? Share your responses with Jesus.

SCRIPTURE:
Thou shalt not steal. (Exodus 20:15)

PRAYER:
Father, I come to listen to your words and discover how to live them daily in my actions. Lord, I remember *Ephesians 4:28: Anyone who has been stealing must steal no longer, but must work, doing something useful with their own hands, that they may have something to share with those in need*. Help me put my hands to work and be a conduit of care. Let your energy flow through me so that when I go forth from here, I will be the living embodiment of the words in *Matthew 5:42: Give to anyone who asks of you, and do not turn away from the one who wants to borrow from you.* Amen.

೧৩

Day 11
FIRST LIMB: FOURTH MORAL RESTRAINT – BRAHMACHARYA

Brahmacharya translates to 'walk with God'. It is thought of as continence, self-restraint, chastity, moderation and temperance. It means the practical daily application of *Leviticus 11:44: Be holy, because I am holy*. It is not necessarily seeking holiness; it is simply letting go of whatever is not holy, and in doing so, you trust holiness to find you. It is walking and acting with utmost reverence to the Lord and by doing so, you restrain yourself from anything ungodly. Reflect on *Luke 12:15: Then he said to them, "Watch out! Be on your guard against all kinds of greed; life does not consist in an abundance of possessions."* Do you let moderation and temperance play a role in your lifestyle choices? As it relates to chastity and holiness, whether married or single, reflect on how you channel your sexual energy. Commune with Jesus on how you 'walk with God' in holiness.

SCRIPTURE:
Enoch walked faithfully with God; then he was no more, because God took him away. (Genesis 5:24)

PRAYER:
Lord, you give me more than enough, more than I could ask or imagine. I come to walk, breathe, and move with you here on the mat with deepest reverence, sacredness and continence. Please forgive me for the ways I have been too excessive in my lifestyle choices and for the times when I have lacked self-restraint. Help me to make choices in life and with my body that align with your will. I remember *1 Corinthians 6:19-20: Do you not know that your bodies are temples of the Holy Spirit, who is in you, whom you have received from God? You are not your own; you were bought at a price. Therefore honor God with your body.* Holy One, my body is your temple, so please teach my how to treat it as such here on the mat. I know you will provide for me *'according to each day's need' (1 Kings 8:59)* so help me practice moderation and walk faithfully like Enoch in each facet and element of my life. I trust in your timing and ways.

Sweep me up in your love, quieted in your truth and awe me in your beauty here on the mat. Amen.

∽

Day 12
FIRST LIMB: FIFTH MORAL RESTRAINT – APARIGRAHA

It means non-hoarding or non-grasping. What to you cling to in life? Reflect on your relationships—be it with a spouse, significant other, your child(ren), parents, friends or coworkers. Can you identify any sense of attachment in them? Now reflect on your body; consider the relationships you have with foods and substances like sugar or coffee, and note any attachments. Do this with your financial choices and the decisions you make in your professional life. What could you let go of in order to be lighter, freer and more fully committed to the Lord? Share your responses with Jesus.

SCRIPTURE:

Jesus said to him, you still lack one thing. "Sell everything you have and give to the poor and you will have treasure in heaven. Then come, and follow me." (Luke 18:22)

PRAYER:

Sovereign Lord, I come to surrender my spirit into your holy hands. I trust that you will wrap me in your love. Help me to understand that I don't need to strive or struggle to experience your unconditional love. Please forgive me for the times I have lost sight of this truth, and help me remember *Matthew 17:33: Whoever tries to keep his life will lose it, and whoever loses his life will preserve it.* Hear this prayer:

Take my life, and let it be consecrated, Lord, to Thee.

Take my moments and my days; let them flow in ceaseless praise.

Take my hands, and let them move at the impulse of Thy love.

Take my feet, and let them be swift and beautiful for Thee.

Take my voice, and let me sing always, only, for my King.

Take my lips, and let them be filled with messages from Thee.
Take my silver and my gold; not a mite would I withhold.
Take my intellect, and use every power as Thou shalt choose.
Take my will, and make it Thine; it shall be no longer mine.
Take my heart, it is Thine own; it shall be Thy royal throne.
Take my love, my Lord, I pour at Thy feet its treasure store.
Take myself, and I will be ever, only, all for Thee.
--Frances R. Havergal, February 1874
Amen.

༄

Day 13
SECOND LIMB OF THE EIGHT LIMB PATH: NIYAMAS

The niyamas are inward observances or applications of truth. They include:

1. *Saucha*—purity or cleanliness
2. *Santosha*—contentment
3. *Tapas*—self-discipline
4. *Svadhyaya*—self-study
5. *Isvara Pranidhara*—devotion to higher power

Reflect on these inner observances. Note where your attention has been directed and what emotions you've been experiencing. Commune with Jesus about any ways you may need to be renewed—body, mind, heart, or spirit.

SCRIPTURE:
Therefore we do not lose heart. Though outwardly we are wasting away, yet inwardly we are being renewed day by day. (2 Corinthians 4:16)

PRAYER:
Lord, I am so thankful that you are inwardly renewing me every day, even when I do not see it. I want to become more fully aware of your presence and the ways you are

refreshing me from the inside out. I remember *2 Corinthians 4:17-18: For our light and momentary troubles are achieving for us an eternal glory that far outweighs them all. So we fix our eyes not on what is seen, but on what is unseen, since what is seen is temporary, but what is unseen is eternal.* Here I fix my eyes on what is unseen and focus my attention on the Spirit-filled life-giving energy that you continuously place inside me. Amen.

∽

Day 14
SECOND LIMB: FIRST INNER OBSERVANCE – SAUCHA

Suacha is cleanliness or purity. As you ponder this principle, note any areas of your life that could use a cleanup, whether these are physical areas (your workspace or home), mental areas (your thoughts) or emotional areas (your relationships). Also note any area where you might be too focused on cleanliness—being paranoid of germs, feeling the compulsive need to ask for forgiveness over and over for the same thing, or using only squeaky clean language so as not to offend anyone. Commune with Jesus about this principle in your life.

SCRIPTURE:
Woe to you, teachers of the law and Pharisees, you hypocrites! You clean the outside of the cup and dish, but inside they are full of greed and self-indulgence. Blind Pharisee! First clean the inside of the cup and dish, and then the outside also will be clean. Woe to you, teachers of the law and Pharisees, you hypocrites! You are like whitewashed tombs, which look beautiful on the outside but on the inside are full of the bones of the dead and everything unclean. In the same way, on the outside you appear to people as righteous but on the inside you are full of hypocrisy and wickedness. (Matthew 23:25-28)

PRAYER:
Lord, help me to see any areas where I may struggle with cleanliness—areas where I am too focused on external cleanliness when I am not being pure in the things that matter. Clean me inside out—body, mind and spirit. I am refreshed by *Acts 10:28: But God has shown me that I should not call any man impure or unclean.* Help

me to see the goodness you have placed in all things and acknowledge the areas I need to grow in purity so that I do not become like a whitewashed tomb. Amen.

ᏇᎧ

Day 15
SECOND LIMB: SECOND INNER OBSERVANCE – SANTOSHA

Santosha means contentment. What are you grateful for in this moment? How do you feel at peace? Reflect on Paul's words in *Philippians 4:11: I am not saying this because I am in need, for I have learned to be content whatever the circumstances.* Commune with Jesus about contentment.

SCRIPTURE:

Thou shall not covet your neighbor's house. You shall not covet your neighbor's wife, or his manservant or maidservant, his ox or donkey, or anything that belongs to your neighbor. (Exodus 20:17 KJV)

PRAYER:

Father, thank you for giving me all that I have—it is more than enough! Help me to meditate on *Mark 8:36: What good is it for someone to gain the whole world, yet forfeit their soul?* I come to seek your kingdom and to love you. Help me to put aside anything petty, anything that hinders my devotion. I hear *Hebrews 13:5: Keep your lives free from the love of money and be content with what you have, because God has said, "Never will I leave you; never will I forsake you."* Faithful Lord, let me abide in this truth. Amen.

ᏇᎧ

Day 16
SECOND LIMB: THIRD INNER OBSERVANCE – TAPAS PART 1

Tapas is self-discipline, commitment or elimination of anything that is not beneficial, good or true. How do you physically stay active and in shape so that you have the physical stamina for the Lord's service? Do you pay attention to your posture? How do you confront your inner urges? What inner urges are you currently addressing? Share your responses with Jesus.

SCRIPTURE:

Therefore, I do not run like someone running aimlessly; I do not fight like a boxer beating the air. No, I strike a blow to my body and make it my slave so that after I have preached to others, I myself will not be disqualified for the prize. (1 Corinthians 9:26-27)

For the grace of God has appeared that offers salvation to all people. It teaches us to say "No" to ungodliness and worldly passions, and to live self-controlled, upright and godly lives in this present age. (Titus 2:11-12)

PRAYER:

Father, I come to physically engage with you and *'put on the new self, created to be like God in true righteousness and holiness' (Ephesians 4:24).* Help me to live a godly life and focus my attention on you with every cell and sinew of my being. I hear *Acts 3:19: Repent, then, and turn to God, so that your sins may be wiped out, that times of refreshing may come from the Lord.* By your great grace that offers salvation, please forgive me for the ways I have been undisciplined, and for neglecting to express the fruits of your Spirit and the inner urges that have arisen that are not in alignment with your truth. I thank you that, as your Word says in *Psalm 103:12: as far as the east is from the west, that is how far you have removed our transgressions from us.* In gratitude I move and breathe for you, oh Lord. Amen.

❧

Day 17
SECOND LIMB: THIRD INNER OBSERVANCE – TAPAS PART 2

Tapas, the intentional, disciplined use of your energy, can be likened to burning what is not pure. Core engagement in yoga is associated with this principle, because by activating your core, you develop internal heat. The belly is associated with digestive fire—breaking down food for energy and eliminating anything unnecessary. Likewise, your mind processes thoughts and digests concepts. How do you test everything and hold the good—physically, mentally and spiritually? How do you burn what is not pure? Commune with Jesus about your disciplined use of energy.

SCRIPTURE:

Do not put out the Spirit's fire, test everything; don't treat prophesies with contempt. Test everything. Hold on to the good. (1 Thessalonians 5:19-20)

PRAYER:

Lord, I come to be intentionally grounded in your Word—physically engaged, mentally alert and spiritually ready to test everything and hold the good. I remember John's words in *Luke 3:16-17: I baptize you with water. But one more powerful than I will come, the thongs of whose sandals I am not worthy to untie. He will baptize you with the Holy Spirit and with fire. His winnowing fork is in his hand to clear his threshing floor and to gather the wheat into his barn, but he will burn up the chaff with unquenchable fire.* Lord, as I engage my core in this practice and develop internal heat, purify me with your holy fire. Burn away any bad habits, thoughts and actions in my life. Refine me through the fire and illuminate my being with your soul-nourishing truth. I thank you for placing this blazing light inside me—your sacred Spirit that cleanses me from the inside out. I position myself to marshal my energy to you. Amen.

ᡣ

Day 18
SECOND LIMB: FOURTH INWARD OBSERVANCE – SVADHYAYA

Svadhyaya means self-study or self-awareness. Are you aware of your actions as they are happening? Do you reflect on them through prayer, journaling and/or in meditation with God? Reflect on your intentions in your yoga practice and your intentions in life, with your family, work and self. Are they self-serving or God-serving intentions? Share your responses with Jesus.

SCRIPTURE:

We demolish arguments and every pretension that sets itself up against the knowledge of God, and we take captive every thought to make it obedient to Christ. (2 Corinthians 10:5)

PRAYER:

Father, I repent for all the times I have thought and acted in self-serving ways instead of God-serving ways. I fall short time and time again. In your mercy, please forgive me and enable me to take every thought and action captive and obedient to your truth. I remember *Psalm 4:4: Tremble and do not sin; when you are on your beds, search your hearts and be silent.* Here on the mat, I search my heart and am silent. Help me cultivate awareness of your indwelling light. Amen.

၆၅

Day 19
SECOND LIMB: FIFTH INWARD
OBSERVANCE – ISWARA PRANIDHANA

Iswara Pranidhana represents devotion and surrender. Reflect on all the things you own, from your car(s) to your kitchen gadgets, and ponder the space and freedom you would gain in your life if you were willing to let go all your material possessions. Now examine the big life memories, both positive and negative, you hold—from the mistakes you cannot seem to forget to the accomplishments that may have fostered pride within you. How do you really let go of the past and stay present in your life right now, at this time and in this place, wherever you may be? Silently commune with Jesus.

SCRIPTURE:

However, I consider my life worth nothing to me, if only I may finish the race and complete the task the Lord Jesus has given me--the task of testifying to the gospel of God's grace. (Acts 20:24)

PRAYER:

Lord, I come in devotion, reverence and awe of your holy presence and truth. I also come in humility and a spirit of repentance for all the moments I have dwelt on the past and have forgotten about your grace in my life. Please forgive me. Open my eyes and direct my gaze to the task at hand, for I am here to run the race you have marked for me. I am ready and willing to let go of anything that hinders my complete dedication to your mighty truth. I remember Paul's words from *Philippians 3:13-14: But one thing I do: Forgetting what is behind and straining toward what is ahead, I press on toward the goal to win the prize for which God has called me heavenward in Christ Jesus.* Here I am, ready and willing to serve and love you fully and faithfully; restore, rebuild and renew me in you, oh Lord. Amen.

෨

Day 20
THIRD LIMB OF THE EIGHT LIMB PATH: ASANAS

Asana is translated as 'seat'. It is a position that helps you meditate in a steady and easy manner. Asanas are designed to purify and strengthen you, and to teach you deep truths. Physically, take note of your body right now: is your back arched or straight? Are your shoulders slumped or upright? How often are you aware of your physical positioning? Take a moment to get comfortable, sit up straight and meditate on *Hebrews 6:19-20: We have this hope as an anchor for the soul, firm and secure. It enters the inner sanctuary behind the curtain, where our forerunner, Jesus, has entered on our behalf.*

SCRIPTURE:
Now when Jesus saw the crowds, he went up on a mountainside and sat down. His disciples came to him, and he began to teach them. (Matthew 5:1)

PRAYER:
Jesus, thank you for being my forerunner. With my soul anchored in holy hope, teach me through asanas on the mat. Let my body be grounded in truth, connected in love, revitalized in grace and open to discipline. I hear *Matthew 6:6 (MSG): Here's what I want you to do: Find a quiet, secluded place so you won't be tempted*

to role-play before God. Just be there as simply and honestly as you can manage. The focus will shift from you to God, and you will begin to sense his grace. I come to the mat to consciously place myself in asanas to be attentive to your presence. Help me stay postured in alignment on your narrow path of Life so that I may approach the *'throne of grace with confidence' (Hebrews 4:16).* Amen.

∾

Day 21
FOURTH LIMB OF THE EIGHT LIMB PATH: PRANAYAMA – PART 1

Pranayama is mindful breathing. Traditional yoga breathing is called ujjayi, and is also referred to as the victorious breath. To do it seal your lips, slightly restricting the back of your throat, and then deeply, slowly and audibly inhale and exhale through your nose. The Greek word for Spirit, pneuma, is also translated as breath. Do you feel connected to God's Spirit through your breath? When was the last time you stopped and just listened to your breath? Take a few minutes to breathe slowly and listen.

SCRIPTURE:
The LORD God formed the man from the dust of the ground and breathed into his nostrils the breath of life, and the man became a living being. (Genesis 2:7)

PRAYER:
Father, thank you for putting breath in me and enabling me to get in touch with your living Spirit through it. I remember *Job 27:3: All the while my breath [is] in me, and the spirit of God [is] in my nostrils.* Focus my awareness on the victorious breath of life flowing through me. With each inhale, let me breathe in your presence, and with each exhale, help me to push out anything that does not serve my body as your living temple. Let my breath be a constant reminder of your indwelling presence. Amen.

∾

Day 22
FOURTH LIMB: PRANAYAMA – PART 2

Breathing slowly and deeply has many physical benefits including soothing and toning the nervous system, warming the body, aerating the lungs, relieving chest pain and increasing confidence. Take a long, full breath right now. What physically did you just experience? Have you ever noticed that when your breath is steady and deep, your emotions tend to be steady and calm, and when your breath is short and shallow, you tend to feel anxious, fearful or distracted? Take a few moments to attend to your breathing.

SCRIPTURE:
The Spirit of God has made me, and the breath of the Almighty has given me life. (Job 33:4)

PRAYER:
Spirit of the living Lord, I thank you for creating me and giving me life. I remember *John 6:63: The Spirit gives life; the flesh counts for nothing. The words I have spoken to you—they are full of the Spirit and life.* Thank you for speaking words of Spirit and Life to me, Jesus. I come to connect with you through my breath and rejoice in *Psalm 150:6: Let everything that has breath praise the lord. Praise the Lord.* Amen.

ᆼᴗᴗ

Day 23
FOURTH LIMB: PRANAYAMA – PART 3

Deep, conscious breathing has a centering and calming effect and often helps to heighten your level of concentration. Open your Bible and read a few verses slowly while focusing on your breath coming in and out of your nostrils. What message did you read? How can you apply that message in your life? Read the verse(s) again and focus on the words that particularly strike you; repeat them for a few minutes as you continue to breathe deeply.

SCRIPTURE:

All Scripture is God-breathed and is useful for teaching, rebuking, correcting and training in righteousness. (2 Timothy 3:16)

PRAYER:

Lord, I come to the mat to be trained by your words, steadied in spirit and corrected in truth. As I breathe into these postures with my body, let me breathe your sacred words with the same sort of intentionality, purpose and discipline. Help me not to skip passages or poses that seem challenging or routine, but to find gratitude for each opportunity to grow. I listen to *Proverbs 13:3: He who guards his lips guards his life.* Yes, before I speak or act, please help me to seek your will by connecting to you through my breath. Amen.

ᏈᎧ

Day 24
FIFTH LIMB OF THE EIGHT LIMB PATH: PRATYAHARA – PART 1

Pratyahara is turning inward, withdrawing, or moving beyond the senses. In what ways have you withdrawn from worldly senses? Have you learned how to let go of worries? Reflect on *Matthew 6:25-30: Therefore I tell you, do not worry about your life, what you will eat or drink; or about your body, what you will wear. Is not life more than food, and the body more than clothes? Look at the birds of the air; they do not sow or reap or store away in barns, and yet your heavenly Father feeds them. Are you not much more valuable than they? Can any one of you by worrying add a single hour to your life? And why do you worry about clothes? See how the flowers of the field grow. They do not labor or spin. Yet I tell you that not even Solomon in all his splendor was dressed like one of these. If that is how God clothes the grass of the field, which is here today and tomorrow is thrown into the fire, will he not much more clothe you—you of little faith?*

SCRIPTURE:

So do not worry, saying, 'What shall we eat?' or 'What shall we drink?' or 'What shall we wear?' For the pagans run after all these things, and your heavenly Father knows that you need them. But seek first his kingdom and his righteousness, and all these things will be given to you as well. (Matthew 6:31-33)

PRAYER:
Father, I let go of all distracting thoughts from to-do-lists to my latest conversations. I am here to focus entirely on you, seeking first your kingdom. By placing my trust in you, I know you will take care of all my needs both great and small. Compassionate Lord, who nourishes me on your words, I recite *Isaiah 61:10: I delight greatly in the LORD; my soul rejoices in my God. For he has clothed me with garments of salvation and arrayed me in a robe of righteousness.* Thank you, living Father, my Lord, my Light! Amen.

༄

Day 25
FIFTH LIMB: PRATYAHARA – PART 2

Shut your eyes and think of all the places where you see God's beauty reside. Ponder what the Lord's beauty looks like in another person—in a facial expression, an act of kindness, or a word of encouragement. Where else can you sense His beauty? In what sounds can you hear Him? In what fragrance can you smell His beauty? In what tastes and touches does it reside? Finally, how may you experience it in your own heart?

SCRIPTURE:
The Lord does not look at the things man looks at. Man looks at the outward appearance, but the Lord looks at the heart. (1 Samuel 16:7)

PRAYER:
Lord, you look into my heart and see all; thank you for your indwelling Spirit and its beauty. I understand, Father, that you look far beyond my physical positioning. What is on the inside of me really matters to you. Please, God of grace, purify my heart during this practice. I commune *Psalm 139:23-24: Search me, God, and know my heart; test me and know my*

anxious thoughts. See if there is any offensive way in me, and lead me in the way everlasting. Amen.

ᢕᢳ

Day 26
FIFTH LIMB: PRATYAHARA – FOCUS ON SIGHT

As you focus on moving towards a higher perspective in your sense of sight, reflect on ways you can move beyond physical, external sights to interior realms of light. What things act as visual distractions in your daily life? Reflect on ways you can stop looking at what is around you and see what is important within. Commune with the Lord about true seeing.

SCRIPTURE:
So Moses thought, "I will go over and see this strange sight—why the bush does not burn up." (Exodus 3:3)

PRAYER:
Lord, I come to focus my eyes on you. I close my eyes at times throughout this practice to be completely present with your indwelling Spirit. I remember Paul in *Acts 9:4: He fell to the ground and heard a voice say to him, "Saul, Saul, why do you persecute me?"* Jesus, you revealed yourself to Paul. For three days he was blind, then scales dropped from his eyes, his sight was restored and he walked boldly in faith. Remove the scales from my eyes and help me to see as you see. Amen.

ᢕᢳ

Day 27
FIFTH LIMB: PRATYAHARA – FOCUS ON SOUND

There is a type of yoga that focuses exclusively on sound. It is called nada yoga, and it taps into the natural energies that harmonize sounds like breath. Note any ways you may have experienced sound synchronization. Also note how you move beyond the realm of sound—both the internal noise of your mind and the external noise in the world around you. When you enter this quietness, you can truly listen to the Lord. Commune with Jesus about the sound.

SCRIPTURE:

He who has an ear, let him hear. (Revelation 13:9)

PRAYER:

Lord, here to listen to you, I take heart in *Numbers 20:16: when we cried out to the LORD, he heard our cry and sent an angel.* Thank you for your divine intercession, peace and protection. Please forgive me for the ways I get distracted by noises. I hear *1 Kings 19:11-13: The LORD said, "Go out and stand on the mountain in the presence of the LORD, for the LORD is about to pass by." Then a great and powerful wind tore the mountains apart and shattered the rocks before the LORD, but the LORD was not in the wind. After the wind there was an earthquake, but the LORD was not in the earthquake. After the earthquake came a fire, but the LORD was not in the fire. And after the fire came a gentle whisper. When Elijah heard it, he pulled his cloak over his face and went out and stood at the mouth of the cave. Then a voice said to him, "What are you doing here, Elijah?"* Please keep my ears alert to your gentle whisper. Throughout this practice I ask, 'what am I doing here on the mat and in life'? With a focus to listen intently and lovingly, I say Amen.

༄

Day 28
FIFTH LIMB: PRATYAHARA – FOCUS ON SMELL

As you draw your attention to smell, identify what smells you find pleasing, and what smells you find repelling. Have you ever noticed that after spending a certain amount of time in a place that first had a distinctive smell, it gradually became less noticeable? Some people live in garbage dumps, others live in poorly maintained elderly care facilities, while still others work in rundown hospital wards. People also work at perfume counters, bakeries and car showroom floors. All of them reach to a point where they don't smell their environments as acutely as someone who's walking into them for the first time. Outside of environmental smells, what are some ways you can take note of the spiritual aromas of others? Commune with Jesus about your sense of smell.

SCRIPTURE:

Pleasing is the fragrance of your perfumes; your name is like perfume poured out. No wonder the young women love you! (Song of Solomon 1:3)

PRAYER:

Lord, let my yoga practice be a fragrant offering to you. I hear *Song of Solomon 2:13: The fig tree forms its early fruit; the blossoming vines spread their fragrance. Arise, come, my darling; my beautiful one, come with me.* I come to spread your aroma of justice, mercy, and love. Where stench is present, let me replace it with the smell of holy hope. Your aroma is so truly pleasing, it draws me in and stimulates and excites me. I imbibe the words of *Song of Solomon 4:10: How delightful is your love, my sister, my bride! How much more pleasing is your love than wine, and the fragrance of your perfume more than any spice!* Let me extend aromatic love to you, oh Lord. Amen.

∽

Day 29
FIFTH LIMB: PRATYAHARA – FOCUS ON TOUCH

Ponder your sense of touch, noting any blessings that physical touch has sparked in your life and any distractions it has caused. Throughout the gospels, Jesus heals with touch. How have you felt touched by the Lord? How can you touch others in a way that blesses them? Commune with Him about touch.

SCRIPTURE:

She said to herself, "If I only touch his cloak, I will be healed." Jesus, turned and saw her. "Take heart, daughter," he said, "your faith has healed you." And the woman was healed from that moment. (Matthew 9:21-22)

PRAYER:

Thank you, Jesus, for your powerful, healing and glorious touch. I imagine my feet in your basin of living water, my fingers gracing the edge of your garment and my hair caressing your feet. Holy Lord, I reach out my hands to dance with you, and I feel my heart beat against your righteous chest. Let me be swooped up into your Spirit. Touch me in the inmost spheres of my essence throughout this practice. I hear *Acts 19:12: so that even handkerchiefs and aprons that had touched him [Paul] were taken to the sick, and their illnesses were cured and the evil spirits left them.* Holy Spirit, fill me completely as I stretch here on the mat so that everything that touches me may also experience your blessing. Amen.

〜

Day 30
FIFTH LIMB: PRATYAHARA – FOCUS ON SPEECH

Pratyhara embodies words and the vibrational energy they carry. Pondering speech, note any recent distractions in your life that were spurred by the words of others; then think of words that have seemed to carry power, blessing and/or hope. Identify the various ways you speak—your words, your tone, your body language, and so on. What are some ways you can practice brevity and gentleness in your language? How can you experience peace, love and truth beyond what can be translated into words? Commune with Jesus about speech.

SCRIPTURE:

Above all, my brothers, do not swear—not by heaven or by earth or by anything else. Let your "Yes" be yes, and your "No," no, or you will be condemned. (James 5:12)
I said, "I will watch my ways and keep my tongue from sin; I will put a muzzle on my mouth as long as the wicked are in my presence." (Psalm 39:1)

PRAYER:

Lord, thank you for the gift of speech and for all the wondrous ways you communicate with me. I remember *Psalm 139:4: Before a word is on my tongue you know it completely, O LORD.* Speak to me during this time on my mat, and when I pick up my mat and follow you in my daily life, may I experience *Jeremiah 1:9: Then the LORD reached out his hand and touched my mouth and said to me, "Now, I have put my words in your mouth."* I commune *Psalm 19:14: May the words of my mouth and the meditation of my heart be pleasing in your sight, O LORD, my Rock and my Redeemer.* Amen.

༄

Day 31
FIFTH LIMB: PRATYAHARA – FOCUS ON TASTE

Reflect on sense of taste. What tastes tempt you, and how you can withdraw from unwholesome taste cravings *'now that you have tasted that the Lord is good'* (1 Peter 2:3)? Meditate on the following verses:

> *Sweet are your words to my taste, sweeter than honey to my mouth! (Psalm 119:103)*
> *Taste and see that the LORD is good; blessed is the man who takes refuge in him. (Psalm 34:8)*
> *And he said to them, "I tell you the truth, some who are standing here will not taste death before they see the kingdom of God come with power." (Mark 9:1)*

SCRIPTURE:
Then Jesus declared, "I am the bread of life. Whoever comes to me will never go hungry and he who believes in me will never be thirsty. (John 6:35)

PRAYER:
Lord, I thank you for each experience of taste, but especially for the taste of your goodness and salvation. Jesus, enhancer of nourishing experiences, turning water to wine, transforming a few fish to many, offering bread that lasts and living water; help me to follow your example. I come to the mat to move beyond physical cravings and to focus instead on spiritual tastes. I remember *Matthew 5:6: Blessed are they which do hunger and thirst after righteousness: for they shall be filled* and focus my belly on rumbling for your righteousness. Please give me my daily bread here on the mat so that I may share your manna of Life with others. Amen.

༄

Day 32
SIXTH LIMB OF THE EIGHT LIMB PATH: DHARANA – PART 1

Dharana is concentration or focus. How do you concentrate on God and what causes you to loose focus? Like Paul, do you feel that there is a war being waged in your mind? What fleshly desires are you struggling with at this time in your life? What thoughts come up for you both on and off the mat that make you feel as though you are living under the law of sin? Share your responses with Jesus.

SCRIPTURE:

So I find this law at work: Although I want to do good, evil is right there with me. For in my inner being I delight in God's law; but I see another law at work in me, waging war against the law of my mind and making me a prisoner of the law of sin at work within me. What a wretched man I am! Who will rescue me from this body that is subject to death? Thanks be to God, who delivers me through Jesus Christ our Lord! So then, I myself in my mind am a slave to God's law, but in my sinful nature a slave to the law of sin. (Romans 7:21-25)

PRAYER:

Lord, thank you for saving me from the law of sin waging a war in my mind. Help me to take every thought captive and make it obedient to your living words. I am here to concentrate my mind, spirit and body completely on you. I remember *Romans 8:5-6: Those who live according to the flesh have their minds set on what the flesh desires; but those who live in accordance with the Spirit have their minds set on what the Spirit desires. The mind governed by the flesh is death, but the mind governed by the Spirit is life and peace.* Setting my mind on what your Spirit desires, I say Amen.

෴

Day 33
SIXTH LIMB: DHARANA – PART 2

Reflecting on your sense of focus, how do you set your mind on things above? How do you tune out earthly distractions, feelings of inadequacy and/or fears of not being accepted that may be manifested through certain lifestyle choices? What relationships, or the desire to be in a particular type of relationship, distract you? What earthly temptations are present for you at this time? Commune with Jesus about anything that may be shifting your focus away from what is good, pure, lovely and admirable.

SCRIPTURE:

Since, then, you have been raised with Christ, set your hearts on things above, where Christ is seated at the right hand of God. Set your minds on things above, not on earthly things. For you died, and your life is now hidden with Christ in God. When Christ, who is your life, appears, then you also will appear with him in glory. (Colossians 3:1-4)

PRAYER:

Lord, I come to focus on your presence and hear *James 3:17: But the wisdom that comes from heaven is first of all pure; then peace-loving, considerate, submissive, full of mercy and good fruit, impartial and sincere.* Sovereign Father, help me to concentrate entirely on things above and not things here on earth. Please forgive me for the times I have lost focus. Lord, you are my life. Thank you for being in me and the wondrous blessing that I am in you. I cannot grasp this union, but I believe your divine nature is more expansive and embracing than my mind can comprehend. Nourish me on the fruits of your Spirit as I place my complete focus on you. Amen.

൭

Day 34
SIXTH LIMB: DHARANA – PART 3

Continuing to focus on concentration, do you eagerly examine the Scriptures to see if what you hear is true? Do you first turn to the Bible for validation, and to discern what is true and what is not true? Take a Bible in one hand and a magazine, newspaper, email or text message in the other; then, close your eyes and ask Jesus to help you make sense of the messages shared in the texts.

SCRIPTURE:

Now the Berean Jews were of more noble character than those in Thessalonica, for they received the message with great eagerness and examined the Scriptures every day to see if what Paul said was true. (Act 17:11)

PRAYER:

Lord, I come to practice with your holy book open and actively engage with you—examining, learning, discovering and verifying. Inscribe your words on my heart as I move on the mat. I remember *Romans 12:12: Do not conform to the pattern of this world, but be transformed by the renewing of your mind. Then you will be able to test and approve what God's will is—his good, pleasing and perfect will.* Focused on renewing my mind in truth so that I may be able to test and approve your holy, pleasing and perfect will, I say Amen.

෬෨

Day 35
SEVENTH LIMB OF THE EIGHT LIMB PATH: DHYANA – PART 1

Dhyana means mediation. Prayer is a time to talk to God, while mediation is a time to listen to God. Do you spend as much time quietly listening for the Lord's voice as you do praying? Take a moment to heighten your attention to hear His voice.

SCRIPTURE:

I meditate on your precepts and consider your ways. Oh, how I love your law! I meditate on it all day long. (Psalm 119:15, 97)

PRAYER:

Jesus, help me to position myself as your student, disciple and intimate friend forever and always. I recognize I am often anxious and break silence with you by talking or by letting 'loud' thoughts pop into my head. Compassionate One, please forgive me. I hear the teaching *'do not be anxious in anything'* *(Philippians 4:6)*, yet sometimes I cannot seem to carry it out! I remember 'the more words, the less meaning' (Ecclesiastes 6:11). Still me in your presence. I commune *Psalm 119:48: I reach out for your commands, which I love, that I may meditate on your decrees*. Amen.

∽

Day 36
SEVENTH LIMB: DHYANA – PART 2

Reflect on what you pray for and what you ask the Lord to do for you. What were your intentions behind the last things you asked, and how do you truly believe the Lord will answer? Ponder *Jeremiah 29:13: You will seek me and find me when you seek me with all your heart*. What are some ways you can seek the Lord with your whole heart? Finally, on what door are you knocking? Commune with Jesus.

SCRIPTURE:
Ask, and it will be given to you; seek, and you will find; knock, and it will be opened to you. (Matthew 7:7)

PRAYER:
Father, I come to make each movement a wholehearted expression of seeking your divine presence. Jesus, let my heartbeat be a knocking of love in you, and Spirit, let my breath be an intimate prayer in your essence. Help me to find, discover and grow in your radiant light. I muse *Matthew 21:22: If you believe, you will receive whatever you ask for in prayer*. Believing, I say, Amen.

∽

Day 37
EIGHTH LIMB OF THE EIGHT LIMB PATH: SAMADHI

Samadhi means union with the object of mediation. Pondering this sort of union, reflect on how you feel 'in' Christ? Read *John 14:20: On that day you will realize* that I am in my Father, you are in me and I am in you. Do you feel this sort of deep, intimate connectedness? Commune with Jesus.

SCRIPTURE:
Therefore, if anyone is in Christ, he is a new creation; the old has gone; the new has come! (2 Corinthians 5:17)

PRAYER:
Father, thank you for transforming me into a new creation in Christ. I remember *Galatians 2:19-20: For through the Law I died to the Law, that I might live unto God. I have been crucified with Christ, and it is no longer I who live, but Christ lives in me; and the life which I now live in the flesh I live by faith in the Son of God, who loved me and delivered Himself up for me* and *Galatians 6:15: Neither circumcision nor uncircumcision means anything; what counts is the new creation.* How glorious it is to be dead to sin and alive through Spirit in you. With deepest gratitude, I say Amen.

෧෨

Day 38
EIGHTH LIMB: SAMADHI – PART 2

Pondering this beautiful concept of union, explore your heart and the kingdom of God within you. Can you see it? What are some ways you can live from that point of awareness? Do you treat yourself as the Lord's holy dwelling place? Close your eyes and seek to feel a sense union of your heart with His.

SCRIPTURE:
Nor will people say, 'Here it is,' or 'There it is,' because the kingdom of God is within you. (Luke 17:21)

PRAYER:
Jesus, I cannot even comprehend the kingdom goodness of the Living Father inside me, yet I believe it. Please open my eyes to see what it means when your word says that your kingdom is within me. I recite the sacred words "the Kingdom of God is within you" and draw inward to understand and seek you

with all my heart. I hear *1 Corinthians 3:16: Don't you know that you are God's temple and that God's Spirit lives in you?* Jesus, help me to grasp this truth on the mat and express it in my life. Amen.

∽

Day 39
CHAKRAS

There are seven main energy centers within the body called chakras. The word chakra can be translated to disk or wheel. Understanding the chakras is a key element of yoga theory. The first chakra is thought to reside in your pelvic floor, and each successive one is positioned a little higher in the body with the top one radiating through the crown of your head. These chakras act as hubs where three primary channels—ida, pingala, and sushumna—intersect. The ida and pingala ascend and descend in a spiral pattern while the sushumna travels straight up. The ida is perceived as the feminine channel and is associated with the moon, coolness and the left nostril. The pingala is perceived as the masculine channel and is associated with the sun, heat and the right nostril. Additionally, there are more subtle channels called nadis, and the human body is thought to have 72,000 in total. To explore the chakras and learn how to sense your internal energy, close your eyes and draw awareness to your tailbone and as you inhale, move the breath up your spine all the way up the middle of your forehead, the spot between your eyes. Then exhale as you extend the breath out and up from there around your head and back down your spine. Visualize the breath as light as you do this breathing exercise a few times, and then quietly commune with Jesus.

SCRIPTURE:
I pray that out of his glorious riches he may strengthen you with power through his Spirit in your inner being, so that Christ may dwell in your hearts through faith. (Ephesians 3:16-17)

PRAYER:
Lord, I marvel at your streams of living water and Spirit bathing me in life-giving energy. Your thoughts are higher than my thoughts, and I am amazed when I

consider how carefully and wonderfully you made me. I come to my mat to be grounded in your truth and to feel you at work in my inner being. I draw your Spirit in as I breathe in and lift your holy Name on high as I breathe out. Let the breath concentrate me. I hear *Ezekiel 40:4: Look with your eyes and hear with your ears and pay attention to everything I am going to show you, for that is why you have been brought here*. Help me to be aware of why I am here and what you desire for my life. Ready to learn, I say Amen.

※

Day 40
FIRST CHAKRA: MULADHARA

The first chakra is located at the base of the spine. It is associated with earth, the waking state, the color red and the sense of smell. Yoga postures that focus on this chakra include standing and seated cross-legged poses. It is related to the desire to satisfy basic needs and to feel grounded, secure, healthy and prosperous. Reflect on your life right now. Do you feel safe and secure? Do you feel grounded in your faith? Do you feel healthy, prosperous, and connected with the world around you? Commune with Jesus about this chakra.

SCRIPTURE:
Therefore everyone who hears these words of mine and puts them into practice is like a wise man who built his house on the rock. The rain came down, the streams rose, and the winds blew and beat against that house; yet it did not fall, because it had its foundation on the rock. (Matthew 7:24-25)

PRAYER:
Sovereign Lord, my Rock and my Redeemer, I come to be completely rooted in your truth so that I may rise up and live according to your will for my life. I remember *1 Corinthians 3:11: For no one can lay any foundation other than the one already laid, which is Jesus Christ*. Father, with deepest gratitude for a foundation in Christ, I come to abide in this divine truth. I begin this class by drawing attention to the tip of my tailbone and securing myself in your provision, grace and love. Amen.

※

Day 41
SECOND CHAKRA: SWADHISTHANA

The second chakra is located in your lower abdomen by your reproductive organs. Its essence is dreams, emotions and water. It is considered the doorway to relationships and is associated with the color orange and the sense of taste. Postures that resonate with this chakra include forward folds, splits and the hero's pose. As you do these poses to connect with this chakra, reflect on whether you feel fluidity and harmony in your life right now. Are you able to respond to changes with grace? How do you feel about your current state of intimacy in your relationships with others as well as with the Lord? Commune with Jesus about this chakra.

SCRIPTURE:
All beautiful are you, my darling, there is no flaw in you. (Song of Solomon 4:7)

PRAYER:
Lord, thank you for your intimacy and for placing your wondrous beauty in me. I recite *Song of Solomon 8:7: Many rivers cannot quench love, rivers cannot wash it away.* Thank you for this abiding love—sweet, strong, sensual and steadfast. As I obey your covenants and keep your commands, I remember your promise in *Deuteronomy 28:11: The LORD will grant you abundant prosperity--in the fruit of your womb.* I aim to remain in you that I may bear fruit that will last. Feeling your divine presence bloom within me, I say Amen.

෮෯

Day 42
THIRD CHAKRA: MANIPURA

The third chakra is located in the solar plexus. It is known as the power center, the place of will, ego and autonomy. It is associated with digestive fire, the color yellow, the sense of sight and twisting postures. Being balanced in this chakra has to do with your relationship with power and effectiveness. As you do twisting poses to connect with this chakra, reflect on how you feel the Lord's power working through you. Do you feel effective in your life, job and interests? How do you display a healthy level of self-confidence and at the same time humility? Commune with Jesus about this chakra.

SCRIPTURE:
The Spirit of the LORD will come powerfully upon you, and you will prophesy with them; and you will be changed into a different person. (1 Samuel 10:6)

PRAYER:
O Lord, your kingdom come, your will be done. I surrender myself completely to your holy power. Please cleanse me of my inequity; nourish me on your word and fill me with the life-giving energy of your Spirit. I remember *Matthew 4:4: It is written: 'Man shall not live on bread alone, but on every word that comes from the mouth of God,'* and *Ezekiel 3:1: Eat this scroll.* Let my being be filled with your words of Life as I move through this practice. Amen.

∽

Day 43
FOURTH CHAKRA: ANAHATA

The fourth chakra is located at the heart, and the hands are an outreach of this chakra. It is the center of compassion and love. It is associated with air, the sense of touch, the color green and backbends and arm balancing poses. Its essence is selflessness, and it is the sphere for uniting opposites such as male/female, mind/body, and so on. As you do these poses to connect with this chakra, assess your sense of inner peace. In what ways have you been acting compassionate and working for the welfare of others? Does your heart cry on behalf of others? Is it pliable to be shaped by the Lord? Commune with Jesus about this chakra.

SCRIPTURE:
The LORD is gracious and righteous; our God is full of compassion. (Psalm 116:5)
Be kind and compassionate to one another, forgiving each other, just as in Christ God forgave you. (Ephesians 4:32)

PRAYER:

Compassionate Lord, thank you for your grace and righteousness. I take heart in *John 11:33: When Jesus saw her weeping, and the Jews who had come along with her also weeping, he was deeply moved in spirit and troubled*. Jesus, help me to care for people with the same sort of tender heart. Forgive me for the times I failed to respond in such a fashion. I recognize *John 13:35: By this everyone will know that you are my disciples, if you have love for one another*. Guide me in your holy love here on the mat, for I desire to live out the words of *1 Peter 3:8: All of you, be like-minded, be sympathetic, love one another, be compassionate and humble*. Amen.

∽

Day 44
FIFTH CHAKRA: VISHUDDHA

The fifth chakra is located at the throat and encompasses the neck, ear and mouth area. Its essence is ether, the color blue and the sense of hearing. Related postures include the shoulder stand and the plow. It is symbolic of how we experience life through vibrations and sounds. It is related to creativity and communication. As you do poses associated with this chakra, think about how you express yourself through your speech. Take note of how comfortable you are praying aloud, communicating in groups and in one-on-one conversations. What spoken words make you feel loved? What words seem to hurt you? Do you listen to others and really hear what their heart is trying to say? Commune with Jesus about this chakra.

SCRIPTURE:

Then you will know the truth, and the truth will set you free. (John 8:32)

PRAYER:

Lord, I quiet myself on the mat to hear to your voice. Enable me to discern what is true because it comes from your heavenly realm, and what is false. Please teach me to communicate in a way that is pleasing to you. I commune *Psalm 25:5: Guide me in your truth and teach me, for you are God my Savior, and my hope is in you all day long,* and *Proverbs 23:16: My inmost being will rejoice when your lips speak what is right.* Let your light direct my step, and be expressed creatively and caringly here on the mat and in my life. Amen.

∽

Day 45
SIXTH CHAKRA: AJNA

The sixth chakra is located in the middle of the brow and is also referred to as your third eye or the seat of enlightenment; it relates to seeing intuitively. Its essence is beyond pulsation, and it is the transcendence of dual realities. Its color is indigo, and an associated posture is the child's pose. As you do the child's pose to connect with this chakra, think of how the Lord has granted you vision in terms of what to do and who to be in life. Consider how you can think more expansively to experience vision beyond that which meets the eye. Read these verses and then take a moment to commune with Jesus.

> *Do not harm the land or the sea or the trees until we put a seal on the foreheads of the servants of our God.* (Revelation 7:3)
> *Then the LORD called to the man clothed in linen who had the writing kit at his side and said to him, "Go throughout the city of Jerusalem and put a mark on the foreheads of those who grieve and lament over all the detestable things that are done in it."* (Ezekiel 9:3-4)
> *I will make your forehead like the hardest stone, harder than flint. Do not be afraid of them or terrified by them, though they are a rebellious people.* (Ezekiel 3:9)

SCRIPTURE:
While I, Daniel, was watching the vision and trying to understand it, there before me stood one who looked like a man. (Daniel 8:15)

PRAYER:
Everlasting Father, who gives great visions to your prophets, I come to seek your perspective and view. I remember *Proverbs 29:18 (KJV): Where there is no vision, the*

people perish: but he that keepeth the law, happy is he. Reveal your vision for me here so that I may live it fully and faithfully. Amen.

༼༽

Day 46
SEVENTH CHAKRA: SAHASRARA

The seventh chakra is located at the top of your head—the crown area. It is related to consciousness, pure awareness, spiritual connection, wisdom and understanding. It is considered a place where only unconditional love exists and is associated with the color violet. It is explored in mediation or in the headstand posture. Read *1 Thessalonians 2:19-20: For what is our hope, our joy, or the crown in which we will glory in the presence of our Lord Jesus when he comes? Is it not you? Indeed, you are our glory and joy.* Reflect on how you feel spiritually connected. How conscious and aware are you of the Lord in your daily activities? How conscious and aware are you of your connectedness to others? Commune with Jesus about this chakra.

SCRIPTURE:
The soldiers twisted thorns into a crown, and put it on his head, and dressed him in a purple garment. (John 19:2)

PRAYER:
Lord, be a crown of light for all my thoughts and actions. I hear *James 1:12: Blessed is the one who perseveres under trial because, having stood the test, that person will receive the crown of life that the Lord has promised to those who love him.* Holy One, I love you. Please strengthen my inner being so that I may live in you and persevere through any difficulties I may encounter in life. I acknowledge the prophetic words of *Isaiah 28:5 (MSG): At that time, God-of-the-Angel-Armies will be the beautiful crown on the head of what's left of his people: Energy and insights of justice to those who guide and decide, strength and prowess to those who guard and protect.* Focused on guiding what is good, deciding what is true, guarding what is pure and protecting what is holy, I say. Amen.

༼༽

Day 47
YOGA MALA

A yoga mala is a string of 108 counting beads in a circle used for reciting mantras. The number 108 has many sacred qualities identified in cultures and traditions around the world. Using a mala for mediation and prayer originates further back in history than the rosary. Reflecting on prayer beads, note any verses or prayers you like to repeat and their significance to you. Taking a moment to recite one, pause after every word or two and meditate on its meaning.

SCRIPTURE:
He said to them, "When you pray, say: 'Father, hallowed be your name, your kingdom come. Give us each day our daily bread. Forgive us our sins, for we also forgive everyone who sins against us. And lead us not into temptation.'" (Luke 11:2-4)

PRAYER:
Jesus, I come to my mat to pray the prayer you taught us in Matthew 6:9-13 This, then, is how you should pray: 'Our Father in heaven, hallowed be your name, your kingdom come, your will be done, on earth as it is in heaven. Give us today our daily bread. And forgive us our debts, as we also have forgiven our debtors. And lead us not into temptation, but deliver us from the evil one.' Amen.

༄

Day 48
THE RADIANCE SUTRAS

The Radiance Sutras are a compilation of 112 yoga teachings, known as tantras, set as a conversation between lovers. Reflect on the beauty of these two verses found in the beginning of the tantras: 'Beloved, my attention is ensnared by a myriad of forms, the innumerable individual entities everywhere. Lead me to wholeness that is beyond all these parts.' In what ways can you find a spirit of union in the various areas of your life—work, home, groups and activities?

Next, reflect on your relationships, is there someone you feel at one with in spirit? What are some ways you can show deep respect for all others? Share your responses with Jesus.

SCRIPTURE:
After David had finished talking with Saul, Jonathan became one in spirit with David, and he loved him as himself. (1Samuel 18:1)

PRAYER:
Lord, I come to learn about union by yoking myself in your Spirit and loving others as myself. I desire to be the embodiment of your love in my relationships. I recite *1 John 4:11: If we love one another, God lives in us and his love is made complete in us.* To know that I can have your complete love within me as I love others—what an indescribably wonderful gift! As your love pours into me, let me pour it out into others. Amen.

༄

Day 49
METAPHOR OF YOGA BRANCHES

Yoga is frequently described as a tree—a living entity with roots, a trunk, branches, blossoms, and fruit. Hatha is considered to be one branch of yoga; others include raja, karma, bhakti, jnana and tantra. Similarly, Scripture has many references to this concept:

> *For I tell you I will not drink again from the fruit of the vine until the kingdom of God comes.* (Luke 22:18)
> *Remain in me, as I also remain in you. No branch can bear fruit by itself; it must remain in the vine. Neither can you bear fruit unless you remain in me.* (John 15:4)
> *Everyone will sit under their own vine and under their own fig tree, and no one will make them afraid, for the LORD Almighty has spoken.* (Micah 4:4)

Commune with Jesus about how you can relate to this analogy of a tree.

SCRIPTURE:

I am the true vine, and my Father is the gardener. He cuts off every branch in me that bears no fruit, while every branch that does bear fruit he prunes so that it will be even more fruitful. (John 15:1-2)

PRAYER:

Jesus, vine of the Living Father, I come to remain in you that I may bear the fruit of *'love, joy, peace, patience, goodness, kindness, gentleness, and self-control' (Galatians 5:22-23).* I remember the beginning verses of the Joy of the Redeemed, found in *Isaiah 35:1-2: The desert and the parched land will be glad; the wilderness will rejoice and blossom. Like the crocus, it will burst into bloom; it will rejoice greatly and shout for joy. The glory of Lebanon will be given to it, the splendor of Carmel and Sharon; they will see the glory of the LORD, the splendor of our God.* O Lord, let me blossom here on the mat and in life and as I do, keep me on your Vine of Life! Amen.

∽

Day 50
HATHA YOGA

Hatha yoga is a major branch of yoga, established by Goraksha and other practitioners around 1000 C.E. Hatha is comprised of two words, "ha" meaning "sun" and "tha" meaning "moon." Together they imply the word "forceful"— suggesting a powerful focus required to purify the body. Hatha yoga emphasizes the physical aspects of the yogic path, including postures and breath control. It calls for physical strength, mental concentration and spiritual energy. In what ways do you stay disciplined as it relates to physical fitness and nutrition? How do you treat your body as the Lord's vessel and focus your energy on connecting with his presence? Commune with Jesus about how you relate to this branch of yoga.

SCRIPTURE:

No discipline seems pleasant at the time, but painful. Later on, however, it produces a harvest of righteousness and peace for those who have been trained by it. Therefore, strengthen your feeble arms and weak knees. (Hebrews 12:11-12)

PRAYER:

Lord, thank you for placing your Spirit within me. I come to strengthen my arms and knees. Please guide me in tending to my body as your holy vessel and expressing the fruit of self-control here on the mat. Harness my energy and help me to focus my attention on you. I hear *1 Thessalonians 5:23-24 (MGS): May God himself, the God who makes everything holy and whole, make you holy and whole, put you together—spirit, soul, and body—and keep you fit for the coming of our Master, Jesus Christ. The One who called you is completely dependable. If he said it, he'll do it!* Thank you, Lord! My trust is in you. Amen.

୧୨

Day 51
TANTRIC YOGA

The tantric branch of yoga is one of ritual. A key element of tantric yoga is found in the word 'consecrated', which means to make sacred, or to set apart as hallowed or holy. A reverential attitude to all elements of life is encouraged. Draw to mind *Luke 12:2: There is nothing concealed that will not be disclosed, or hidden that will not be made known.* Often tantric yogis are deeply moved by ceremonies and spiritual rituals such as Holy Communion, confirmation, marriage, Easter and Christmas. Most schools of tantric yoga recommend a celibate life and those who practice tantric yoga often connect with the feminine aspects of holiness as well as the masculine. Take a moment to reflect on the recitation of the Hail Mary prayer and Virgin of Guadeloupe vigils. Where do you see holiness, and what rituals and ceremonies have meaning to you? Commune with the Lord about what makes you feel consecrated to Him.

SCRIPTURE:

"Haven't you read," he replied, "that at the beginning the Creator 'made them male and female,' and said, 'For this reason a man will leave his father and mother and be united to his wife, and the two will become one flesh'? So they are no longer two, but one flesh. Therefore what God has joined together, let no one separate." The disciples said to him, "If this is the situation between a husband and wife, it is better not to marry." Jesus replied, "Not everyone can accept this word, but only those to whom it has been given. For there are eunuchs who

were born that way, and there are eunuchs who have been made eunuchs by others—and there are those who choose to live like eunuchs for the sake of the kingdom of heaven. The one who can accept this should accept it." (Matthew 19:4-6, 10-12)

PRAYER:

Lord, I thank you for holy sacraments—times to gather with loved ones, praise your Name, remember your wonders, listen for your voice, repent, love you and love others. I remember *Matthew 26:26-28: While they were eating, Jesus took bread, and when he had given thanks, he broke it and gave it to his disciples, saying, "Take and eat; this is my body." Then he took a cup, and when he had given thanks, he gave it to them, saying, "Drink from it, all of you. This is my blood of the covenant, which is poured out for many for the forgiveness of sins."* Let each breath and action mark my consecration to you. Amen.

ᖇ᧏

Day 52
RAJA YOGA

Raja means royal. The focus of this branch of yoga is meditation and involves adherence to the eight 'limbs' of yoga as shared in the Yoga Sutras. Raja yoga typically attracts individuals who are introspective in nature. How inclined are you to spend time meditating? While pondering this royal path, read *Isaiah 55:5: Surely you will summon nations you know not, and nations you do not know will come running to you, because of the LORD your God, the Holy One of Israel, for he has endowed you with splendor.* Commune with Jesus about how you relate to this branch of yoga.

SCRIPTURE:

Moreover, Solomon has taken his seat on the royal throne. (1 Kings 1:46)
I will establish your royal throne over Israel forever, as I promised David your father when I said, 'You shall never fail to have a successor on the throne of Israel.' (1 Kings 9:5)

PRAYER:

Lord, thank you for endowing me with your holy splendor. I commune *Psalm 104:1: Praise the LORD, my soul. LORD my God, you are very great; you are clothed with splendor and majesty,* and rejoice in *2 Timothy 2:12: If we endure, we will also reign with him.* Thank you for your mighty love, and for clothing me with salvation, the spirit of endurance and the blessing of grace. These gifts are greater than I can fathom; *2 Corinthians 9:15: Thanks be to God for his indescribable gift!* Amen.

∽

Day 53
KARMA YOGA

Karma is the branch of yoga denoted by a path of service. The principle of karma yoga is that what we experience today is a result of the ways we have acted in the past. Read and reflect on *John 5:14: Later Jesus found him at the temple and said to him, "See, you are well again. Stop sinning or something worse may happen to you."* Karma is rooted in self-transcending action—it is to *'go and sin no more' (John 8:11 KJV).* Ponder *Matthew 6:18: Your Father, who sees what is done in secret, will reward you openly,* and *Matthew 10:42: And if anyone gives even a cup of cold water to one of these little ones who is my disciple, truly I tell you, that person will certainly not lose their reward.* Missionaries are examples of people who dedicate their lives to serving others, modeling Jesus' love in practical ways, as it says in *Matthew 20:28: Just as the Son of Man did not come to be served, but to serve.* Consider how your time on the mat may be a time of service. Commune with Jesus about how you relate to this branch of yoga.

SCRIPTURE:
You, my brothers and sisters, were called to be free. But do not use your freedom to indulge the flesh; rather, serve one another humbly in love. (Galatians 5:13)

PRAYER:
Lord, thank you for each opportunity you give me to love others and to act as your hands and feet. I remember *Ephesians 6:8: Because you know that the Lord will reward each one for whatever good they do, whether they are slave or free. Each branch will be recognized by its fruit.* Lord, help me to be of service to you and bear good

fruit. I hear *Philippians 2:3: Do nothing out of selfish ambition or vain conceit. Rather, in humility value others above yourselves.* Help me put those holy words into practice, as well as what you teach us *John 15:12: My command is this: Love each other as I have loved you,* and remember *Romans 13:8: Let no debt remain outstanding, except the continuing debt to love one another, for whoever loves others has fulfilled the law.* I repent of my sin, Lord, and aim to sin no more. Help me to move at the impulse of your commands. Amen.

∽

Day 54
BHAKTI YOGA

Bhakti is the devotion branch of yoga. It is about seeing the divine in all of creation. Bhakti yoga offers a way to positively direct your emotions and provides an opportunity to accept everyone you encounter. Those who practice this branch of yoga seek to express their devotional spirit with every thought and action. Reflect on *Colossians 3:17: And whatever you do, whether in word or deed, do it all in the name of the Lord Jesus, giving thanks to God the Father through him.* What are some ways you can find opportunities to express devotion with every thought, word and action? Do you accept others just the way they are? Have you accepted yourself? Commune with Jesus about wholehearted devotion.

SCRIPTURE:
Hezekiah turned his face to the wall and prayed to the LORD, "Remember, LORD, how I have walked before you faithfully and with wholehearted devotion and have done what is good in your eyes." And Hezekiah wept bitterly. (2 Kings 20:2-3)

PRAYER:
Lord, I come here to express my devotion to you physically, emotionally and spiritually. I hear *Romans 15:7: Accept one another, then, just as Christ accepted you, in order to bring praise to God. This is a spiritual act of worship.* What a powerful act—devotional love! Keep me on the straight and narrow path you have designed for me, oh Lord, for I know *1 Corinthians 7:35: I am saying*

this for your own good, not to restrict you, but that you may live in a right way in undivided devotion to the Lord. Aiming to be in synch with your Spirit, I listen to *2 Chronicles 29:31:You have now dedicated yourselves to the LORD. Come and bring sacrifices and thank offerings to the temple of the LORD.* I dedicate myself as your temple. Please guide me in living devotional love here on the mat and off it in my daily life. Amen.

∽

Day 55
JNANA YOGA

Jnana is the branch of yoga that focuses on the mind and wisdom. It is the path of the scholar and calls for the study of holy texts, and with its emphasis on intellectual pursuit, it is often perceived as the most difficult path. Reflect on *1 Corinthians 1:19-20: For it is written: "I will destroy the wisdom of the wise; the intelligence of the intelligent I will frustrate." Where is the wise person? Where is the teacher of the law? Where is the philosopher of this age? Has not God made foolish the wisdom of the world?* Seek to identify how wisdom plays a role in your spiritual beliefs, your daily life, and your yoga practice? Commune with Jesus about this branch of yoga.

SCRIPTURE:
Blessed are those who find wisdom, those who gain understanding. (Proverbs 3:13)
If any of you lacks wisdom, you should ask God, who gives generously to all without finding fault, and it will be given to you. (James 1:5)

PRAYER:
Lord, as Solomon requested in 2 Chronicles 1:11, I ask for a spirit of wisdom and discernment that I may do your will and live out the calling you have for my life. I rejoice in *Ephesians 1:8: that he lavished on us.With all wisdom and understanding.* Thank you, Sovereign King. Seal your words on my heart; fasten them to my feet and let them be an ever-active vehicle for transforming my mind. Ever, only and all for you, I say Amen.

∽

Day 56
AYURVEDA

Ayurveda is the practice of balancing your energy and creating optimal health in your being. It is often considered the sister science of yoga and dates back approximately 5,000 years. Ayurveda considers there to be three main qualities, known as doshas—vata, pitta and kapha—expressed in all things, yet each person has a unique composition of these three. Reflect on how you are physically, mentally and spiritually unique. Everything from your personality type to the times of day when you feel most energized factor into your unique dosha makeup. Commune with Jesus about your natural tendencies, preferences and characteristics.

SCRIPTURE:
There are different kinds of gifts, but the same Spirit distributes them. (1 Corinthians 12:4)

PRAYER:
Lord, I praise you for all the subtle ways you have made me unique and remember *Song of Solomon 6:9: But my dove, my perfect one, is unique, the only daughter of her mother, the favorite of the one who bore her. The young women saw her and called her blessed; the queens and concubines praised her.* Thank you for purposely and distinctively designing and shaping me. Help me explore this uniqueness here on the mat. Amen.

༄

Day 57
AYURVEDA: VATA DOSHA

The vata dosha is considered the lightest of the Ayurvedic elements and the main mover of the body. The vata dosha is associated with the elements air and ether, the seasons of fall and winter, and the times of day from 2 am to 6am and 2 pm to 6pm. People with lots of this dosha tend to have a light, thin body frame and are quick minded, and they perform activities at a fast pace. They often are light sleepers and have an aversion to cold weather. Ayurveda principles may suggest balancing these qualities by keeping warm, playing calm music, finding creative outlets, getting consistent sleep and having routine eating and exercise patterns. Where do you feel you fall on the vata spectrum? Think about Peter eagerly getting out of the boat to walk on water to Jesus and then quickly getting scared. Does Peter's action seem to align with how you may have acted the situation, or like the other disciples, would have you most likely stayed seated on the boat? Commune with Jesus.

SCRIPTURE:

"Lord, if it's you," Peter replied, "tell me to come to you on the water." "Come," he said. Then Peter got down out of the boat, walked on the water and came toward Jesus. But when he saw the wind, he was afraid and, beginning to sink, cried out, "Lord, save me!" (Matthew 14:28-30)

PRAYER:

Lord, I thank you for all the moments when you have reached out your hand and calmed the winds in my life. Excited to spring into action for you, I remember *1 Samuel 25:18: Abigail acted quickly. She took two hundred loaves of bread, two skins of wine, five dressed sheep, five seahs of roasted grain, a hundred cakes of raisins and two hundred cakes of pressed figs, and loaded them on donkeys.* Abigail's quick action in righteousness saved her life. Like Abigail, help me to be quick minded and to spring into action whenever the situation calls for it yet stay calm in trying times. Help me to harmonize these energies here on the mat. Amen.

෴

Day 58
AYURVEDA: PITTA DOSHA

Where there is transformation, there is pitta energy. Pitta applies to metabolism, body heat, vision and intelligence. Elements associated with pitta energy include fire and water, the seasons of spring and summer, and the times of day from 10 pm to 2am and 10 am to 2 pm. Some characteristics of those with lots of pitta energy include a medium body frame, a good memory and an aggressive nature. They often have a tendency to anger easily and favor order. To bring balance, Ayurveda may suggest relaxing, not overworking; spending time in nature; and diffusing intensity with moderation. Do any of these attributes resonate with you? Reflect on Paul, and how he describes himself in *1 Timothy 1:12-13: Even though I was once a blasphemer and a persecutor and a violent man, I was shown mercy because I acted in ignorance and unbelief. The grace of our Lord was poured out on me abundantly, along with the faith and love that are in Christ Jesus.* Paul redirected that passion and fire-filled energy towards loving Jesus! How are channeling your passion? Which activities and relationships fire you up? Where do you fall on the passion spectrum? Are you filled with lots of fiery energy, or do you tend to be mellow? How might you further be drawn in alignment in this area? Commune with Jesus.

SCRIPTURE:

Here is a trustworthy saying that deserves full acceptance: Christ Jesus came into the world to save sinners—of whom I am the worst. (1 Timothy 1:15)

PRAYER:

Lord, I thank you for baptizing me with *the Holy Spirit and fire (Luke 3:17)*, and for blessing me with a passion for you. Like Paul, I have been blind, yet you have continuously opened my eyes to truth. I come to the mat to be guided in obedience to you. Holy One, I am reminded of when you spoke to Paul in *Acts 22:7: I fell to the ground and heard a voice say to me, 'Saul! Saul! Why do you persecute me?'* Your light blinded Paul for three days. Then his eyes were opened and he used his great scriptural knowledge to share the fullness of Life with others. What an amazing transformation you brought about in his life! Just as you did with Paul, provide me with fresh boldness and holy fire-filled energy here on the mat. Amen.

෮

Day 59
AYURVEDA: KAPHA DOSHA

Kapha is the heaviest of the doshas. It is thought to provide structure to the body and is associated with strength, grounding and fertility. Its elements are water and earth; its seasons are winter and spring; and its times of day are from 6 am to 10 am and 6 pm to 10 pm. High Kapha types typically have larger body frames, a steady walking pace, are heavy sleepers and have a calm and understanding disposition. Reflect on *1 Kings 4:29: God gave Solomon wisdom and very great insight, and a breadth of understanding as measureless as the sand on the seashore. Solomon was steady and grounded in godly wisdom in his council.* Do some of Solomon's attributes resonate with you? To balance Kapha qualities, Ayurveda may suggest invigorating exercise, playing energizing music and avoiding over-sleeping. From sleep patterns to a steadiness in your step—how do you relate to these qualities? How may they be brought further into alignment in you? Commune with Jesus.

SCRIPTURE:

Nevertheless, God's solid foundation stands firm, sealed with this inscription: "The Lord knows those who are his," and, "Everyone who confesses the name of the Lord must turn away from wickedness." (2 Timothy 2:19)

PRAYER:

Lord, thank you for blessing me with a solid foundation in you, steadying my step and guiding me in understanding. I hear Jacob's blessing to Joseph as writ-ten in *Genesis 49:24-25: But his bow remained steady, his strong arms stayed limber, because of the hand of the Mighty One of Jacob, because of the Shepherd, the Rock of Israel, because of your father's God, who helps you, because of the Almighty, who blesses you with blessings of the skies above, blessings of the deep springs below, blessings of the breast and womb.* Like Joseph, keep me strong and limber in Spirit and here on the mat and in life. Amen.

∽

Day 60
MEANINGLESS

The poses are simply tools to physically exert the body, quiet the mind and prepare the heart for union with God's Spirit. It is a wonderfully beauti-ful thing! Selah. Reflect on *Ecclesiastes 1:14: I have seen all the things that are* done under the sun; all of them are meaningless, a chasing after the wind. What are you chasing after, and how might it be meaningless? Scan your thoughts and examine your heart; note what really counts and has meaning in your life and being.

SCRIPTURE:

"Meaningless! Meaningless!" says the Teacher. "Utterly meaningless! Everything is meaningless." (Ecclesiastes 1:2)

PRAYER:

Name above all Names, knower of all and in all—your fullness and glory is beyond my comprehension yet eminently present. I acknowledge that some things I put so much emphasis on are actually meaningless. There are postures that I exert much energy into 'achieving' that you consider insignificant. Holy One, often I fail to see the significance in things you deem praiseworthy. Please forgive me. I listen to Ecclesiastes 1:9: What has been will be again; what has been done will be done again; there is nothing new under the sun. Please help me to keep a holy perspective and rest in the truth that there is nothing you cannot heal, restore and redeem. Thank you for your mighty power and sovereign nature. I remember Solomon's reflection in Ecclesiastes 3:22: So I saw that there is nothing better for a person than to enjoy their work, because that is their lot. For who can bring them to see what will happen after them? I remember Ecclesiastes 8:15: So I commend the enjoyment of life, because there is nothing better for a person under the sun than to eat and drink and be glad. Focused on enjoying the positions that I find myself in, I say Amen.

༂

Day 61
TURIYA

In yoga, turiya is a term used to describe the beautiful silence that can happen in moments of complete peace; it is a sense of peace that transcends all understanding. Ponder Revelation 8:1: When he opened the seventh seal, there was silence in heaven for about half an hour. Turiya is often thought to come after meaningful activity or sound. Have you experienced a time when suddenly something opened up or subtly shifted and you felt the Lord's presence? Have you ever had such a strong connection with another person or in a particular place that no words needed to be spoken to share an intimate experience? What have you learned through times of silence? Take a moment in solitude.

SCRIPTURE:

And the peace of God, which transcends all understanding, will guard your hearts and your minds in Christ Jesus. (Philippians 4:7)

PRAYER:

Lord, quiet my mind and heart here on the mat. With my head bowed, I listen to *Lamentations 3:28-29 (MSG): When life is heavy and hard to take, go off by yourself. Enter the silence. Bow in prayer. Don't ask questions:Wait for hope to appear.* Waiting in hope, I quietly thank you for the moments I have felt intimately connected to You and moments I have felt intimately connected to others. Sovereign King, I come to cultivate closeness with you through inner stillness. Please guard my heart, body and mind here on the mat. Amen.

৩৩

Day 62
SANKALPA

Sankalpa is a yoga term that means sacred intention. It is a belief that you have everything you need in the current moment. It may also be translated as resolution, free will or imagination. What is your sacred intention in your yoga practice? What is your sacred intention in life? What is the secret of contentment for you? Do you feel like you have everything you need in the current moment? Commune with Jesus.

SCRIPTURE:

I know what it is to be in need, and I know what it is to have plenty. I have learned the secret of being content in any and every situation, whether well fed or hungry, whether living in plenty or in want. (Philippians 4:12)

PRAYER:

Lord, my sacred intention is to love you and love others—here on the mat and in each moment in life. Thank you for placing your spirit in me as a deposit. I desire to more deeply understand, treasure and illuminate this holy truth. I ponder *Psalm 23:1: The LORD is my shepherd, I lack nothing.* To feel, experience and live this verse is my sacred intention and commune *Psalm 131:1-2: My heart is not proud, LORD, my eyes are not haughty; I do not concern myself with great matters or things too wonderful for me. But I have calmed and quieted myself, I am like a weaned child with its mother; like a weaned child I am content.* Selah. Shalom. Amen.

∾

Day 63
SUKHASANA – EASY OR SIMPLY SEATED POSE

Sukhasana is a seated position with legs crossed and hands resting on the knees, cradled together in your lap or pressed together in front of your heart. In the beginning, all 'yoga' was done from this pose. Remember asana means seat. Come into this position and reflect on the beginning markers in your life—birth, introduction to faith, introduction to yoga, and so on. How does this moment right now mark a beginning?

SCRIPTURE:

In the beginning God created the heavens and the earth. Now the earth was formless and empty, darkness was over the surface of the deep, and the Spirit of God was hovering over the waters. And God said, "Let there be light," and there was light. God saw that the light was good, and he separated the light from the darkness. (Genesis 1:1-4)

PRAYER:

Lord of beginnings, you constantly bring new moments into being. I remember *John 1:1-2: In the beginning was the Word, and the Word was with God, and the Word was God. He was with God in the beginning.* I thank you for your divine nature. From this simple seated posture, may it be your Will that directs my motion, your Word that keeps my path straight, and your Spirit that transforms me into your likeness. Amen.

∾

Day 64
TOE EXPANSION POSE

The toe expansion pose helps create space between your toes, thus allowing fresh blood to flow to all the inner places of your feet. The opening sensation this pose spurs may create a revitalizing feeling throughout your body. To do this posture, come to a kneeling position with your toes curled under and then sit back on your heels. As you fan your toes, reflect on fanning the flame—putting the gifts and talents God has given you into practice. How do you do this in a physical as well as in an intellectual and spiritual sense? Commune with Jesus about the ways you're actively developing and utilizing your talents.

SCRIPTURE:
For this reason I remind you to fan into flame the gift of God, which is in you through the laying on of my hands. (2 Timothy 1:6)

PRAYER:
Lord, thank you for placing your holy flame inside of me. I come here to let it shine. As I fan my toes, Jesus, I am reminded of you washed your disciples' feet—cleansing their bodies and their hearts. Thank you for that purifying touch. I hear *1 Corinthians 12:12: Just as a body, though one, has many parts, but all its many parts form one body, so it is with Christ.* Revitalize me in this holy truth as I move on the mat so that at the end of the practice I may go forth to spread Light, for we are all one in you. Amen.

ᕼᎧ

Day 65
AGNISTAMBHASANA – FIRE LOG POSE

The fire log pose is very similar to the double pigeon pose (dwi pada rajaka-potasana); the main difference is the positioning of the hands and chest, which may move forward in the double pigeon. To do the fire log pose, start in a seated position and slide your right leg on top of your left so that your right knee is on top of your left foot and your right ankle is on top of your left knee. Lift your chest, then draw your shoulders down and back. Keep your arms by your sides with the pads of your fingers pressing downward onto the mat. You may hold a few breaths then work your hands and chest forward, deepening the stretch in the hips and groin. Remember to reverse sides and do this with the left leg over the right. While you're in the fire log position, reflect on what it was like for Moses to experience God's presence in an unexpected place—a burning bush—and recall the unexpected places and times when you have felt illumined by the Lord's light. Have you ever felt the presence of an angel? Commune with Jesus about light and revelation.

SCRIPTURE:
There the angel of the LORD appeared to him in flames of fire from within a bush. Moses saw that though the bush was on fire it did not burn up. (Exodus 3:2)

PRAYER:
Father, I thank you for the wondrous ways you appear and reveal yourself. I thank you for angels, heavenly hosts and holy fire. I am grateful for your presence that protects, guides, and radiates indescribable heat and light. I remember *Judges 13:20: As the flame blazed up from the altar toward heaven, the angel of the LORD ascended in the flame. Seeing this, Manoah and his wife fell with their faces to the ground.* Lord, in the fire log pose I work my face forward to the ground in reverence. Help me to become further aware of your radiant presence here on the mat. Guide me into a more intimate and reverential relationship with you. Amen.

Day 66
SIMHASANA – LION POSE

To do the lion pose, start by kneeling with your knees together, then lift your gluts to cross your right foot over your left one and sit back on right heel. Place your palms down on your thighs with your fingers spread. Inhale deeply through your nose and stretch your tongue out wide and slowly breath out through your mouth making a 'ha' sound. Repeat a few times then switch sides. Lions are often a symbol of strength. Think about Sampson in *Judges 14:6: The Spirit of the*

LORD came powerfully upon him so that he tore the lion apart with his bare hands as he might have torn a young goat. But he told neither his father nor his mother what he had done. For David, lions were symbolic of trusting in the Lord's mighty hand. As David says to Saul in *1 Samuel 17:36:Your servant has killed both the lion and the bear; this uncircumcised Philistine will be like one of them, because he has defied the armies of the living God.* For Daniel, lions were symbolic of faithfulness, for he was thrown into a den of lions and yet he came out unharmed. *Daniel 6:22: My God sent his angel, and he shut the mouths of the lions. They have not hurt me, because I was found innocent in his sight. Nor have I ever done any wrong before you, Your Majesty.* Reflect on how the Lord has enabled you to be victorious over your enemies and/or has provided you with strength to overcome unfavorable circumstances or threats. How may you need the Lord to help rise above whatever you are facing now? Commune with Jesus.

SCRIPTURE:

You are a lion's cub, Judah; you return from the prey, my son. Like a lion he crouches and lies down, like a lioness—who dares to rouse him? (Genesis 49:9)

PRAYER:

All-Powerful Holy Father, thank you for strengthening me from the inside out, shielding me from harm, and letting your holy energy flow through me. I re-member *Hosea 11:10: They will follow the LORD; he will roar like a lion. When he roars, his children will come trembling from the west.* Lord, I come trembling to you in complete awe and wonder. Knowing you will transform my awe-stricken fear into lion-like courage, I say Amen.

༄

Day 67
UPAVISTHA KONASANA – WIDE-ANGLE SEATED FORWARD BEND

To do this asana, start in a seated position with legs straight out and as wide as you can get them; rotate your thighs outward and elongate your upper body through the crown of your head. Walk hands forward hinging at hips with a flat back. Arms may extend wide towards your feet or straight forward. This pose stretches the entire backside of your body. Solidly grounded on the mat with arms and legs postured wide, ponder whether your heart is wide open in all of life's situations. What bad reports have you faced and what good reports have your received? How have you been known and also seemingly unknown? Have you lived through dire situations? Made others rich? Had nothing? Possessed everything? Commune with Jesus.

SCRIPTURE:

Through glory and dishonor, bad report and good report; genuine, yet regarded as impostors; known, yet regarded as unknown; dying, and yet we live on; beaten, and yet not killed; sorrowful, yet always rejoicing; poor, yet making many rich; having nothing, and yet possessing everything. We have spoken freely to you, Corinthians, and opened wide our hearts to you. (2 Corinthians 6:8-11)

PRAYER:

Lord, thank you for knowing me and providing me with just what I need in each moment. I come in gratitude for the ways you have carried me through life's situations whether I noticed and acknowledged it at the time on not—I do now. Thank you for your constant presence. Help me to extend your love wide. I remember *2 Corinthians 6:12-13: We are not withholding our affection from you, but you are withholding yours from us. As a fair exchange—I speak as to my children—open wide your hearts also.* Lord, please forgive me for any ways I have withheld affection. Here on the mat, I open my heart wide to love you and to love others. Amen.

⤳

Day 68
ARDHA MATSYENDRASANA – HALF LORD OF THE FISHES POSE, SEATED TWIST

To do this asana, start in a seated position with legs extended, then bend your knees and draw your right foot up by your left glut while keeping your right knee down on the mat. Your left knee stays up and your left foot is planted by your right hip. Your left arm is planted down behind your right glut with fingers facing away from you, and your right arm is raised up, then bends at the elbow, and your right hand rests on the outside of your left knee. Hold a few breaths and reverse sides. How has the Lord displaced fear in you and made you into a 'fisher' for others? Commune with Jesus about how and where you are drawing a net of love.

SCRIPTURE:

Then Jesus said to Simon, "Don't be afraid; from now on you will fish for people." (Luke 5:10)

PRAYER:

Lord, here I am: your fisher. I hear *John 21:5-6: He [Jesus] called out to them, "Friends, haven't you any fish?""No," they answered. He said, "Throw your net on the right side of the boat and you will find some."When they did, they were unable to haul the net in because of the large number of fish.* Thank you for teaching me how to fish. I trust in your directions, and I desire to cast my net into the world in kindness, goodness, generosity and love when and where you lead me. Amen.

∾

Day 69
MARICHYASANA A OR MARICHI'S POSE

Marichi in Sanskrit literally means a ray of light. To do this pose start seated with your legs straight out in front of you; then bend your right leg, with your right knee up and over the ankle and your right foot down by your right glut. Lift chest up then bow head forward. Reach your right arm forward and rotate it inwardly; next, wrap your arm around your leg and back. Your left arm reaches back as you aim to bring your fingertips together. Hold for a few breaths and reverse sides. Marichi's pose stretches your shoulders and spine, and stimulates your abdominal organs. Close your eyes and reflect on physical, emotional and spiritual darkness as well as light. Ponder the various ways that darkness and light interact in your life. Could you stand in complete light for twenty-four hours a day, seven days a week? Could you stand in darkness for that long? Consider how you can find harmony between the two in your life and commune with Jesus.

SCRIPTURE:

Your sun will never set again, and your moon will wane no more; the LORD will be your everlasting light, and your days of sorrow will end. (Isaiah 60:20)

PRAYER:

God, who created light and saw that it was good, and who separated from darkness, I am thankful for both light and darkness; I come here to ponder both these elements and their roles. I remember *John 12:36: Believe in the light while you have the light, so that you may become children of light. When he had finished speaking, Jesus left and hid himself from them.* Lord, when it feels like you are hidden, please draw me back and illumine me as a child of light. Teach me to radiate your fruits of the light, *goodness, righteousness and truth* as it says in *Ephesians 5:9.* Amen.

༄

Day 70
MARICHYASANA B, C, AND D

These poses in traditional yoga circles are thought to be dedicated to the Sage Marichi. He is considered the Vedic father, similar to Adam's role in the Bible. As a quick refresher on position A, start in the seated pose with one leg extending straight out and the other leg bent at the knee with the foot down, parallel to the extended leg. Draw your chest forward and wrap your arm around the inside of your bent leg. Aim your hands to connect behind your back. In pose B, instead of extending one leg, place that leg in lotus on the leg with the knee up. In pose C, start with pose A, but place the opposite arm of your bent knee on the outside of the knee and gaze backward. Pose D starts with pose B, but the opposite arm is placed on the outside your knee and your back. As you do these poses with all their varying options, think of how many animals Adam had to name! (See Genesis 2:20). Reflect on Adam, 'made in God's image' and how you've been made in God's image. The first thing the Lord does with Adam and Eve is to bless them; what are some ways the Lord has blessed you? Continuing to ponder Adam's story, when he and Eve chose to eat from the tree, they immediately felt naked and hid themselves, but God understood this and cared for them as we read in *Genesis 2:21: The LORD God made garments of skin for Adam and his wife and clothed them*. How does the Lord care for you even through the various choices you make—good and bad alike? Commune with Jesus.

SCRIPTURE:

So God created mankind in his own image, in the image of God he created them; male and female he created them. God blessed them and said to them, "Be fruitful and increase in number; fill the earth and subdue it. Rule over the fish in the sea and the birds in the sky and over every living creature that moves on the ground." (Genesis 1:27-28)

PRAYER:

Lord, I want to thank you for forming and fashioning me just the way I am. Thank you for the blessing of your presence. I come before you and repent of the ways I have not heeded your instructions. Please forgive me. Thank you for caring for me and calling me to you even when I attempt to hide. I remember *Job 30:18: In his great power God becomes like clothing to me; he binds me like the neck of my garment*. Yes Lord, as I move about in my life and on the mat, let me feel your presence surround me and abide within me. Amen.

᧑

Day 71
JANU SIRSASANA – HEAD TO KNEE FORWARD BEND

To do this pose, start in the seated with your legs straight out in front of you; bend your right knee and place the bottom of your right foot on the inside of your left leg. Your right knee is down on the mat. Lift both arms up, then bend forward until your forehead touches your straightened left leg; hold a few breaths and reverse sides. This asana stretches your back, hamstrings and groin. It is thought to help calm the mind and relieve stress and anxiety. Bringing your forehead to your knee, reflect on how you feel loved through your close relationships with friends and family members. Who do you feel deeply connected to, and in what relationships is a spirit of disconnection present? Share with Jesus any close relationships and areas of your life that could use healing.

SCRIPTURE:

Israel said to Joseph, "I never expected to see your face again, and now God has allowed me to see your children too." Then Joseph removed them from Israel's knees and bowed down with his face to the ground. (Genesis 48:11-12)

PRAYER:

Father, I bring my head to my knees in gratitude to you for strengthening my faltering knees and for receiving me in your holy family. Oh, great I AM, who lifts up those who are bowed down, I rejoice in *Isaiah 66:12: For this is what the LORD says: "I will extend peace to her like a river, and the wealth of nations like a flooding stream; you will nurse and be carried on her arm and dandled on her knees. As a mother comforts her child, so will I comfort you; and you will be comforted over Jerusalem."* Lord, thank you for your comfort. Please help me to act as a comforter, connector and family peacemaker here on earth. Amen.

༄

Day 72
GOMUKHASANA – COW FACED POSE

To do this asana, start seated; bend your knees, then draw your left foot by your right hip and set your knee down; then work your right foot over to your left hip. Your right knee draws down and stacks on top of the left. Your left arm goes up and reaches behind your back, and your right arm goes down and back and bends, with your fingers reaching up to touch the fingers on your left hand. You may use a band if your fingertips do not meet. Hold for a few breaths and reverse sides. As you do this pose, consider how the Lord has brought you to a fertile place and provided you with opportunities to grow. In what ways have you tasted the Lord's goodness—His 'milk and honey'? In what ways has the Lord set you apart and given you unique blessings? What can you feel the Lord doing in your life now? Commune with Jesus.

SCRIPTURE:

But I said to you, "You will possess their land; I will give it to you as an inheritance, a land flowing with milk and honey." I am the LORD your God, who has set you apart from the nations. (Leviticus 20:24)

PRAYER:

Lord, like a cow in green pastures, you nourish me on your word. Thank you for choosing me and setting me apart to be consecrated to you. Help me to direct this time to grow in spiritual understanding. I remember the sign of Immanuel in *Isaiah 7:21-22: In that day, a person will keep alive a young cow and two goats. And because of the abundance of the milk they give, there will be curds to eat. All who remain in the land will eat curds and honey.* Lord, thank you for blessing me with both physical and spiritual food, and for giving me an inheritance that comes from being your child. Help me to express your nourishing energy on the mat and off it in my life. Amen.

༚

Day 73
VIRASANA – HERO'S POSE

To do the hero's pose, start in a standing position on your knees; draw your knees together and lower your gluts down to the mat, with your heels by your sides and your hands resting on your thighs. An option is to move into the reclining hero, supta virasana, from here. To do so, bring your hands by your heels and work your upper body back until your back is flat on the mat. A final expression is to bring your arms above your head with your biceps next to your ears and with one forearm on top of the other. As you do this pose, think of who is a hero for you—in faith, in yoga, and in life. What heroic moments stand out in your life? Commune with Jesus.

SCRIPTURE:

These are the last words of David: "The inspired utterance of David son of Jesse, the utterance of the man exalted by the Most High, the man anointed by the God of Jacob, the hero of Israel's songs. (2 Samuel 23:1-2)

PRAYER:

Lord, I commune *Psalm 16:1: Keep me safe, my God, for in you I take refuge.* As I move throughout this practice and in my daily life, I do so declaring you as my refuge and stronghold against the foe. How wonderful it is to praise you through asanas like the hero's pose. Father, help me move valiantly for you. Amen.

❧

Day 74
KROUNCHASANA – HERON POSE

To do the heron pose, start in the staff pose and bring the right leg back so that your heel is by the outside of your right hip; lift your left leg straight up in front of you. Reach your arms up around your left leg with your wrists crossed behind your ankle. Work to have a straight spine; hold for a few breaths then reverse sides. The heron pose stimulates the abdominal muscles and heart. Since herons often stand on one leg, they have been associated with inner quietness and wisdom. How has your practice stimulated a sense of inner quietness in you? What does wisdom look like to you? In what areas of your life may you still need to grow in wisdom? Commune your responses with Jesus.

SCRIPTURE:

For this reason, since the day we heard about you, we have not stopped praying for you. We continually ask God to fill you with the knowledge of his will through all the wisdom and understanding that the Spirit gives. (Colossians 1:9)

PRAYER:

Father, thank you for the insights and truths you have revealed to me through the Spirit. Help me continue to grow in knowledge and to cultivate a sense of inner quietness. I remember *Ecclesiastes 8:1:Who is like the wise? Who knows the explanation of things? A person's wisdom brightens their face and changes its hard appearance.* May I not just stretch physically here but also spiritually and intellectually. Fill my inner being with wisdom and understanding so that I may live in accordance with your ways. Amen.

❧

Day 75
PADMASANA – LOTUS POSE

For the lotus pose, start seated and draw your right leg up and place your right ankle on your left thigh; then draw your left leg up and place it on your right thigh. Flex your feet and hold for as long as you like, then reverse the cross of your legs. Ponder a lotus. It rises up out of muddy water and opens into a beautiful flower. Consider how you have grown through 'muddy' times—ones that were tough and challenging. In what ways did you feel the Lord's presence in the midst of those difficulties? Is there a 'muddy' part of your life right now in which you could use some guidance? Commune with Jesus.

SCRIPTURE:

A shoot will come up from the stump of Jesse; from his roots a Branch will bear fruit. (Isaiah 11:1)

PRAYER:

Lord, help me remain on the vine and bear fruit that will last. Thank you for guiding through and out of mud and sin. I long to stay rooted in you—blossoming in light. I remember *Psalm 40:2: He lifted me out of the slimy pit, out of the mud and mire; he set my feet on a rock and gave me a firm place to stand.* Yes, thank you lifting me out of the mud and showering me with grace. Hold me in your integrity and give me a firm place to stand and soar to new heights in you. Budding in love, I breathe into the sensation I feel in this practice and throughout my days. Amen.

ભ

Day 76
GARBHĀSANA – EMBRYO, FETUS POSE

The embryo pose is a challenging asana. To do it, start in a seated position with your legs in lotus and your feet flexed. Slide your arms through your legs and lift your knees up; cross your forearms to make an x shape and hug your hamstrings with your elbows. Keep sitting up straight and remember to switch sides, reversing the cross of your legs and hands. How have you felt God with you even when your faith has been like a fetus, small and not fully developed? Commune with Jesus about any new, budding embryo ideas that may be taking shape in your life.

SCRIPTURE:

Can a mother forget the baby at her breast and have no compassion on the child she has borne? Though she may forget, I will not forget you! (Isaiah 49:15)

PRAYER:

Lord, I come to develop my faith and to tap into your Spirit for nourishment like a fetus connected to and nurtured by its mother. Help me cultivate the new embryo ideas you have been planting in me. I understand that the faith of a mustard seed can move a mountain. Let your holy seed grow in me. Father, I find peace in *Deuteronomy 31:8: The LORD himself goes before you and will be with you; he will never leave you nor forsake you.* I know that even if my faith is smaller than a mustard seed, you will never forsake me. Thank you, Lord. Amen.

∞

Day 77
DANDASANA – STAFF POSE

To do the staff pose, come to a seated position with your legs straight out in front of you, your feet flexed, toes spread, hands by your sides, fingers pointing towards your feet, and shoulders drawn down and back as if at attention. The Lord revealed to Moses that the simple staff in his arms could be used to perform great miracles. *Exodus 4:17: But take this staff in your hand so you can perform the signs with it.* What tools, gifts and abilities have you been given? Commune with the Lord about how He may perform miracles through you.

SCRIPTURE:

Moses answered, "What if they do not believe me or listen to me and say, 'The LORD did not appear to you'?" Then the LORD said to him, "What is that in your hand?" "A staff," he replied. The LORD said, "Throw it on the ground." Moses threw it on the ground and it became a snake, and he ran from it. Then the LORD said to him, "Reach out your hand and take it by the tail." So Moses reached out and took hold of the snake and it turned back into a staff in his hand. "This," said the LORD, "is so that they may believe that the LORD, the God of their fathers—the God of Abraham, the God of Isaac and the God of Jacob—has appeared to you." (Exodus 4:1-5)

PRAYER:

Lord, I come here to you to be your staff and a conduit of care for your people. I hear Jacob's words from *Genesis 32:10-11: I am unworthy of all the kindness and faithfulness you have shown your servant. I had only my staff when I crossed this Jordan, but now I have become two camps.* Father, with humble people and tools you do great things. Thank you for all the miraculous signs you have given me throughout my life to remind me that you love me. Each wonder reaffirms your mighty presence and blessing. In your Holy Name, I say Amen.

᠙

Day 78
BADDHA KONASANA – COBBLER'S POSE, BOUND ANGLE

To do the cobbler's pose, start in a seated position; bring the tops of your feet together with your knees spread wide. Work your feet towards your body. With your hands interlaced and wrapped around your feet, sit upright; then, feel free to lower your chest down with elbows pressing into your knees. The cobbler's position opens your hips and groin area. It helps you to feel grounded in truth, and to be open and humble. Cobblers mend shoes; who mends spirits? What area of your life could use some mending and reconditioning? Commune with Jesus.

SCRIPTURE:

Nevertheless, I will bring health and healing to it; I will heal my people and will let them enjoy abundant peace and security. (Jeremiah 33:6)

PRAYER:

Lord, I come to be grounded in your truth, open to your plans and humbled in my position. I understand that no matter what has happened in my life, you can mend and heal me in the deepest, most intimate way. *Romans 12:1 (MSG): So here's what I want you to do, God helping you: Take your everyday, or-dinary life—your sleeping, eating, going-to-work, and walking-around life—and place it before God as an offering. Embracing what God does for you is the best thing you can do for him.* Jesus, as my fingers embrace my feet in the cobbler's posi-tion, I envision you with a towel around your waist and water by your side, wrapping me in love and washing my feet in peace. Seal me in Spirit here on the mat. Amen.

☙

Day 79
EKA PADA SIRSASANA – TELEPHONE, BACKPACK AND FOOT-BEHIND-THE-HEAD POSE

To do these asanas, start in a seated position with your legs extended straight out in front of you. Draw one leg towards your chest and place your two peace fingers around your big toe. Extend the leg back out as long as your fingers will allow and then draw it back in as if answering a phone. Do this a few times, and when you feel warmed up, draw your leg all the way back and place it over your shoulder, backpack pose. If accessible for you, while keeping your head stable, bring your shin to the backside of your head, foot behind the head pose. Repeat on the other side or 'conference call' your other leg in by bringing it up as well. Foot-behind-the-head is an advanced posture with your heart and head being physically in front of your feet in its full expression. What might this mean spiritually? Think about how you may draw God into your mind and heart before stepping forward. Reflect on your latest phone conversations and your intentionality with your words. How have your words been reflecting what you have been carrying around in your heart? Commune with Jesus.

SCRIPTURE:
And about the matter you and I discussed—remember, the LORD is witness between you and me forever. (1 Samuel 22:23)

PRAYER:

Lord, I desire to let your light shine through all my conversations and motions on and off the mat. Please forgive me for the instances I have neglected to let your righteous truth pour forth from my words and behaviors. I remember *Acts 15:7-8: After much discussion, Peter got up and addressed them: "Brothers, you know that some time ago God made a choice among you that the Gentiles might hear from my lips the message of the gospel and believe.* Jesus, help me to be like Peter: may my lips be a vessel to share knowledge and truth. Reveal to me the people you desire me to call, who you want me to be in relationship with and what I should carry in my heart. Holy Spirit, as I lift my foot in the telephone pose, may it be an outward expression of me calling you inwardly. Jesus, let the backpack pose be symbolic of me picking up my cross and following you anew, every day. Let the foot-behind-the-head pose be an act of total surrender. Putting on Your burden of light, I say Amen.

༄

Day 80
MUDRAS

Mudras are specific hand positions, also referred to as gestures in yoga. Mudra means 'to seal'. They are done to stimulate subtle energy in the body, and often are associated with a particular chakra or energy center. They may be expressed or felt through your whole body. The classic mudra is accomplished by placing the index finger and thumb together with the other fingers extended. It is thought to clarify the mind, to help you concentrate, to develop intuition, to alleviate stress and to banish depression. Take a moment to try doing this mudra and notice any feelings or sensations that arise. How can you feel the Lord's seal on you? Are there any close relationships with others, such as your spouse, children, good friends, or coworkers, with whom you feel sealed? Commune with Jesus about what it means to be sealed.

SCRIPTURE:

Place me like a seal over your heart, like a seal on your arm. (Song of Songs 8:6)

PRAYER:

Lord, I come to be sealed in your Spirit. Thank you for placing it within me as a deposit and for wrapping me in your love. I remember *Ephesians 1:13-14: And you also were included in Christ when you heard the message of truth, the gospel of your salvation. When you believed, you were marked in him with a seal, the promised Holy Spirit, who is a deposit guaranteeing our inheritance until the redemption of those who are God's possession—to the praise of his glory.* Thank you for this indescribable gift! Amen.

❧

Day 81
FIRST, ADI MUDRA

The adi mudra is often the first gesture an infant makes—thumb in with fingers wrapped around making a fist. It is thought to stimulate deep recesses in the mind and is associated with the crown chakra. Reflect on the soft nature of an infant's head, soft and open to God. Place your hands in this position and elongate your body through the crown of your head with your eyes closed; then, as if drawing in spiritual milk through each breath, spend a few minutes holding this position. Ponder how you connect with the Lord in a childlike fashion. Commune with Jesus about anything you experience.

SCRIPTURE:

But Jesus called the children to him and said, "Let the little children come to me, and do not hinder them, for the kingdom of God belongs to such as these. Truly I tell you, anyone who will not receive the kingdom of God like a little child will never enter it." (Luke 18:16-17)

PRAYER:

Lord, I come to receive your love and light like a little child. I thank you for creating me, calling me and loving me. I remember *1 Peter 2:2-3 (ESV): Like newborn infants, long for the pure spiritual milk, that by it you may grow up to salvation–if indeed you have tasted that the Lord is good.* I thirst for spiritual milk and desire to grow up in faith. Please let your teachings fall afresh on me. Amen.

❧

Day 82
FEARLESS, ABHAYA MUDRA

This mudra is meant for displacing fear in others and was often used in Renaissance art by Christian painters. Raise your right hand with fingers up, palm open. Keep your fingers together and hold for a few breaths. This gesture may also be done with your left hand. The fearless mudra is connected to the heart chakra and symbolizes a prayerful and compassionate intent. In what ways have you displaced fears in others? Conversely, how have others alleviated fear in you? What makes you feel protected? Meditate on *Psalm 56:4: In God, whose word I praise—in God I trust and am not afraid. What can mere mortals do to me?*

SCRIPTURE:
There is no fear in love. But perfect love drives out fear, because fear has to do with punishment. The one who fears is not made perfect in love. (1 John 4:18)

PRAYER:
Father, thank you for your divine protection over my life and for displacing my fears with your holy love. I remember *Romans 8:15: For you did not receive a spirit that makes you a slave again to fear, but you received the Spirit of sonship. And by him we cry, "Abba, Father."* Thank you for making me your child and for loving me so expansive that it drives out fear. Abba, let your will be done on this mat, in my life and in this world. I acknowledge *1 Timothy 1:7 (KJV): God hath not given us a spirit of fear; but of power, and of love, and of self-control.* Your Kingdom Come, oh Lord. Amen.

༄

Day 83
FIRE, AGNI MUDRA

To do the fire mudra, draw your thumb to the tip of your middle finger and extend your other fingers out. It is associated with the abdominal chakra and thought to help with digestion and to promote intelligence. Reflect on your digestive patterns. Are they regular and solid? Similarly, consider your nourishment on the Lord's words. Do you digest them slowly and carefully, nourishing yourself fully on them? Place your hands in the fire mudra gesture and meditate on *John 6:35: Jesus said to them, "I am the bread of life. Whoever comes to me will never be hungry, and whoever believes in me will never be thirsty."*

SCRIPTURE:
The blueness of a wound cleanseth away evil: so do stripes the inward parts of the belly.
(Proverbs 20:30 (KJV)

PRAYER:
Lord, thank you for cleansing the inward parts of my belly. I listen to *John 6:48-50 (NRSV): I am the bread of life. Your ancestors ate the manna in the wilderness, and they died. This is the bread that comes down from heaven, so that one may eat of it and not die.* Let Your words penetrate my inmost being in this practice—bringing holy energy into my bones, blood and entire being. Amen.

∽

Day 84
DEER, APAN MUDRA

This mudra is thought to promote patience, serenity, self-confidence and the release of toxins. Second and third fingers touch the thumb while the pinkie and index fingers are extended. In this gesture, your hands are shaped like a deer's antlers. How has the Lord demonstrated patience with you? What calms and comforts you? What strengthens your step? Take a moment in quietness with Jesus.

SCRIPTURE:
Being strengthened with all power according to his glorious might so that you may have great endurance and patience, and joyfully giving thanks to the Father, who has qualified you in sharing the inheritance of the saints of the kingdom of light. (Colossians 1:11-12)

PRAYER:

Lord, I thank you for your patience. Help me cultivate a spirit of serenity and poise here on the mat. I hear *2 Samuel 22:34: He makes my feet like the feet of a deer; he causes me to stand on the heights.* You strengthen my step and lift my spirit. I recite *Psalm 42:1: As the deer pants for streams of water, so my soul pants for you, my God.* Panting for you, I say Amen.

꩜

Day 85
PRAYER, ANJALI MUDRA – NAMASTE

Namaste is a word often spoken at the end of a traditional yoga class while bowing forward with your hands together in a prayer position. It is translated as 'the light in me honors the light in you'. It also may be translated to 'the teacher in me respects the teacher in you'. This is a gesture of humility, appreciation and gratitude toward others for sharing their light. What are some ways you can show consideration for others before yourself? How can you share Christ's light in a humble way? How can you acknowledge that you have something to learn from everybody? Commune with Jesus.

SCRIPTURE:

Do nothing out of selfish ambition or vain conceit. Rather, in humility value others above yourselves, not looking to your own interests but each of you to the interests of the others. (Philippians 2:3-4)

PRAYER:

Jesus, great teacher, rabbi and high priest, I come to learn from you and those you have specially placed in my life. I remember *Philippians 2:5-8: In your relationships with one another, have the same mindset as Christ Jesus:Who, being in very nature God, did not consider equality with God something to be used to his own advantage; rather, he made himself nothing by taking the very nature of a servant, being made in human likeness. And being found in appearance as a man, he humbled himself by becoming obedient to death—even death on a cross!* Jesus, help me to take on your mindset. Let your light shine through me and guide me in recognizing your light in others. I aim to be like the Good Samaritan, handling others' interests with the utmost importance and care. Jesus, guide me in acknowledging your presence in the least and the lowly, and help me learn from each experience you have in store for me. Amen.

෬

Day 86
SECRET PRAYER, PASHCHIMA NAMASKARASANA – REVERSE NAMASTE

To do this gesture, place your hands together with your fingers up in prayer behind your back. Reverse Namaste can be done in a variety of asanas; it serves to open your chest, draw your shoulders down and back, and to enhance the flexibility of your wrists. It is an active position in which you are truly aware of your hands. In what ways do you feel you are the Lord's handiwork? The NLT version of *Ephesians 2:10* reads, *'for we are God's masterpiece.'* Ponder the truth of His Word—you are His masterpiece—and let it resonate within you. In what ways do you feel inimitably talented and like 'secret prayer,' in what ways do you pray in solitary places? Commune with Jesus.

SCRIPTURE:
For we are God's handiwork, created in Christ Jesus to do good works, which God prepared in advance for us to do. (Ephesians 2:10)
But when you pray, go into your room, close the door and pray to your Father, who is unseen. Then your Father, who sees what is done in secret, will reward you. (Matthew 6:6)

PRAYER:
Lord, I come to you privately and alone to thank you for making me your handiwork; I honor you in the uniqueness of my form and talents. Help me to share the gifts you have given me as you intend for them to be used. I hear *Isaiah 64:8: But now, O Lord, You are our Father; we are the clay, and You our potter; and all we are the work of Your hand.* Postured with my hands behind my back in reverse prayer, you take the lead, Father. Reverse any conceptions of 'prayer' I have held in error,

and direct me in your holy light. Here I am, Lord; I'm your handiwork. Do with me what you will. I am ready—let me be your clay. Amen.

෧෪

Day 87
TADASANA – MOUNTAIN POSE

To do the mountain pose, start by standing with your feet together, legs engaged, belly lifted up and in, shoulders drawn down and back and crown of your head reaching high. The mountain pose is traditionally done with your arms down at your sides with your hands palms forward; however, many times it is directed for your arms to be overhead. It is a position where you are completely aware of how you are standing. How often are you aware of your posture? What allows you to feel grounded, confident and poised? Commune with Jesus about being rooted, steady and alert.

SCRIPTURE:
You will bring them in and plant them on the mountain of your inheritance—the place, LORD, you made for your dwelling, the sanctuary, Lord, your hands established. (Exodus 15:17)

PRAYER:
My Rock and Redeemer, I come to stand in faith and love. Postured in vigilance, I hear *1 Kings 19:11: The LORD said, "Go out and stand on the mountain in the presence of the LORD, for the LORD is about to pass by."* Doing so, my heart sings *Psalm 48:1 Great is the Lord, and most worthy of praise, in the city of our God, his holy mountain.* Amen.

෧෪

Day 88
SAMASTHITI – EQUAL STANDING POSE

To do the equal standing pose, start in a standing position with your feet together and hands together in prayer at heart center. This is an active posture with your legs engaged, chest lifted, shoulders drawn back and down and crown of your head high. It is an asana to place the Lord always before you. What reminds you to pray—certain times of day, places, events or certain people? Take a moment in the equal standing pose and reflect on *Romans 8:25-27: But if we hope for what we do not yet have, we wait for it patiently. In the same way, the Spirit helps us in our weakness. We do not know what we ought to pray for, but the Spirit himself intercedes for us through wordless groans. And he who searches our hearts knows the mind of the Spirit, because the Spirit intercedes for God's people in accordance with the will of God.* Quietly commune with Jesus through your breath.

SCRIPTURE:

David said about him: 'I saw the Lord always before me. Because he is at my right hand, I will not be shaken. Therefore my heart is glad and my tongue rejoices; my body also will live in hope, because you will not abandon me to the grave, nor will you let your Holy One see decay. You have made known to me the paths of life; you will fill me with joy in your presence'. (Acts 2:25-28)

PRAYER:

Lord, I come to commune with you in spirit and truth. When I stand in this yoga practice and bring my hands together by my heart, I do so as a reminder to place your presence in front of me and feel it within me. I hear *Psalm 30:7: LORD, when you favored me, you made my royal mountain stand firm.* Holy One, keep me standing firm, alert and at attention; Holy Spirit, please intercede if my knees falter. In gratitude for your mighty, anointing and all-powerful presence, I say Amen.

❧

Day 89
URDHVA HASTASANA – UPWARD SALUTE

To come into the upward salute position, start by standing with your feet and legs together, arms straight up overhead and palms facing each other. Shoulders stay down as arms reach up. This posture may also be referred to as the maintain pose. How do you 'let nothing move you' as the scripture says in I Corinthians 15:58? Ponder the ways you can remain calm and not get rattled when people put you down or when others oppose you or ridicule you. When people ask you to bend the rules for them or to accept something that does not meet your moral code, how do you stay grounded in the truth of God's Word? What does it look like in your life to stand in integrity and give yourself fully to the Lord? Share your responses with Jesus.

SCRIPTURE:
Therefore, my dear brothers and sisters, stand firm. Let nothing move you. Always give your-selves fully to the work of the Lord, because you know that your labor in the Lord is not in vain. (1 Corinthians 15:58)

PRAYER:
Almighty Lord, I have come to stand firm. Please forgive me for the ways I have faltered. Restore and rejuvenate me here on the mat so that I may have the energy and stamina to give myself fully to your work. I remember *Luke 21:19: Stand firm, and you will win life,* and proclaim *Psalm 89:2: I will declare that your love stands firm forever, that you have established your faithfulness in heaven itself.* Amen.

༄

Day 90
ARDHA UTTANASANA – HALFWAY LIFT, STANDING HALF-FORWARD BEND

From the forward fold position, lift halfway up until your back is parallel to the mat; elongate through the crown of your head, engage your core, draw your shoulder blades together and rotate your thighs inward. This posture is often done as a transition, preparing and aligning your body for action. Doing the halfway lift pose, think about how you prepare for action in life. In what ways do you become alert and aware of your surroundings before speaking or moving? How do you position yourself to respond to and engage with your environment? Commune with Jesus about preparation.

SCRIPTURE:

Not until halfway through the festival did Jesus go up to the temple courts and begin to teach. The Jews there were amazed and asked, "How did this man get such learning without having been taught?" (John 7:13-14)

PRAYER:

Lord, thank you for watching over me, observing my actions and preparing me for tasks in accordance with your will. Please forgive me for the times I have failed to prepare; guide me in that disciplinary and important step. I remember Paul's words to the church of Athens in *Acts 17:23: For as I walked around and looked carefully at your objects of worship.* As I do halfway lifts here on the mat, align and straighten me on your path of light. Let me become fully aware of all you desire me to see and learn. Amen.

༄

Day 91
UTKATASANA – CHAIR POSE

To come into the chair pose from a standing position, draw your feet together and your knees together, then sit back in the hips, lift your belly up and in, and draw your arms up. You should be able to see your toe tips. Keep your gaze up. The chair pose requires attention and strength, much like listening to God. It requires alertness and engagement. When do you actively listen for God's voice? What are some ways you can still yourself in the midst of a fast-paced, checklist-driven, results-orientated culture? Take a moment to listen for the Lord's voice.

SCRIPTURE:

I will praise you as long as I live, and in your name I will lift up my hands. (Psalm 63:4)

PRAYER:

Lord, I lift up my hands to you. Please quiet my mind and heart in your presence. Jesus, I am reminded of the story of Mary and Martha in Luke 10. Mary is sitting at your feet actively listening to what you are saying while Martha is focused on the preparations she feels are necessary to have you as a guest. I remember your words in *Luke 10:42: Mary has chosen what is better, and it will not be taken away from her.* Like Mary sitting quietly and attentively at your feet, I seek to do likewise in the chair pose. I lift my hands so that I may not be distracted by other things but instead will focus on listening for your voice. Jesus, guide me through this practice and in my daily life. Amen.

ᕲ

Day 92
TABLETOP POSE

To do this asana, come to all fours, with your shoulders stacked over yours wrists and your hips over your knees. Your hands, knees and the tops of your feet remain on the mat. Think about your table, whether it's your dinner table or a table you share with a friend or coworker. How do you give thanks at your table? Who eats with you? At what tables do you gather around with others? How do you approach the Lord's Table? Commune with Jesus about the breaking of bread.

SCRIPTURE:
When he was at the table with them, he took bread, gave thanks, broke it and began to give it to them. (Luke 24:30)

PRAYER:
Father, I come to reflect on your blessings, to repent of my sin and to give thanks for your grace. Lord, with reverence and humility, help me set the table for you. I remember *Luke 22:27-30: For who is greater, the one who is at the table or the one who serves? Is it not the one who is at the table? But I am among you as one who serves. You are those who have stood by me in my trials. And I confer on you a kingdom, just as my Father conferred one on me, so that you may eat and drink at my table in my kingdom and sit on thrones.* Lord, this gift is beyond my comprehension! Praise to you—your Kingdom come. Amen.

ᕲ

Day 93
TABLETOP POSE WITH ACTION

From the tabletop pose, raise your right hand so that it extends out in front of you, and extend your left leg out behind you, then bring your elbow to your knee and back out again. Repeat this a few times and switch sides. Consider the table of your back in an emotional and spiritual sense. What needs to be overturned? What activities and items need to be cleaned off from the tables of your life? Commune with Jesus about how you give response.

SCRIPTURE:
So he made a whip out of cords, and drove all from the temple courts, both sheep and cattle; he scattered the coins of the money changers and overturned their tables. (John 2:15)

PRAYER:
Father of clean slates and pure intentions, help me to clear off anything you do not deem right in my life, my heart or in the physical spaces I occupy. I remember *1 Corinthians 10:21: You cannot drink the cup of the Lord and the cup of demons too; you cannot have a part in both the Lord's table and the table of demons.* Jesus, I come to your holy table; please overturn anything that needs overturning. Matthew 5 tells that a light should be placed on a table or stand so that everyone in the house may see it. Here I am to be your stand. Please place your light on me and let it shine. Amen.

 ∿

Day 94
MARJARYASANA-BITILASANA – CAT-COW

These asanas are often done together as a way to stretch and strengthen the entire back, heat up the core and prepare the body for further movement. From the tabletop position, lift your chest and tailbone while the belly drops; this is the cow pose. Next, arch your back upward, curling your head and tailbone down; this is the cat pose. Keep alternating back and forth between these postures for several breaths. You may want to try turning your wrist around or add some side-to-side movement for variation. The cat-cow pose physically expresses opening yourself to the Lord and drawing his presence inward. Lifting to truth and bowing in humility—how can you balance these two actions in your life? How can you express reverence to the Lord as you move in and out of your daily activities? Commune with Jesus about transitions, openness and reverence.

SCRIPTURE:

But for you who revere my name, the Sun of righteousness will rise with healing in his wings. And you will go out and leap like calves released from the stall. (Malachi 4:2)

PRAYER:

Lord, who delivers your people to a land of milk and honey, I listen to *Deuteronomy 13:4: It is the LORD your God you must follow, and him you must revere. Keep his commands and obey him; serve him and hold fast to him.* Let each movement I do be an act of reverence. As I develop internal heat in the cat-cow pose, may your holy flame enlighten me from the inside out. Guide me in obedience as I move from one asana to the next. Amen.

༄

Day 95
KUMBHAKASANA, UTTIHITA CHATRUNGA DANDASANA – HIGH PLANK POSE

To come into the high plank pose, start by placing your hands shoulder width apart on the mat and walk your feet back until your body forms a straight line. Elongate through the crown of your head with the palms of your hands pressed evenly on the mat, eyes of elbows directed at each other, your body core engaged, toes curled under and heels pressing back. This position builds strength throughout your entire body. Imagine your mat as a full-length mirror while you hold this posture and offer your body as a living sacrifice. Can you see God's holiness in you when you look in the mirror? How can you love yourself as the Lord loves you? Scan your body parts and find gratitude for each part, starting with your toes and working your way up your body.

SCRIPTURE:

Therefore, I urge you, brothers, in view of God's mercy, to offer your bodies as living sacrifices, holy and pleasing to God--this is your spiritual act of worship. (Romans 12:1)

PRAYER:

Lord of Lords and Kings of Kings, I offer myself up as a living sacrifice to you here on the mat. Thank you for my feet, calves, knees, thighs, hips, stomach, spine, ribs, heart, lungs, shoulders, arms, hands, neck, head, mind, skin and spirit. I recite *Mark 1:3* echoing the prophecy of Isaiah: *'Prepare the way for the Lord, make straight paths for him.'* Lord, let me make straight paths for you during this holy practice and in life. Amen.

༄

Day 96
CHATURANGA DANDASANA – FOUR-LIMBED STAFF, LOW PLANK POSE

This is a low and challenging posture to hold in which hands and toes are on the mat, the body is in a straight line from your heels to the crown of your head, and your elbows are in by your ribs and bent 90 degrees. Chaturanga is the term often used as a cue to move from the high- to the low–plank pose. How can you relate to each of the beatitudes written in Matthew 5 (today's scripture passage)? Take a moment and read each one carefully and its meaning. Reflect on who in your life reveals these qualities. Choose one of the beatitudes you can express more fully in your life and share it with Jesus.

SCRIPTURE:

Blessed are the poor in spirit, for theirs is the kingdom of heaven.
Blessed are they who mourn, for they shall be comforted.
Blessed are the meek, for they shall possess the earth.
Blessed are they who hunger and thirst for justice, for they shall be satisfied.
Blessed are the merciful, for they shall obtain mercy.
Blessed are the pure of heart, for they shall see God.
Blessed are the peacemakers, for they shall be called sons of God.

Blessed are they who suffer persecution for justice sake, for theirs is the kingdom of heaven. (Matthew 5:3-12)

PRAYER:

Lord, I pray that you would pour out blessings on all your saints. As I actively work to keep my body in a straight line while moving from the high to the low plank pose, I want to do likewise with my heart—lowering in meekness and with mercy; developing a hunger for justice and a pure heart. Teach me how to embody these attributes in my life. I thank you for your blessings, oh Lord, which I utterly do not deserve. Guide me, my Rock and Redeemer. Amen.

∽

Day 97
BHUJANGASANA – COBRA POSE

To do this asana, start by lying down in a prone position with your belly down and the tops of your feet down and together; position your hands under your shoulders, your elbows in and your chin in the center. Then lift your chest and let your hands softly graze the mat or hover right above the mat. Cobra is a position where your head and heart rise but your body stays low, your gluts are soft and the tops of your feet are grounded. How do you find harmony between lifting up and staying grounded, engaging and softening, raising your heart and mind while keeping your body solidly set in holy Truth? What area of your life may be out of balance? Share your responses with Jesus.

SCRIPTURE:

The infant will play near the cobra's den, the young child will put its hand into the viper's nest. They will neither harm nor destroy on all my holy mountain, for the earth will be filled with the knowledge of the LORD as the waters cover the sea. (Isaiah 11:8-9)

PRAYER:

Lord, all is safe on your holy mountain; as I lift my head and heart in the cobra pose, may they both be filled with your knowledge and light. I remember Paul's instruction in *Colossians 2:6-7: So then, just as you received Christ Jesus as Lord, contin-ue to live in him rooted and built up in him, strengthened in the faith as you were taught, and overflowing in thankfulness.* Focused on doing so, I say Amen.

༄

Day 98
URDHVA MUKHA SVANASANA – UPWARD FACING DOG

To do this pose, start by lying on your belly with your hands planted on the mat right below your shoulders with your elbows pinned in; lift up by straightening your arms and elevating your chest while your shoulders draw down and back. In the full expression of this pose, your shins, knees and thighs are actively lifted off the mat—just your hands and the tops of your feet are down. While your heart is directed upward, reflect on how you have been lifting your heart in life. What has been the focus of your prayers and attention? Where are you channel-ing love? Commune with Jesus about what has been flowing from your heart as well as from your mouth.

SCRIPTURE:
The good man brings good things out of the good stored up in his heart, and the evil man brings evil things out of the evil stored up in his heart. For out of the overflow of his heart his mouth speaks. (Luke 6:24)

PRAYER:
Lord, I understand that I speak from what is stored in my heart; may my heart be infused with your love and expressed in my speech. Please forgive me for the moments my speech has not been an overflow of your holiness but instead a reflection of my sinfulness. I shine my heart in the upward facing dog pose so that the rays of your glorious light will penetrate and permeate it. I remember *Proverbs 4:23: Above all else, guard your heart, for it is the wellspring of life.* Focused on doing so, I say Amen.

༄

Day 99
ADHO MUKHA SVANASANA – DOWNWARD FACING DOG

To come into this pose from the tabletop pose, curl your toes under, draw your heels down, lift your hips up and straighten out your arms. This is a common inversion often used as a restorative pose. Taking on the position of a submissive dog—with your head down and gluts up—is humbling. Reflect on the woman cited in Matthew 15 essentially describing herself as a dog to Jesus. Through this humility, he sees her great faith. How do you take lowly stances? Read *Luke 18:10-14: Two men went up to the temple to pray, one a Pharisee and the other a tax collector. The Pharisee stood by himself and prayed: 'God, I thank you that I am not like other people—robbers, evildoers, adulterers—or even like this tax collector. I fast twice a week and give a tenth of all I get.' But the tax collector stood at a distance. He would not even look up to heaven, but beat his breast and said, 'God, have mercy on me, a sinner.' I tell you that this man, rather than the other, went home justified before God.* Reflect on how you come to the Lord.

SCRIPTURE:
"Yes, Lord," she said, "but even the dogs eat the crumbs that fall from their masters' table." Then Jesus answered, "Woman, you have great faith! Your request is granted." And her daughter was healed from that very hour. (Matthew 15:27-28)

PRAYER:
Lord, I come to you like the Canaanite women in Matthew 15. Please have mercy on me, a sinner. Thank you for your grace and goodness that I do not deserve yet so deeply appreciate. I remember *Proverbs 15:1: A gentle answer turns away wrath, but a harsh word stirs up anger*. Jesus, as I take the position of a downward facing dog time and again on the mat, please help me increase in faith and understanding and be gentle and humble like you. Amen.

ॐ

Day 100
BEAR POSE

To come into the bear pose from the downward facing dog, lift your heels and place a deep bend in your knees. Here your knees come towards your chest while your back stays flat and your weight is evenly dispersed between your arms and feet. As you maintain the bear pose, ponder how the verb 'to bear' is used in many different contexts in the Bible—to bear fruit, to bear children, to bear the blame, and so on. What do your bear? Reflect on *Colossians 3:13: Bear with each other and forgive one another if any of you has a grievance against someone. Forgive as the Lord forgave you.* How do you bear with others? Commune with Jesus about bearing.

SCRIPTURE:

Then God said, "Let the land produce vegetation: seed-bearing plants and trees on the land that bear fruit with seed in it, according to their various kinds." And it was so. (Genesis 1:11)

Then God said, "Yes, but your wife Sarah will bear you a son, and you will call him Isaac. I will establish my covenant with him as an everlasting covenant for his descendants after him. (Genesis 17:19)

I myself will guarantee his safety; you can hold me personally responsible for him. If I do not bring him back to you and set him here before you, I will bear the blame before you all my life. (Genesis 43:9)

PRAYER:

All merciful Lord, help me to forgive others as you have forgiven me, and to bear fruit that will last. Father, I come to further discern what you desire me to bear remembering *Exodus 16:29: Bear in mind that the LORD has given you the Sabbath; that is why on the sixth day he gives you bread for two days. Everyone is to stay where they are on the seventh day; no one is to go out.* I also come to understand what you do not want me to bear, such as what is written in *Leviticus 19:18: Do not seek revenge or bear a grudge against anyone among your people, but love your neighbor as yourself. I am the LORD.* Finally, I rejoice in *2Peter 3:15 Bear in mind that our Lord's patience means salvation, just as our dear brother Paul also wrote you with the wisdom that God gave him.* Lord, thank you for bearing with me! Amen.

෮ᓙ

Day 101
RUNNER'S LUNGE

From the downward facing dog pose, lift your right leg up and set it down between your hands for an active version of this stretch. For a deeper stretch, bring your forward leg outside your hands and work it to the edge of your mat. In this version, the crown of your head lowers to the mat and you can come onto your forearms and/or drop your back knee down. The runner's lunge embodies humility, a contradiction to the image of the runner perceived by worldly notions. How can you run the race marked out for you by the Lord? What race is marked out for you? In what ways do you feel as though you are in strict training? How do you do it humbly? Share your responses with Jesus.

SCRIPTURE:

Do you not know that in a race all the runners run, but only one gets the prize? Run in such a way as to get the prize. Everyone who competes in the games goes into strict training. They do it to get a crown that will not last, but we do it to get a crown that will last forever. (1 Corinthians 9:24-27)

PRAYER:

Lord, I come to my mat to be in strict training for you—physically, emotionally and spiritually. I am focused on running in such a way as to attain the prize. I rejoice in *Colossians 2:9-10: For in Christ all the fullness of the Deity lives in bodily form, and in Christ you have been brought to fullness.* Jesus, lead me in the way of everlasting life. Amen.

୧୨

Day 102
ARDHA HANUMANASANA – HALF SPLITS

Start in a low lunge, then place your back leg down and straighten your front leg. Lift and elongate through your spine then fold your chest over your front leg. This is an awesome hamstring and hip stretch—no need for full splits today. The half split is enough. While holding a yoga pose, have you ever had the thought, "If I could just ____." It's the same way in life: "If I could just _____," then I would be happy, give more abundantly, and so on. How can you relate to such phrases. Are you satisfied in this moment with what you have? Read *2 Corinthians 12: 9: My grace is sufficient for you.* Now take a minute in solitude with the Lord.

SCRIPTURE:

All things are wearisome, more than one can say. The eye never has enough of seeing, nor the ear its fill of hearing. (Ecclesiastes 1:8)

PRAYER:

Lord, you have truly given me more than enough, and I thank you. Help me not to have a spirit of striving but rather to find contentment in my life and on the mat. May I not find myself forcing my way into any poses but simply allow your grace and goodness to flow through my being. I remember *Matthew 6:34: Therefore do not worry about tomorrow, for tomorrow will worry about itself. Each day has enough trouble of its own.* I come here not worrying about tomorrow or this practice, but focusing on the richness of the moment at hand. Amen.

∽

Day 103
QUAD STRETCH

For the quad stretch, start in a low lunge with the right leg forward and set the back knee down. Bend your back leg, then reach your right arm back to grab the inside of your back foot. Draw your heel in towards your gluts and breathe. Remember to switch sides. An option in this pose is to use a strap to reach your foot. Whether you can get your heel to touch your gluts or you choose to use a strap—your body gets just the right amount of stretching you need as you breathe into the sensation you experience. On the mat, as in life, the right amount for you may not be the right amount for another. How does this concept play out in your life? Your list may include a need for more or less sleep, alone time, exercise time, intake of food, etc. How comfortable are you with this principle? Do you find yourself questioning fairness or simply understanding and acknowledging the differences? Share your responses with Jesus.

SCRIPTURE:

The Israelites did as they were told; some gathered much, some little. And when they measured it by the omer, the one who gathered much did not have too much, and the one who gathered little did not have too little. Everyone had gathered just as much as they needed. (Exodus 16:17-18)

PRAYER:

Lord, I come to thank you providing me with exactly what I need. Help me to fully appreciate and celebrate the unique attributes and blessings you have given to everyone as I practice here on the mat and in go about my daily life. I remember *1 Corinthians 12:4: There are different kinds of gifts, but the same Spirit distributes them,* and recognize *Romans 12:6: We have different gifts, according to the grace given to each of us.* This is a mighty blessing. Selah and Amen.

૭౯

Day 104
SPHINX POSE

To do the sphinx, lie on your belly and keep your legs and feet down as you lift your chest and bring your forearms parallel to one another to rest on mat; keep your hands down, fingers forward and shoulders drawn down and back. The crown of your head reaches upward and your chin stays down. The sphinx symbolically represents a desire to transcend from your natural state to a 'higher' form. The sphinx has the body of a lion and the head of a human. As you do this pose, consider how you are developing physically in your practice. Are you able to stretch farther than when you first started and/or balance for longer durations? How are you growing spiritually? In what ways do you feel like you're maturing in life? Commune with Jesus as you do the sphinx pose.

SCRIPTURE:

To equip his people for works of service, so that the body of Christ may be built up until we all reach unity in the faith and in the knowledge of the Son of God and become mature, attaining to the whole measure of the fullness of Christ. (Ephesians 4:12-13)

PRAYER:

Lord, I thank you for continuously developing me and providing ways for me to grow. I remember *James 1:4: Let perseverance finish its work so that you may be mature and complete, not lacking anything.* Almighty One, please strengthen me from the inside out in body, mind and spirit so that I may be able to accomplish the purpose for which you sent me here. Amen.

∽

Day 105
SHALAMBHASANA – LOCUST POSE

Start by lying on your belly, arms down by your side, and then lift up your chest, your arms and your legs. Reaching up with your head, hands and feet, your heart lifts ever so slightly. Taking the position of a locust, reflect on how the Lord hears your cries from lowly positions. How do you find the stamina to lift your head from places that are emotionally and/or spiritually dark and hard? Share your response with Jesus.

SCRIPTURE:

For I am poor and needy, and my heart is wounded within me. I fade away like an evening shadow; I am shaken off like a locust. My knees give way from fasting; my body is thin and gaunt. (Psalm 109:22-24)

PRAYER:

Lord, I thank you for always hearing my cries and lifting me up when I am down yet keeping me humble and grounded. I remember that in the desert you fed John the Baptist on wild honey and locusts. Father, you provide in wondrous ways! I hear *Joel 2:25-26: I will repay you for the years the locusts have eaten—the great locust and the young locust, the other locusts and the locust swarm—my great army that I sent among you. You will have plenty to eat, until you are full, and you will praise the name of the LORD your God, who has worked wonders for you; never again will my people be shamed.* Let me remember this in the locust pose. Trusting in your deliverance, I say Amen.

❦

Day 106
PARIGHASANA – GATE POSE

For the gate pose, kneel and extend your right leg out to the side with your heel down, foot flexed, right arm reaches long on your right leg and your left arm reaches up and over. This opens up your left side body. Hold a few breaths and then reverse sides. Gates during Biblical times were considered a meeting place for exchanging ideas and socializing, much like how coffee shops are today. They were necessary for the exchanging of resources. Where do you meet with others and where do you commune with the Lord? How can you feel the beautiful exchange of love and life as you confess your sin and let the Lord's grace pour into your heart? Have you felt as though you are being rebuilt in such moments? Scan your body and imagine God rebuilding you with turquoise, lapis lazuli, rubies and precious stones.

SCRIPTURE:
Afflicted city, lashed by storms and not comforted, I will rebuild you with stones of turquoise, your foundations with lapis lazuli. I will make your battlements of rubies, your gates of sparkling jewels, and all your walls of precious stones. (Isaiah 54:11-12)

PRAYER:
Father, thank you for rebuilding me inside out and for making my gates sparkling jewels. I remember *Nehemiah 3:1: Eliashib the high priest and his fellow priests went to work and rebuilt the Sheep Gate.* Yes, the first gate Nehemiah rebuilt was the sheep gate where sacrifices to you entered and exited. Lord, like Nehemiah, may I put sacrifices to you first and offer my body as a living sacrifice to you on this mat. Let your words, grace and light fill me through the gate pose, and let anything that does not serve my body as your temple exit. Amen.

❦

Day 107
ANANTASANA – SIDE-RECLINING LEG LIFT

While lying on your right side, flex your right ankle and draw your right arm straight out with your elbow bent and your right hand resting on your right check. Externally rotate your left leg so that your toes are up, then bend your left knee and grab your big toe with the two peace fingers of your left hand, or place a strap around the arch of your foot, then extend your leg high for a few breathes. Reverse sides. Another variation is to inhale as you lift the leg straight up by itself and exhale as you lower it, repeating slowly through several breath cycles. In the book of Ruth, we read that Boaz marries Ruth after he observes her faithfulness, care and diligence. How have you witnessed faithfulness in others? How have you acted in obedience in your life by caring for another? To what and for whom have you shown loyalty? Commune with Jesus about these experiences.

SCRIPTURE:

In the middle of the night something startled the man; he turned—and there was a woman lying at his feet! "Who are you?" he asked. "I am your servant Ruth," she said. "Spread the corner of your garment over me, since you are a guardian-redeemer of our family." "The LORD bless you, my daughter," he replied. (Ruth 3:8-10)

PRAYER:

Lord, I come in obedience to express my love and loyalty to you, and to rejoice in the truth that you will never leave me or forsake me. Help me to act in accordance with your faithfulness. I reflect on the loyalty of Ruth to Naomi, even when she knew Naomi would have no other sons for her to marry as written in *Ruth 1:16: But Ruth replied, "Don't urge me to leave you or to turn back from you. Where you go I will go, and where you stay I will stay. Your people will be my people and your God my God."* Likewise, here on the mat, teach me how to be faithful to you and to those you have placed in my life. Amen.

৩৯

Day 108
MALASANA – GARLAND POSE, YOGI SQUAT

To do a garland pose, start squatting with your feet hip width apart pointed out at 45 degrees and grounded, hands in prayer position and elbows pressed against your knees opening your hips and stretching your ankles, groin and back. The yogi squat is a position many in third world countries spend significant time doing, especially children. While in the garland pose, pray for those who are destitute and hungry. Think about how this physically low position with your head up expresses your faith. How can you listen to God's instructions? How do you listen to your parents' teaching whether they are 39 or 79? Ponder how you can remember, respect and respond to the callings of others.

SCRIPTURE:
Listen, my son, to your father's instruction and do not forsake your mother's teaching. They are a garland to grace your head and a chain to adorn your neck. (Proverbs 1:8-9)

PRAYER:
Lord, I come to listen to you, and I desire to bless those who are hungry, poor and desperate around the world, those who are squatting right now. Likewise, I desire to bless and learn from my parents and every teacher you place in my life. I commit to gain understanding about how to do these things, treasuring the holy words about wisdom from *Proverbs 4:8-9: Cherish her, and she will exalt you; embrace her, and she will honor you. She will give you a garland to grace your head and present you with a glorious crown.* With this sacred intention, I say Amen.

෩

Day 109
PASASANA – NOOSE POSE

To do the noose pose, place your feet together and knees together, and sit back until your gluts are sitting on your heels, then shift your left shoulder to the right and reach your left arms around your legs and back. Reach your right arm down and back, and work to bring your fingertips together. You can also do this pose with your legs slightly apart and wrap your left arm only around your left leg. Hold for a few breaths and reverse sides. The noose pose stretches your ankles and opens your chest, and is thought to improve your posture. From Sanskrit, pasa may be translated as noose, knot, tie, bind or fetter. In what ways have you felt trapped in a pattern of sin? How have you been freed from destructive habits, patterns or relationships? Commune with Jesus about the areas in your life where you may still need to be set free.

SCRIPTURE:

With persuasive words she led him astray; she seduced him with her smooth talk. All at once he followed her like an ox going to the slaughter like a deer stepping into a noose (Proverbs 7:21-23).

PRAYER:

Lord, as I breathe I feel the words of *2 Corinthians 3:17: Wherever the Lord's Spirit is, there is freedom.* Thank you for your mercy and for freeing me from the bondage of sin. I remember *Galatians 5:1: For it is the freedom of Christ that has set us free. Stand firm then and do not let yourselves be burdened with the yoke of slavery.* Jesus, help me stand firm in truth and light and walk on the straight and narrow path you have set before me. Let the physical release of coming out of the noose pose or any other yoga bind remind me of the freedom I have in you. Thank you breaking the yoke of slavery and sin that leads to death and for offering me your yoke, which is easy and leads to life. Bind me in your love as I take your yoke upon me. Amen.

಄

Day 110
HORSE POSE

To do the horse pose, start by standing with your feet three to four feet apart and toes pointed out about 45 degrees, knees over ankles, hips lowered, tailbone slightly tucked, core engaged, back straight and hands together in prayer. For a challenge, lift your heels. In this pose, which is symbolic of a reined-in horse, reflect on how you keep the Lord's holy day honorable. How do you center yourself on the Lord instead of doing things your own way or following your own plans? How do you keep from speaking idle words—filling quiet moments with chatter? Commune with Jesus about how to uphold the Sabbath.

SCRIPTURE:

"If you keep your feet from breaking the Sabbath and from doing as you please on my holy day, if you call the Sabbath a delight and the LORD's holy day honorable, and if you honor it by not going your own way and not doing as you please or speaking idle words, then you will find your joy in the LORD, and I will cause you to ride in triumph on the heights of the land and to feast on the inheritance of your father Jacob." For the mouth of the LORD has spoken. (Isaiah 58:13-14)

PRAYER:

Lord, horseshoe my feet to your words, and help me keep Sabbaths holy and all my days honorable to you. Forgive me for the times I have filled your holy space with chatter and have done things my own way instead of listening to you. I hear *Proverbs 21:23: Those who guard their mouths and their tongues keep themselves from calamity.* This yoga practice involves no talking on my part, so bridle my mouth and attune my heart to your voice, oh Lord. I remember *2 Thessalonians 2:15: So then, brothers and sisters, stand firm and hold fast to the teachings we passed on to you, whether by word of mouth or by letter.* Here I am, ready to stand firm in you, and like a trained horse, I will move at your command. Amen.

∞

Day 111
WIDE LEGGED SQUAT WITH CACTUS ARMS

For this variation of the horse pose, your arms are extended wide at shoulder height, your elbows are bent 90 degrees and your hands are up. If you like, also try doing cactus arms in the upward salute and warrior 1 positions with a gentle backbend. Cactus arms physically exemplify your thirsting for living water and opening to God's Spirit. How do you raise your hands and open your heart—standing passionately for something you believe in? Through trying times, how has a friend supported you, and how have you supported a friend? Commune to Jesus any loved ones who may need to be lifted up.

SCRIPTURE:

So Joshua fought the Amalekites as Moses had ordered, and Moses, Aaron and Hur went to the top of the hill. As long as Moses held up his hands, the Israelites were winning, but whenever he lowered his hands, the Amalekites were winning. When Moses' hands grew tired, they took a stone and put it under him and he sat on it. Aaron and Hur held his hands up—one on one side, one on the other—so that his hands remained steady till sunset. So Joshua overcame the Amalekite army with the sword. (Exodus 17:10-13)

PRAYER:

Sovereign Lord, when I am weak, you are strong; your grace is made perfect in my weakness. I thank you for bringing people into my life that support me as I strive to live in your truth and power. I also thank you for the opportunity to return the blessing and support others. As I practice cactus arms, I recite *Psalm 143:6: I spread out my hands to you; my soul thirsts for you like a parched land.* Living water, quench me. Amen.

∾

Day 112
STAR POSE

To do the star pose, stand with your feet about three to five feet apart and keep them parallel to each other, legs active and arms straight up and out. Star is an invigorating static posture. When you do the star pose, do you feel the Spirit's expansive energy moving through you? Where do you need to bring the Lord's light into your body so that you do not move with grumbling and complaining? Likewise, where do you need to bring His light in your life? Finally, like stars in the sky, how may you connect with other people to form constellations of love?

SCRIPTURE:

Do everything without grumbling or arguing, so that you may become blameless and pure, "children of God without fault in a warped and crooked generation." Then you will shine among them like stars in the sky. (Philippians 2:14-15)

PRAYER:

Lord, I desire to be your star. Please forgive me for the ways I have grumbled or complained, for I desire to stop it and shine for you once again. In the star pose, I actively express this intention. I remember *Daniel 12:3: Those who are wise will shine like the brightness of the heavens, and those who lead many to righteousness, like the stars forever and ever.* Father, please grant me wisdom, clarity and perspective to act in a grateful and benevolent way to my body and others around me. Guide me in your holy light and lead me into position with the right constellation. Amen.

෧෨

Day 113
PRASARITA PADOTTANASANA – STANDING STRADDLE BEND, WIDE LEGGED FORWARD FOLD

To the wide legged forward fold pose, start standing and step one foot back about three feet. Keeping your feet, hips and shoulders parallel to your sides with your hands to your hips or stretched out, fold forward leading with your chest and with the crown of your head moving towards the floor. There are many hand options in this asana. A few include placing them between your legs, around your ankles or taking your two peace fingers and wrapping them around your great toes. Postured wide in expansive love and head down in humility in the standing straddle bend, ponder how you consider others better than yourself. Examine your relationships. How do you live this principle of humility on the mat, in your job, at home, and in every facet of your life? Share your response with Jesus.

SCRIPTURE:

Do nothing out of selfish ambition or vain conceit, but in humility consider others better than yourselves. (Philippians 2:3)

PRAYER:

Lord, I come to humble myself at your feet and apologize for all the ways I have carried pride within my heart—ways I have not been quick to admit my error or guilt or have held myself in false esteem in relation to others. Please forgive me, Sovereign King. I hear *Romans 12:10: Be devoted to one another in brotherly love. Honor one another above yourselves.* In this wide legged forward fold with my head down, teach me how to honor others above myself. Amen.

༺ ༻

Day 114
FALLEN WARRIOR

To do the fallen warrior pose, start in a high plank and draw your right leg through so that it positions straight out on your left side with your foot flexed. Left toes stay curled under with your left heel drawing back. Hands walk over to the right and arms and chest may lower to the mat. Reverse sides. In this asana, ponder the harmony between being proactive and surrendered. This pose physically expresses being a warrior of God yet acknowledges you are fallen and in need of grace. How can you attain this balance in your life? Take a moment to commune with Jesus about any of the ways you may feel out of balance physically, emotionally or spiritually.

SCRIPTURE:
Better a patient person than a warrior, one with self-control than one who takes a city. (Proverbs 16:32)

PRAYER:
Lord, I come to align myself with your holy will. I understand I fall short time and time again, yet every time I repent, listen to your will and act in self-control, I feel Your Spirit rising and building me up again as a warrior for you. I believe *John 5:17: My Father is always at his work to this very day, and I too am working.* Holy One, alive and active in me, let this practice be an expression of praise to you. Amen.

༺ ༻

Day 115
CRESCENT MOON POSE

For the crescent moon pose, start in a low lunge, keep your back knee down and reach your arms straight up overhead. Draw hands into a steeple grip and gently arch your back as your heart lifts and your throat opens. You may lift the back knee up for an additional challenge while keeping the top of that foot on the mat. Reverse sides. Like Rebekah's unbridled kindness to Abraham's servant, even when she didn't know who he was, how have you shown kindness to a stranger? How did it feel? What, if anything, transpired as a result of it? Commune with Jesus about this type of kindness.

SCRIPTURE:

May it be that when I say to a young woman, 'Please let down your jar that I may have a drink,' and she says, 'Drink, and I'll water your camels too'—let her be the one you have chosen for your servant Isaac. By this I will know that you have shown kindness to my master. (Genesis 24:14)

PRAYER:

Lord, I come to lift up my arms in thankfulness. I feel steadied by your truth, arched in compassion and postured as your sacred temple as I hold a steeple grip in the crescent moon pose. As I open my heart to you, help me to learn how to serve your people even when they are strangers to me. I commune *Genesis 32:10: I am unworthy of all the kindness and faithfulness you have shown your servant,* and remember *Ruth 3:10: "The LORD bless you, my daughter," he replied. "This kindness is greater than that which you showed earlier: You have not run after the younger men, whether rich or poor."* Help me to follow Ruth's example of loyalty and devotion to those you have placed in my life. I celebrate you placing eternity in my heart. As I move on the mat and feel my heartbeat, help me to feel connected to your heartbeat and the heartbeat of all your people. Amen.

෭෨

Day 116
ANJANEYASANA – CRESCENT LUNGE

To do crescent lunge from the downward facing dog, lift the right leg forward, engage your back leg and lift up; your back heel is lifted, back knee is up and front knee is over your front ankle. Both hands are extended overhead. Remember to reverse sides. The crescent lunge strengthens your legs and tones your arm muscles. The word crescent comes from the Latin verb *crescere*, which means 'to grow'. How have you been growing in your faith? How are you growing your perspective, skills and talents in life? How are your relationships with others growing? Commune with Jesus as you ponder your spiritual growth.

SCRIPTURE:

But the seed on good soil stands for those with a noble and good heart, who hear the word, retain it, and by persevering produce a crop. (Luke 8:15)

PRAYER:

Lord, I come to hear your Word, retain it and persevere in order to produce a crop. I remember *1 Corinthians 3:7: I planted a seed, Apollos watered it, but God made it grow. So neither he who plants nor he who waters is anything, but only God, who makes things grow.* Righteous Father, who makes things grow, let me grow in faith on the mat as well as in each area of my life and relationship as you so desire it. Amen.

⁂

Day 117
VIRABHADRASANA 1 – WARRIOR 1

For the warrior 1 pose, stand with your left leg back about three feet from your right, keeping heel-to-heel alignment. Your back leg is straight with your foot facing forward, toes out about 45 degrees. Your front leg is bent 90 degrees with your front knee over your front ankle. Work your hips and shoulders square to the front and draw your arms up. Hold a few breaths and switch sides. In warrior 1, all four corners of your feet are grounded down; especially focus on the back edge of the back foot. Think about how you keep your feet outfitted in peace. Reflect also on your belt of truth. How can you keep your core engaged physically and in God's truth spiritually? Do you walk with your shoulders drawn back and down, confident because your breastplate of righteousness is in place? Warrior positions support these things! Commune with Jesus about how your spiritual feelings may manifest themselves physically in your body.

SCRIPTURE:

Stand firm then, with the belt of truth buckled around your waist, with the breastplate of righteousness in place, and with your feet fitted with the readiness that comes from the gospel of peace. (Ephesians 6:14-15)

PRAYER:

Lord, I come to my mat to be a warrior of your truth, righteousness and peace. Equip me as I prepare for movement. I remember *Romans 13:12: The night is nearly over; the day is almost here. So let us put aside the deeds of darkness and put on the armor of light.* As my heart lifts, my gaze goes up and fingers reach to your holy heavens in the warrior 1 pose. Let your light descend on me and radiate out through my being. Amen.

୬~୭

Day 118
BADDHA VIRABHADRASANA – HUMBLE WARRIOR

For humble warrior, from the warrior 1 position with the right leg forward, interlace your hands behind your back, lift your chest then bow forward. Both shoulders work to the inside of the front knee while drawing away from your ears, and the crown of your head gently lowers toward the mat. Hold a few breaths, then return to warrior 1 and switch sides. How do you reflect humility in your practice and outside your practice, in your professional and personal life? Also reflect on how you exemplify humility in your relationship with the Lord.

SCRIPTURE:

Humble yourselves before the Lord, and he will lift you up. James 4:10

PRAYER:

Father, I remember *Proverb 3:34: He mocks proud mockers but shows favor to the humble and oppressed*, and *Psalm 146:8: The Lord lifts up those who are bowed down*. I come to my mat to submit to your words and to your will. Please remove any pride in me. Lord, I repent as I bow down in the humble warrior position. Doing so, I feel you remove that yoke of sin and replace it with your yoke of light as I lift back up. Praise to You! Amen.

෴

Day 119
VIRABHADRASANA 2 — WARRIOR 2

For the warrior 2 pose, start in the low lunge with your right foot forward, right heel over your front ankle, back leg bladed down and back toes forward and out about 45 degrees. Rise up with your right arm extending forward and left arm extending back. Your shoulders are stacked directly over the hips, both open evenly to the side. Hold a few breaths and reverse sides. Use the warrior 2 pose to direct your attention to the Lord. Gaze over your front fingers in the warrior 2 pose and imagine your extended hand holding the sword of the Spirit. On your back arm, picture a shield of faith and around your head, a helmet of salvation protecting your mind. Reflect on how you hold onto God's Word and use it in your daily life. Also reflect how your faith has acted as a shield from a verbal, spiritual or other type of attack. Commune with Jesus about these pieces of spiritual armory.

SCRIPTURE:

In addition to all this, take up the shield of faith, with which you can extinguish all the flaming arrows of the evil one. Take the helmet of salvation and the sword of the Spirit, which is the word of God. (Ephesians 6:16-17)

PRAYER:

Lord, I come before you as your warrior with a shield of faith, the sword of the Spirit and the helmet of salvation in place. Please direct my tongue and actions. I recite *John 3:14-15: Just as Moses lifted up the snake in the wilderness, so the Son of Man must be lifted up, that everyone who believes may have eternal life in him.* Jesus, I believe in you and trust you to lift me in your love and light. I move at the battle horn of your calling. Hallelujah! Amen.

∽

Day 120
UTTHITA PARSVAKONASANA – EXTENDED SIDE ANGLE

For extended side angle from warrior 2 with your right leg forward, draw the right arm forward and down and the left arm high with your fingertips pointing up or forward; your chest is lifted and your gaze is up. Hold for a few breaths and switch sides. An advanced option is to take a half or full bind. For the half bind, the left arm wraps around and rests on your right thigh. For the full bind, your right arm glides over your right thigh and goes under your leg. Your hands meet behind your gluts and your arms work to straighten while your chest remains over your thigh and your heart is up. As you hold this pose, ponder how you can extend the Lord's grace, love and light to others. What are some ways you can extend a hand to help a neighbor, help on a work project or support a child? Can you feel Christ's power working in and through you when you extend love to others? Share your responses with Jesus.

SCRIPTURE:

To this end I strenuously contend with all the energy Christ so powerfully works in me. (Colossians 1:29)

PRAYER:

Lord, I come to my mat and extend my limbs in love. I feel light radiating out of my fingertips as I reach and extend. Stretch me in my understanding of your almighty grace. I recite *1 Corinthians 15:10: But by the grace of God I am what I am, and his grace to me was not without effect. No, I worked harder than all of them—yet not I, but the grace of God that was with me.* Let my yoga practice be a reflection of these holy words expressed through my entire being. I am here to strenuously contend with all your holy energy that is so powerfully at work in me. Amen.

೧౨

Day 121
VIPARITA VIRABHADRASANA – EXALTED WARRIOR, REVERSE WARRIOR

For exalted warrior pose with from the warrior 2 position with the right leg forward, bring your left arm back to your left straight leg and lift your right arm high. Direct your chest and gaze upward as you open through your side body. As an option, work a half bind with your left arm wrapping around your back and being set on your right front thigh, or for a more intense side body stretch, reach both arms up and back. Make sure to do both sides. This is a pose to exalt the Lord's Name above all names with your body. Ponder the ways you exalt the Lord on your mat and in your life—through your words, actions and thoughts.

SCRIPTURE:
Be exalted, O God, above the highest heavens! May your glory shine over all the earth. (Psalm 57:5)

PRAYER:
Lord, exalted on high, I recite with joy *Psalm 148:13: Let them praise the name of the LORD, for his name alone is exalted; his splendor is above the earth and the heavens.* I do exalted warriors and every position as a physical exaltation to you! Here I am to praise you with my entire body and being. Thank you for calling me and loving me. Reign in me, Lord. Amen.

೧౨

Day 122
TRIKONASANA – TRIANGLE POSE

For the triangle pose, start in a standing position, then draw one leg back about three feet, keeping your legs straight and with heel-to-heel alignment. Both feet are directed forward with back toes out about 45 degrees. Reach your front fingertips forward as far as they can go, then down, and lift your other arm straight up. Advanced options include drawing your hands together out in front of you, working a half bind with your top arm or a full bind with arms coming to meet behind your front leg. Make sure to keep your chest lifted and in line with your front leg. Hold a few breaths and reverse sides. How do you connect with the Father, Son and Holy Spirit? What do they each signify for you and your faith? Take a moment to ponder the Trinity.

SCRIPTURE:
May the grace of the Lord Jesus Christ, and the love of God, and the fellowship of the Holy Spirit be with you all. (2 Corinthians 13:14)

PRAYER:
Alpha and Omega, I give praise to you. I marvel at your nature, which is beyond my comprehension yet is intimately present—Father, Son and Spirit. I hear *John 14:17: The Spirit of truth. The world cannot accept him, because it neither sees him nor knows him. But you know him, for he lives with you and will be in you.* Like a cord of three strands, your love is harnessed to me. I come into the triangle pose to physically express being rooted in peace, tied in love and sealed in grace. Glory to you! Amen.

∞

Day 123
VIPARITA TRIKONASANA – REVERSE TRIANGLE

For reverse triangle, start in the triangle pose with the right leg forward a few feet from the left in heel-to-heel alignment, back toes forward and out about 45 degrees, then draw your left arm back and down and your right arm up. Hold a few breaths and reverse sides. The reverse triangle is like a tent: your legs are forming the tent body, your lower arm is like an opening flap and your top arm is like a pole that provides structure. Have you ever slept in a tent? Could you feel its fragility and its strength? How can you experience your body being like a tent? How can you grasp this earthly tent/heavenly tent concept shared in today's scripture, 2 Corinthians 5:1? Share your responses with Jesus.

SCRIPTURE:
For we know that if the earthly tent we live in is destroyed, we have a building from God, an eternal house in heaven, not built by human hands. (2 Corinthians 5:1)

PRAYER:
Lord, thank you for transforming my 'earthly tent' into your heavenly likeness. I remember *Romans 6:10-11: The death he died, he died to sin once for all; but the life he lives, he lives to God. In the same way, count yourselves dead to sin but alive to God in Christ Jesus.* Jesus, please make me alive in you and draw me into your tent in this practice. Amen.

෧ఎ

Day 124
PARSVOTTANASANA – INTENSE SIDE STRETCH, PYRAMID POSE

For the pyramid pose, start in a standing position and step your left foot back about two to three feet, toes forward with left toes out 45 degrees; maintain heel-to-heel alignment. Legs engage and hands level your hips to the front then go up and with flat back fold forward. Lower your head to your front shin, bring your arms down to the mat, then stretch your hands back. This posture is said to calm your mind and improve digestion. What calms your mind? How does the peace of Christ rule in your heart? How do you feel at peace with your life and with others right now? Share your responses with Jesus.

SCRIPTURE:

Let the peace of Christ rule in your hearts, since as members of one body you were called to peace. And be thankful. (Colossians 3:15)

PRAYER:

Lord, I remember the words in one of Paul's letters to the church of Thessalonians in *2 Thessalonians 3:16: Now may the Lord of peace himself give you peace at all times and in every way. The Lord be with all of you.* Yes Lord, may your presence be with all. Help me cultivate a spirit of peace here on the mat. I hear *Jude 1:2: Mercy, peace and love be yours in abundance.* Please let your divine mercy rule in my heart as I practice with others and throughout all my daily interactions. Amen.

∽

Day 125
PARIVRTTA UTKATASANA – PRAYER TWIST

For the prayer twist, start in chair pose and bring your hands to your heart center; then, lift your chest and twist so your left elbow goes outside of the right knee. You can keep your hands at your heart center, open them up, or take a half or full bind. Hold a few breaths and then switch sides. While you're in the prayer twist, imagine what it would have been like trying to stay up and pray with Jesus in the Garden of Gethsemane right before he was arrested. Remember, his friends fell asleep on him three times that very night! What are some things you can do to sit still and pray at night? Have you ever fallen asleep while praying? Have you not stayed by someone's side when they needed you? Conversely, has a friend not stayed by you when you needed it? Commune with Jesus about these experiences.

SCRIPTURE:

Then Jesus went with his disciples to a place called Gethsemane, and he said to them, "Sit here while I go over there and pray." He took Peter and the two sons of Zebedee along with him, and he began to be sorrowful and troubled. Then he said to them, "My soul is overwhelmed with sorrow to the point of death. Stay here and keep watch with me." (Matthew 26:36-38)

PRAYER:

Lord, here I am with alertness to admit and apologize for all the times I have fallen asleep on you, and the times I have forgotten to be your hands and feet and have fallen asleep on others. In your great mercy, Father, please forgive me. Cleanse me of my iniquity in the twist. I remember *Matthew 26:41: Watch and pray so that you will not fall into temptation. The spirit is willing, but the flesh is weak.* Strengthen me with your supernatural strength so that I may stay alert and bless your sheep; keep me away from temptation. Amen.

၆၀

Day 126
PARIVRTTA ANJANEYASANA – REVOLVING CRESCENT LUNGE

For revolving crescent lunge from the crescent lunge with your right leg forward and your left leg back, bring your hands to your heart center, lift your chest, and place your left elbow outside of your right knee. As you inhale, lengthen through the crown of your head and draw your chest upwards; then, as you exhale, deepen the twist by drawing your belly button towards your spine. If you prefer, drop your back knee down to the mat for stability. Advanced options are to open your arms or take a bind. Hold for several breaths, then reverse sides. This is a cleansing posture because it compresses your internal organs as you twist and draws fresh blood to those organs as you come out of the twist. You move into this pose with your hands at your heart, symbolizing an engagement with the Lord. How do you draw in God's presence throughout your day and let the Spirit heal and bind you in any areas where you need mending? Commune with Jesus about any areas that may need binding now.

SCRIPTURE:

Come, let us return to the LORD. He has torn us to pieces but he will heal us; he has injured us but he will bind up our wounds. (Hosea 6:1)

PRAYER:

Sovereign Lord, I come to the mat to return to you and draw near you. I thank you for your healing presence. Every time I draw my hands to my heart and twist, I hear *Isaiah 1:18: "Come now, let us settle the matter," says the LORD. "Though your sins are like scarlet, they shall be as white as snow; though they are red as crimson, they shall be like wool."* Thank you, great healer and redeemer. Please bathe me in your love and grace, and purify me from the inside out. Amen.

∾

Day 127
PARIVRTTA PARSVOKANASANA – REVOLVED WARRIOR 1, REVOLVED EXTENDED SIDE ANGLE

For the revolved warrior 1 pose, start in warrior 1 with your right leg forward, knee in line with the ankle and the left leg back with your foot bladed down and toes pointed as far forward as is accessible for you. Arms come to the prayer position at heart center and twist so that your left elbow is outside your right knee. Hold a few breaths and then reverse sides. How can you find stillness in this challenging asana and trust the Lord will work in you, through you and for you? What battles has the Lord fought for you? Can you think of an unfavorable situation where the Lord gave you a sense of victory despite the outward circumstances? Ponder where in your life you are in need of His presence now.

SCRIPTURE:

You will not have to fight this battle. Take up your positions; stand firm and see the deliverance the LORD will give you, Judah and Jerusalem. Do not be afraid; do not be discouraged. Go out to face them tomorrow, and the LORD will be with you. (2 Chronicles 20:17)

PRAYER:

Lord, thank you for fighting for me and staying present with me through each sensation and experience. I remember *Joshua 1:9: Have I not commanded you? Be strong and courageous. Do not be afraid; do not be discouraged, for the LORD your God will be with you wherever you go.* Thank you for your constant presence. I still myself in the revolved warrior 1 pose assured that you will fight for me on the mat and in life. Amen.

꩜

Day 128
PARIVRTTA TRIKONASANA – REVOLVED TRIANGLE

For the revolved triangle pose from the warrior 1 with your right foot forward and in heel-to-heel alignment, straighten your front leg, reach your left hand forward and down to the outside of the right foot, and draw your right hand up. You may use a block to support your bottom hand and help you hold the twist. Remember to do both sides and in this challenging pose, reflect on the areas of your life where you've stumbled. Commune with Jesus about where you may be stumbling now, whether in a certain relationship or with a certain practice, aspect of your job or habit.

SCRIPTURE:
Though he may stumble, he will not fall, for the LORD upholds him with his hand. (Psalm 37:24)

PRAYER:
Lord, thank you for upholding me in your hand. Infuse every part of my body and life with Spirit. Please forgive me for the areas where I have lost sight of your presence and help me draw it back in fullness. As I stretch, twist, engage and soften here on the mat, I fall in and out of postures. I try to gaze upward but am afraid of falling, I quickly look down. In such moments I hear the words of *1 Samuel 2:4: The bows of the warriors are broken, but those who stumbled are armed with strength*. Lord, in so many ways I stumble as I aim to obey your words, yet you continue to re-arm me with strength. I give all praise to you! Amen.

꩜

Day 129
NAVASANA – BOAT POSE

For the boat pose, start in a seated position with your legs forward and your knees bent. Draw your chest back until you feel your core engage, then reach your legs up and hold your arms out parallel to the floor, palms up. Continue to lift your chest and draw your shoulders back. In the boat pose reflect on how has the Lord guided you through 'storms' in your life, calmed waters that were raging around you and shown you dry ground. How have you been strengthened through these sorts of experiences? Commune with Jesus about any current 'storms' you're facing now.

SCRIPTURE:
When the dove returned to him in the evening, there in its beak was a freshly plucked olive leaf! Then Noah knew that the water had receded from the earth. (Genesis 8:11)

PRAYER:
Father, just as you had the dove carry fresh hope to Noah, you continuously provide fresh signs of hope to me. Thank you for your calming presence and shower of divine grace. Strengthen me through storms. I open my hands heavenward in the boat pose to offer up the fruits of my practice. With deepest gratitude for your abiding presence and for bring to me the fullness of Life, I say Amen.

೦౪

Day 130
LOW BOAT POSE

For the low boat pose, start in the high boat and lower your legs until they are hovering a few inches from the mat and your upper body back until it is a few inches off the mat. Keep both arms and legs straight. The low boat is a full body engagement pose with many variations to explore—paddling your boat by moving arms together from side to side or splitting your legs and then criss-crossing them one on top of the other. You may want to move from high to low boat and then from low to high boat. All these motions strengthen you from the inside out! What creative, unexpected ways has God steered you and/or delivered you? Who has helped part the waters in your life, defended you and protected you? How have you acknowledged them? Commune with Jesus about these experiences.

SCRIPTURE:

Then Moses stretched out his hand over the sea, and all that night the LORD drove the sea back with a strong east wind and turned it into dry land. The waters were divided, and the Israelites went through the sea on dry ground, with a wall of water on their right and on their left. (Exodus 14:21-22)

PRAYER:

Lord, who parts waters and rescues people, thank you for rescuing me time and time again and for placing others in my life to redirect me back to your holy truth when I get off track. Great Shepherd, I remember *Jeremiah 3:22: "Return, faithless people; I will cure you of backsliding." "Yes, we will come to you, for you are the LORD our God."* Lord, I come to listen to you, return to you, and to engage on the path you are leading me on through your holy words. Amen.

ᔕ

Day 131
ABDOMINAL CRUNCHES

Abdominal crunches are core strengthening movements done in power-styled classes. Start by lying on your back with your knees up and your feet hip-width apart planted on the mat by your gluts. Then lift your upper body as you exhale and lower it as you inhale. Continue with this alternating motion for a minute or two. Crunches can help in your practice because most asanas stem from core strength. Core muscles stabilize your frame, protect vital organs and support proper spinal alignment. Similarly, placing holy words in the core of your being protects, supports and strengthens you from the inside out in a spiritual sense. Identify your core values and beliefs, and commune with Jesus about keeping your core strong.

SCRIPTURE:

I am the vine; you are the branches. If a man remains in me and I in him, he will bear much fruit; apart from me you can do nothing. (John 15:5)

PRAYER:

Lord, I thank you for your presence. Please reside in the core of my being. I hear *Jeremiah 17:7-8: But blessed is the one who trusts in the LORD, whose confidence is in him. They will be like a tree planted by the water that sends out its roots by the stream. It does not fear when heat comes; its leaves are always green. It has no worries in a year of drought and never fails to bear fruit.* I place my trust and confidence in you. As I perform crunches, align my core with the core of your ministry, Jesus—to love the Father and love others. Amen.

◦◦

Day 132
ABDOMINAL TWISTS, BICYCLE, CRISSCROSS

To do abdominal twists, start in a supine position with your hands interlaced behind your head and your knees up. Next, draw your left elbow to your right knee and extend your left leg, then come back to your center and reverse directions—right elbow to left knee and extend your right leg. Keep alternating back and forth for a minute or two. The closer your extended leg goes to the mat, the more challenging it becomes. You can also do abdominal twists with straight legs (scissoring the legs) for added difficulty if desired. Abdominal twists strengthen your external and internal oblique muscles. Reflecting on King Solomon's words in 1 Kings 3, he was able to tell which woman was the mother of the child by placing the women in a trying situation. How has the Lord provided you with a spirit of discernment in a difficult situation? When presented with two different viewpoints, how do you determine which side to believe? Commune with Jesus about any areas in your life where you need to foster a spirit of discernment.

SCRIPTURE:

The king said, "This one says, 'My son is alive and your son is dead,' while that one says, 'No! Your son is dead and mine is alive.'" Then the king said, "Bring me a sword." So they brought a sword for the king. He then gave an order: "Cut the living child in two and give half to one and half to the other." (1 Kings 3:23-25)

PRAYER:

Lord, I love you and seek to express it on the mat. I remember that when Solomon first took the throne, he asked for wisdom. *1 Kings 3:9: So give your servant a discerning heart to govern your people and to distinguish between right and wrong. For who is able to govern this great people of yours?* Like Solomon, enliven me with a spirit of discernment and insight, that I may walk in your ways, follow your commands and provide justice and mercy where needed. As I scissor my legs in the crisscross pose, cut out any area of my life where I'm not serving you, and strengthen the core of my being in Truth. Amen.

∽

Day 133
CORKSCREW POSE

To do the corkscrew, start in a seated position and place your feet on the ground, knees over your ankles and hands planted under your shoulders with your fingers pointing towards your feet. Lift your hips up, then them down and back up. Your knees may shift from side to side. Continue with this motion for about a minute or two. This pose can also be done laying supine, feet straight up and hips lifting to the right, left and down, then left, right and down. When it comes to core work like the corkscrew—do you sow consistent work so that you may attain a stronger body? Do you keep with it and not give up? Think about how you pour energy, cheerfulness and effort into your practice and in your daily life. Commune with Jesus about what you desire to give.

SCRIPTURE:

He told them, "The harvest is plentiful, but the workers are few. Ask the Lord of the harvest, therefore, to send out workers into his harvest field." (Luke 10:2)

PRAYER:

Lord, here I am to sow generously and harvest faithfully. I come excited to try any new postures cued and to do my routine ones with passion. When I give my all it brings me joy, inner peace and cheer. Lord, you make it fun! Let me not just cultivate goodness and kindness on the mat but in all aspects and areas of my life. Infused with your glorious light, I say Amen.

✹

Day 134
CORE EXERCISES FROM THE DOWNWARD FACING DOG POSE

Start in the downward facing dog pose and draw your right knee to your right elbow then to left elbow, back to right and then to the downward facing dog again. You might also want to hold your knee at one elbow or at your nose for a few breaths for extra core strengthening. Make sure to reverse sides. Your knee is making the motion of opening a door as it draws from elbow to elbow. How have you opened the door of your heart and how do you open all the 'rooms' of your life to the Lord—inviting Him into each relationship and activity? Commune with Jesus about where you may still need to open the door.

SCRIPTURE:

Here I am! I stand at the door and knock. If anyone hears my voice and opens the door, I will come in and eat with that person, and they with me. (Revelation 3:20)

PRAYER:

Jesus, thank you for asking the Father to send me a Counselor, the Spirit of Truth to be with me always. Lord, I am here to keep the door of my heart, mind and spirit open and receptive to your light and to be attentive to your presence. I remember *John 14:19-20 Before long, the world will not see me anymore, but you will see me. Because I live, you also will live.* I move as an active expression of gratitude for this mighty blessing here on the mat. Let it stem in my core and radiate out through all my limbs. Amen.

✹

Day 135
DOLPHIN POSE

For the dolphin pose from the downward facing dog, come down onto your forearms and keep them parallel to each other or draw your hands together and interlace your fingers in front of you. Lower your hips until they form a straight line from your heels to the crown of your head. Then raise and lower your hips—essentially moving like a dolphin. Jonah was swallowed by the fish when he was running away from God. In what ways have you rebelled, and like with Jonah, how did the Lord save and restore you through the experience? Commune with the Lord about any ways that you may be 'running away' from Him or from something that He wants to bring you through in your life.

SCRIPTURE:
Now the LORD provided a huge fish to swallow Jonah, and Jonah was in the belly of the fish three days and three nights. (Jonah 1:17)

PRAYER:
Lord, please forgive me for the times and ways I have run away. Draw me back to you. I remember that after Jonah had been spat out by the big fish, he listened to you and went to Nineveh to preach, and you saved more than 120,000 people through this act! Oh gracious and compassionate Father, deliver me from my rebellion. I come to engage with you on my mat that I my further live out Your calling for my life. Amen.

෴

Day 136
VIRABHADRASANA 3 – WARRIOR 3

For the warrior 3 pose, start standing with your arms straight up over your head; stabilize yourself on one leg and extend the other back while your chest and arms reach forward in proportion to your extended leg lifting. Your hips stay square and your legs are straight and active. Hold a few breaths and switch sides. The warrior 3 pose is a challenging balancing posture that requires focus. Likewise, it requires focus to stand in God's love, light and compassion and not succumb to fleshly instincts to complain, criticize, condemn or gossip. Reflect on *Ephesians 4:29 Do not let any unwholesome talk come out of your mouths, but only what is helpful for building others up according to their needs, that it may benefit those who listen.* In what situations do you find it hard not to criticize or complain? How does acting in alignment with the Lord in these situations challenge you? Take a moment to commune with Jesus.

SCRIPTURE:

Therefore put on the full armor of God, so that when the day of evil comes, you may be able to stand your ground, and after you have done everything, to stand. (Ephesians 6:13)

PRAYER:

Lord, I come to be steadied in your truth, grace and peace so that it may be evident in my actions. Thank you for the blessing of each dialogue and conversation I have with others; there is so much to learn from each interaction. Please forgive me for the times when I have neglected to build others up according to their needs and instead have been critical or self-absorbed. I earnestly desire to learn how to communicate with others according to your word, remembering Colossians 4:6 *Let your conversation be always full of grace, seasoned with salt, so that you may know how to answer everyone.* Help me live out Ephesians 6:18 *pray in the Spirit on all occasions with all kinds of prayers and requests. With this in mind, be alert and always keep on praying for all the Lord's people.* With this sacred intention, I say Amen.

~

Day 137
TULANDANDASANA – BALANCING STICK POSE

To do the balancing stick pose, start by standing with your hands together in prayer and shift your weight to one foot; lift your other leg back while your torso moves forward proportional to your back leg lifting. Form a steeple grip with your index fingers and extend your arms outward in front of you while your biceps hug your ears. Hold for a few breaths and switch sides. This asana requires focus, and may serve as a physical expression of an inner positioning of your body as a temple for the Holy Spirit. In the balancing stick pose, reflect on your relationship with your body. How do you perceive it? What is your attitude about it? Speak freely to Jesus about your body.

SCRIPTURE:

You are altogether beautiful, my darling; there is no flaw in you. (Song of Solomon 4:7)

PRAYER:

Father, I bring my hands together in prayer and thank you for forming and fashioning me. You see me as beautiful. As I seek balance here in your light, help me to perceive my body as you do. I desire to treat my body as your holy vessel so that I may have the stamina and strength to live out your calling in my life. I rejoice in *Song of Solomon 7:6 How beautiful you are and how pleasing, my love, with your delights!* Delighting in You, I say Amen.

❧

Day 138
DAKASANA – AIRPLANE POSE

To do the airplane pose start in a standing position and draw one leg back with your chest moving forward proportionately. Both arms reach straight back in line with your body. Aim for a straight line from the crown of your head to your lifted back foot, and keep both legs straight and active. Hold for a few breaths and reverse sides. The airplane pose is thought to have an elevating effect. How has the Lord given you the strength to rise above any unfavorable circumstances in life? Who or what helps to elevate your thoughts, attitude and perspective? Commune with Jesus about any ways you need to elevate your vantage point.

SCRIPTURE:

I can do all things through Him who gives me strengthen. (Philippians 4:13)

PRAYER:

Lord, thank you for strengthening me from the inside out, and for being my strength when I am weak. You lift my spirits even when they feel as physically heavy as an airplane. Praise to You! I remember Joseph's words to his brothers in *Genesis 45:7 But God sent me ahead of you to preserve for you a remnant on earth and to save your lives by a great deliverance.* Your ways are higher than my ways, Lord. Please shift my perspective and draw me into alignment with your Spirit in the airplane pose. Like Joseph, use me to show others the good you bring to all situations; even the situations that appear to have been intended for bad, Father, you can use them for good. Hallelujah! Amen.

∾

Day 139
ARDHA CHANDRASANA – HALF MOON POSE

For the half moon pose, from extended side angle with your right leg forward, draw your right hand to the floor, straighten your right leg and lift your left leg up to be parallel to the mat. Your top hip opens and your left arm reaches high. Work your gaze upward and your right fingers to lift off the mat. Hold for a few breaths and reverse sides. An advanced option is to dance your half moon by reaching your top arm around and grabbing the ankle of the extended leg, further opening your top hip. The half moon pose is thought to harmonize and expand your internal energy. Do you know where the moon is in its cycle? When was the last time you watched the sunrise or sunset? How do you balance your time gazing outward at God's beauty in nature and inward on His Spirit dwelling in you? Share your responses with Jesus.

SCRIPTURE:

The moon will shine like the sun, and the sunlight will be seven times brighter, like the light of seven full days, when the LORD binds up the bruises of his people and heals the wounds he inflicted. (Isaiah 30:26)

PRAYER:

Lord, I marvel at the ways you adorn nature—the moon, sun, stars, mountains, hills, valleys, animals, plants and people, and I thank you for all the ways you adorn me with your holy grace. In the half moon pose, I remember *Proverbs 4:18 The path of the righteous is like the first gleam of dawn, shining ever brighter until the full light of day*. Lord, please guide me in your everlasting light so that I may gleam like the dawn and extend your grace to others *'not seven times, but seventy-seven times' (Matthew 18:22)*. Stretching in your luminous glow, I say Amen.

ᏜᏜ

Day 140
PARIVRTTA ARDHA CHANDRASANA – REVOLVED HALF MOON

To do the revolved half moon pose, start standing and draw your right leg straight up behind you as your arms go forward. Then bring your right arm down to the mat so that your fingertips grace it. Raise your left arm and direct your gaze upward. Hold for a few breaths and then switch sides. An advanced option is to reach your lowered hand around your grounded ankle. Reflect on *Isaiah 51:5 My righteousness draws near speedily, my salvation is on the way, and my arm will bring justice to the nations. The islands will look to me and wait in hope for my arm*. In this challenging posture, in which you try to keep your gaze upward and fixed on your extended fingertips, ponder how you can extend your arms to those who are in need of justice and deliverance. Commune with Jesus about where justice may be needed now and how you may help.

SCRIPTURE:
Who has measured the waters in the hollow of his hand, or with the breadth of his hand marked off the heavens? Who has held the dust of the earth in a basket, or weighed the mountains on the scales and the hills in a balance? (Isaiah 40:12)

PRAYER:
Lord who measures the waters in the hollow of your hand, I am awed by your majesty and strength. In gratitude for your deliverance, help me extend justice. *Proverbs 16:11 Honest scales and balances belong to the LORD; all the weights in the bag are of his making*. As I aim to balance on the mat, I place my hope in Your arms of righteousness and salvation and offer up this time as a prayer for those in need. I

remember *John 3:17 For God did not send his Son into the world to condemn the world, but to save the world through him,* and *James 2:13 Mercy triumphs over judgment.* Help me to focus on extending love and mercy. I rejoice in *Ezekiel 34:16 I will search for the lost and bring back the strays. I will bind up the injured and strengthen the weak, but the sleek and the strong I will destroy. I will shepherd the flock with justice.* In gratitude, I say Amen.

∽

Day 141
URDHVA PRASARITA EKA PADASANA – STANDING SPLITS

To do the standing splits pose, from a standing forward fold shift your weight to one leg and lift your other leg straight up as high as you can. Work your hands in toward your grounded foot, possibly wrapping them around your ankle. Straighten your back as the crown of your head goes toward the mat and your forehead draws to your shin. Hold for a few breaths and reverse sides. With one leg lifted high to the heavens in standing splits, ponder how you place the Lord first in your financial decisions. Reflecting on your spending, saving, investing and giving habits, commune with Jesus about how you show devotion through financial stewardship.

SCRIPTURE:

No servant can serve two masters. Either he will hate the one and love the other, or he will be devoted to the one and despise the other. You cannot serve both God and Money. (Luke 16:13)

PRAYER:

Lord, I come to serve you with the financial resources you have entrusted to me and with my body. I trust You to provide for my all of needs. I give freely to You by giving to others out of the love that springs in my heart. Please forgive me for the times I have neglected to do so. As I stretch physically on my mat, stretch my perspective, especially as it relates to money. Help me to be a good steward. Open me to the joys of giving, saving and investing, and provide me with a spirit of encouragement and discipline that I may multiply the talents and treasures You have so graciously given me. I remember the parable of the talents, *Matthew 25:23 The man with the two talents also came. 'Master,' he said, 'you entrusted me with two talents; see, I have gained two more.'"His master replied, 'Well done, good and faithful servant! You have been faithful with a few things; I will put you in charge of many things. Come and share your master's happiness!'* Jesus, I desire to be a faithful and good servant; help me to give to 'Caesar' what is 'Caesar's' (my financial responsibilities such as paying taxes) and to God what is God's. Amen.

∽

Day 142
EXTENDED HAND-TO-BIG-TOE POSE, UTTHITA HASTA PADANGUSTASANA

To do the extended hand-to-big-toe pose from a forward fold, bring your left hand to your hip and your right index and middle fingers (peace fingers) around your right big toe, then lift your right leg straight up and out in front of you and hold for a few breaths. Next draw your right foot out to the right side and gaze left; take a few breaths while holding this position, then move your leg back to the center and down; reverse sides. As an option, you can use a strap instead of grabbing your foot with your fingers. This asana strengthens your ankles and legs, and improves your sense of balance. Can you feel all your limbs working together? Similarly, can you feel all elements of your life working together? Do you feel united and connected to your family, those at work, at church, and in your organizations and groups? Where may the spirit of unity be lacking? Share your responses with Jesus.

SCRIPTURE:
The eye cannot say to the hand, "I don't need you!" And the head cannot say to the feet, "I don't need you!" On the contrary, those parts of the body that seem to be weaker are indispensable. (1 Corinthians 12:21-22)

PRAYER:
Lord, I come to this mat to unite myself in spirit, body and truth, reciting *1 Corinthians 12:24-27 But God has put the body together, giving greater honor to the*

parts that lacked it, so that there should be no division in the body, but that its parts should have equal concern for each other. If one part suffers, every part suffers with it; if one part is honored, every part rejoices with it. Now you are the body of Christ, and each one of you is a part of it. Jesus, guide me in this type of unity in all the various elements of my life and relationships. Lead me in wholeness and holiness here on the mat. Amen.

∽

Day 143
VRKSASANA – TREE POSE

To do the tree pose, start standing with your hands in prayer. Kickstand your right leg and place the bottom of your right foot on your left leg next to your ankle, calf or upper thigh. Direct your right knee outward to the side. You may keep your arms at your heart center or extend them upward as though you are 'growing your branches'. Work your gaze upward, or try closing your eyes for a challenge. As you think about your life, in what ways are you growing in your faith? What 'seeds' (ideas/skills/talents) are growing within you? Who is taking note and helping to develop them? Conversely, what seeds are you planting in others? Share your responses with Jesus.

SCRIPTURE:

Jesus entered Jericho and was passing through. A man was there by the name of Zacchaeus; he was a chief tax collector and was wealthy. He wanted to see who Jesus was, but because he was short he could not see over the crowd. So he ran ahead and climbed a sycamore-fig tree to see him, since Jesus was coming that way. When Jesus reached the spot, he looked up and said to him, "Zacchaeus, come down immediately. I must stay at your house today." So he came down at once and welcomed him gladly. All the people saw this and began to mutter, "He has gone to be the guest of a sinner." But Zacchaeus stood up and said to the Lord, "Look, Lord! Here and now I give half of my possessions to the poor, and if I have cheated anybody out of anything, I will pay back four times the amount." Jesus said to him, "Today salvation has come to this house, because this man, too, is a son of Abraham. For the Son of Man came to seek and to save the lost." (Luke 19:1-10)

PRAYER:

Jesus, like Zaccheus, I want to see you. I form the tree pose so that I may catch a glimpse of your presence. As a tree, please nourish me with your light and living waters. Help me to remain on your holy vine and creatively express my faith here on the mat. Jesus, do yoga with me and stay in my house. I welcome you into my heart! Amen.

༄

Day 144
ARDHA BADDHA PADMOTTANASANA – HALF BOUND LOTUS STANDING FORWARD BEND

To do the half bound lotus standing forward bend, start standing and bring your left leg up; position it in the half lotus, foot flexed and secured on right thigh, knee down. An advanced option is to reach your left arm around your back and grab the big toe of the left foot with your two peace fingers, and then hinge at your lower hips with a flat back. Your right arm may wrap around your right ankle. Hold for a few breaths, then reverse these steps to come out of the pose and switch sides. As you seal your peace fingers around your toe and bow forward, this posture expresses an awesome prostration to the Lord. It physically expresses being bound in the Lord's love, sealed in peace and surrendered in light. Reflect on how can you recognize God's presence in your life and read *Exodus 34:5-6 Then the LORD came down in the cloud and stood there with him and proclaimed his name, the LORD. And he passed in front of Moses, proclaiming, "The LORD, the LORD, the compassionate and gracious God, slow to anger, abounding in love and faithfulness."*

SCRIPTURE:

You, Lord, are forgiving and good, abounding in love to all who call to you. (Psalm 86:5)

PRAYER:

Name above all names, Holy One, thank you for abounding in love and faithfulness. I rejoice in *Psalm 86:15 But you, Lord, are a compassionate and gracious God, slow to anger, abounding in love and faithfulness,* and in *Numbers 14:18 The LORD is slow* to anger, abounding in love and forgiving sin and rebellion. Yet he does not leave the guilty unpunished. Let this practice be an act of reverence to You. Amen.

∽

Day 145
PADA ANGUSHTHASANA – TIPTOE POSE

To do the tiptoe pose, start in the standing position and bring your right leg up with your right ankle positioned on your left thigh, knee down (half lotus). Next, bring your hands heart center and, if your balance is steady, bend forward with a flat back. Your left leg stays straight as you fold forward, and your arms come down. Then bend the left leg and lower your gluts until your tailbone makes contact with your left heel. Your left toes and fingertips are the only body parts touching the mat. A final expression would be to bring one arm to your heart and then the other into the prayer position. Hold for a few breaths, then return your arms to the mat; straighten your left leg and come up slowly to stand. Reverse sides. This challenging and stimulating posture requires your full attention. Developing intimate relationships in our lives also takes care and attention. Intimacy is a subject often tiptoed around in faith communities, but it need not be this way. How has physical intimacy and love factored into your life? In what ways have those intimate experiences connected you with the Lord? In what ways do you feel like you are His beloved? Commune with Jesus about intimacy.

SCRIPTURE:

Look! Listen! There's my lover! Do you see him coming? Vaulting the mountains, leaping the hills. My lover is like a gazelle, graceful; like a young stag, virile. Look at him there, on tiptoe at the gate, all ears, all eyes—ready! My lover has arrived and he's speaking to me! (Song of Solomon 2:8 MSG)

PRAYER:

Lord, thank you for calling me and embracing me in your love. I hear Isaiah 54:5: For your Maker is your husband—the LORD Almighty is his name—the Holy One of Israel is your Redeemer; he is called the God of all the earth. Holy One, I am yours;

caress me in your hands. Let this time on the mat be a dance with you. Though I may stumble as I turn my gaze upward to see you, I know you will keep the rhythm with your Spirit and waltz me back into your righteous arms. Lord, lead me in this practice and life. Amen.

∽

Day 146
FIGURE FOUR POSE

To do the figure four pose from the chair position, bring your right leg up, place your right ankle on the left thigh while your right knee stays out to the side, foot flexed. Hands may stay raised or come to your heart, and if so, draw your elbows towards the right knee and ankle. Hold a few breaths and reverse sides. As you explore the figure four pose, reflect on how the Lord has made things holy in your life; consider the acts of submission you have chosen to do as a way to draw near the Lord. What may need to be made holy in your life now? Commune with Jesus.

SCRIPTURE:
When you enter the land and plant any kind of fruit tree, regard its fruit as forbidden. For three years you are to consider it forbidden; it must not be eaten. In the fourth year all its fruit will be holy, an offering of praise to the LORD. (Leviticus 19:23-24)

PRAYER:
Lord, thank you for making things holy in my life, and for your presence on the four corners of the mat. I am deeply grateful for your healing, restoring and redeeming touch. Jesus, I remember the story of how you raised Lazarus, described in *John 11:39-40:"But, Lord,"said Martha, the sister of the dead man,"by this time there is a bad odor, for he has been there four days."Then Jesus said,"Did I not tell you that if you believe, you will see the glory of God?"*Surrendered and believing all things are possible through you, I say Amen.

∽

Day 147
EKA PADA GALAVASANA – FLYING CROW, FLYING FIGURE FOUR POSE

To do the flying crow pose, start in figure four (right ankle placed on left knee, right foot is flexed and right knee is out to the side) and slowly draw your arms down to the mat. Hook your right foot around your right bicep, bend your elbows slightly and shift your weight forward so that you are balancing on your hands. Note your right shin is balancing on your upper arms. From here, extend your left leg up and work to straighten it. For those with an extremely advanced practice, draw your head to the mat for a one-legged tripod headstand. Hold for a few breaths, then reverse the steps to come out safely and switch sides. Think of the wondrous mystery of flying. Whether or not you can get into this challenging posture, the Lord can lift you up and that is a glorious thing! In what ways have you soared with the Lord—be it physically, emotionally or spiritually? What sensations did it evoke? Meditate on *Habakkuk 3:11 Sun and moon stood still in the heavens at the glint of your flying arrows, at the lightning of your flashing spear.*

SCRIPTURE:
Who are these that fly along like clouds, like doves to their nests? (Isaiah 60:8)

PRAYER:
Lord, I thank you for enabling me to soar in your light and love. Help me to see things from a higher vantage point so that I may further understand your holy perspective. I remember *Zechariah 5:1: I looked again, and there before me was a flying scroll.* Lord, as I shift my focus to you, let me see any 'flying scrolls' you place in front of me. I am here to fly to you, Lord. Guide me in the shadow of your wings. Amen.

༄

Day 148
YOGI DANDASANA – GRASSHOPPER POSE

To do the grasshopper pose, start in the figure four pose (right leg up with right ankle on your left thigh, right foot flexed and knee out to the side) and draw your hands to prayer. Then twist your torso left and lower your hands to the floor. Place the bottom of your right foot on the backside of your right arm; shift your weight forward, engage your core and lift your left leg up and out. This asana requires focus, balance and belief. It is an extremely challenging asana to do. Like the Israelites in Numbers 13, how can you maintain your belief that the Lord will carry you through each experience (including attempting the grasshopper pose)? How do you place your confidence in His strength in the face of opposition? Like the Nephilim, reflect on any external opposition you may be facing now, as well as any internal opposition, like doubts in your own mind. Commune with Jesus about how you give response.

SCRIPTURE:

They said, "The land we explored devours those living in it. All the people we saw there are of great size. We saw the Nephilim there (the descendants of Anak come from the Nephilim). We seemed like grasshoppers in our own eyes, and we looked the same to them." (Numbers 13:32-33)

PRAYER:

Lord, I come to place my trust fully in you. Taking the position of a grasshopper on my mat, I realize how little it takes to get out of alignment and fall. I rejoice that in the midst of my weakness and fragility, your strength prevails. Help me to face opposition with courage. I remember *1 Corinthians 1:27: But God chose the foolish things of the world to shame the wise; God chose the weak things of the world to shame the strong.* I place my confidence in you and know you will deliver me in wondrous and glorious ways. Praise to you! Amen.

⁓

Day 149
GARUDASANA – EAGLE POSE

To do the eagle from chair pose, your right arm goes under and around your left arm and your right leg goes up and around your left leg. Work to keep your back straight as if sitting in a chair. Ankles, knees, elbows, wrists and fingertips align straight up. Hold a few breaths and switch sides. The eagle pose is thought to increase your ability to concentrate. How has the Lord renewed your vision at various stages of your life? Commune with Jesus about any ways you may need to reestablish hope.

SCRIPTURE:

But those who hope in the LORD will renew their strength. They will soar on wings like eagles; they will run and not grow weary, they will walk and not be faint. (Isaiah 40:31)

PRAYER:

Good Shepherd, I come to reaffirm my hope in you. Thank you for always providing me with the endurance and vision I need to rise above any opposition. I remember you told Moses to tell the people in *Exodus 19:4 You yourselves have seen what I did to Egypt, and how I carried you on eagles' wings and brought you to myself.* Praise and glory to you in the Highest! Rock and Redeemer, I soar in hope during this practice and in life. Help me to keep my eyes on the prize, the prize of being with you now and forever and always. Amen.

ᢉᢦ

Day 150
FLYING EAGLE POSE

From the eagle pose, your elbows draw down to your knees, your belly lifts up and in, and your back arches as you curl. Hold steady for a few breaths or draw your elbows up and down a few times strengthening your core. When you are ready, unwrap your legs and arms and switch sides. Another option is to simply unwrap your leg and extend it back and up. This is the warrior 3 pose with eagle arms. You are balancing on one straight leg with the other held up at a 90–degree angle and your hips square to the mat. After a few breaths, come into the crescent lunge with eagle arms by setting your extended leg down a few feet behind the already standing leg and lift your elbows high, creating a gentle back bend. Stay here a few breaths then unwrap your arms, come to stand at the front of the mat and do the same motions on your other side. As you flow from one posture to the next, reflect on how you find refuge in the Lord in the motions of your life. What are some ways you can keep from getting wrapped up in the emotions of different events and situations and keep your focus steady on the Lord despite whatever is happening around you or in you? Commune with Jesus.

SCRIPTURE:

He will cover you with his feathers, and under his wings you will find refuge; his faithfulness will be your shield and rampart. (Psalm 91:4)

PRAYER:

Lord, who shields me with faith, delivers me from evil and clothes me in salvation, thank you for your divine protection. I remember *Deuteronomy 31:6: Be strong and courageous. Do not be afraid or terrified because of them, for the LORD your God goes with you; he will never leave you nor forsake you.* Thank you for this mighty blessing. I come to the mat to breathe, flow and soar as I trust in you. I rejoice in *Psalm 36:7: How priceless is your unfailing love, O God! People take refuge in the shadow of your wings,* and *Psalm 63:7: Because you are my help, I sing in the shadow of your wings.* Hallelujah and Amen.

∽

Day 151
NATARAJASANA – DANCER'S POSE, LORD OF THE DANCE

To do the dancer's pose, start by standing with your arms straight up overhead. Bring your right arm to your side, palm up and thumb back; bend your right knee and reach for the inside of your foot. Draw your knees together and reach up through your extended left fingertips and kick into your hand. Your left hand will come forward in proportion to how high your right leg is extended upward. Hold this pose for a few breaths and switch sides. This asana is a beautiful expression of the Lord's saving right hand. How has the Lord parted waters in your life and provided you with safe passage when you felt an enemy of sorts was after you? How have friends and family members protected and shielded you? Likewise, how have they come around you and celebrated victorious moments? Commune with Jesus.

SCRIPTURE:

Then Miriam the prophetess, Aaron's sister, took a tambourine in her hand, and all the women followed her, with tambourines and dancing. (Exodus 15:20)

PRAYER:

Lord who parts waters, what an indescribable, glorious blessing it is to be led in your light and holy power. I joyfully declare *Psalm 150:4: Praise him with tambourine and dancing, praise him with the strings and flute, rings in my ears.* As I balance like a dancer here on my mat, I acknowledge it is you who keeps me from stumbling. You lift me up when I fall down and draw me into community with other believers so that we may be mutually encouraged. Thank you, Father. Amen.

∽

Day 152
DHANURASANA – BOW POSE

To do the full bow pose, start in the standing position and shift your weight to one foot, then raise the other up and back, and reach behind with both arms to grasp the foot. Lift your heart as you draw your elevated leg up higher, hold for a few breaths and switch sides. To do the floor bow, lie on your belly with your knees bent and reach both arms back to take hold of your outer ankles. Lift your chest and kick your feet into your hands for a few full breaths. You may use a strap in either of these postures to reach your feet if needed. Reflect on King Joash while you're in the bow pose; how can you keep 'firing arrows', showing perseverance through difficult times both on your mat and in your life? Commune with Jesus about perseverance and where your may need to cultivate a spirit of commitment to stay with the tasks at hand.

SCRIPTURE:

"Open the east window," he said, and he opened it. "Shoot!" Elisha said, and he shot. "The LORD's arrow of victory, the arrow of victory over Aram!" Elisha declared. "You will completely destroy the Arameans at Aphek." Then he said, "Take the arrows," and the king took them. Elisha told him, "Strike the ground." He struck it three times and stopped. The man of God was angry with him and said, "You should have struck the ground five or six times;

then you would have defeated Aram and completely destroyed it. But now you will defeat it only three times." (2 Kings 13:17-19)

PRAYER:

Lord, Great Archer, Your angels are equipped with flaming arrows. I remember *Lamentations 3:12-13: He drew his bow and made me the target for his arrows. He pierced my heart with arrows from his quiver.* Pierce my heart with your love and help me to continuously shoot flaming arrows of your holy light out to others. I desire to be an ever-arching bow drawn by your mighty, righteous arms. Amen.

⁂

Day 153
BAKASANA – CROW, CRANE POSE

To do the crow pose, start in a yogi squat and place your hands down, six to eight inches apart, with your fingers spread wide. Gaze about a foot in front of you, activate your core, bring your knees onto your upper arms and begin to shift your weight forward until you are balancing on your hands. This is a pose of finesse, coordination and focus; it is thought to help develop mental tranquility. Reflect on how the Lord provided for Elijah in 1 Kings 17:4 (today's scripture) and think about how He has blessed you through surprising sources. Take a moment to identify as many of these as you can. How might you still need to hone this sense of trust in the Lord's provision in your life? Pause and commune with Jesus.

SCRIPTURE:

You will drink from the brook, and I have directed the ravens to supply you with food there. (1 Kings 17:4)

PRAYER:

Lord, thank you for always providing for me. Please forgive me for the times I have lost sight of this holy blessing. I come to this practice mat to actively focus on you. I remember *Luke 12:24: Consider the ravens: They do not sow or reap, they have no storeroom or barn; yet God feeds them. And how much more valuable you are than birds!* As I aim to balance on my hands in this pose, let it be an outward expression of gratitude for your caring touches. Trusting in your glorious provision, I say Amen.

༄

Day 154
PARSVA BAKASANA – SIDE CROW, SIDE CRANE POSE

To do the side crow pose, start in a squat with your feet and knees together, then bring your hands down to the mat; your arms are shoulder width apart and your gaze is about a foot in of you. Come up onto your toe tips and swivel your knees to the outside of your left upper arm, and then draw your legs up. Hold for a few breaths and reverse sides. The side crow pose strengthens your arms and sense of balance. It requires steady attention and patience. How are you patient as you learn new yoga moves, and more importantly, in your life? How do you keep yourself from envying what others have? Conversely, how do you keep your pride in check? Share your responses with Jesus.

SCRIPTURE:

Love is patient, love is kind. It does not envy, it does not boast, it is not proud. (1 Corinthians 13:4)

PRAYER:

Jesus, thank you for serving as a role model for love during your ministry here on earth; please help me express that same love to others. I remember *2 Peter 3:9: The Lord is not slow in keeping his promise, as some understand slowness. Instead he is patient with you, not wanting anyone to perish, but everyone to come to repentance.* Lord, thank you for your active demonstration of love through your patience with me. I am so grateful for it. Like yoga poses, I fall out of obedience to your word time and time again; please forgive me. I so desperately want to keep it but often stumble. Good Shepherd, please lift me back up in your grace and help me show the fruits of your love. Help me to show patience to all your sheep. Amen.

༄

Day 155
VASISTHASANA – SIDE PLANK POSE

To do the side plank pose, start with your feet together in the high plank, then move your left hand to the center of your mat, tip your heels to the left and lift your right hand straight up, keeping your shoulders, hips and feet stacked. Option to drop the inside knee down and/or raise the top leg up. Break forth like the dawn as you lift your gaze and stabilize your body in a straight line perpendicular to the mat. Hold this pose for a few breaths then reverse sides. How are you engaging and growing stronger in the various sides of your life—spiritual, professional, personal, financial, social and emotional? Share your response with Jesus.

SCRIPTURE:
Then your light will break forth like the dawn, and your healing will quickly appear; then your righteousness will go before you, and the glory of the LORD will be your rear guard. (Isaiah 58:8)

PRAYER:
Lord, I am here to engage with you. I hear *Deuteronomy 5:32: So be careful to do what the LORD your God has commanded you; do not turn aside to the right or to the left.* Let the side plank pose be a reminder to keep my whole body and spirit focused on you. Though I turn my body physically on the mat, spiritually I aim to keep my focus directly, straightly and upwardly to you. Thank you for letting your light break forth from me and for strengthening my frame. Amen.

ᖇᕐ

Day 156
EKA PADA KOUNDINYASANA 1 – HUDDLERS 1, ONE-LEGGED SAGE POSE 1

To do the huddlers 1 pose, from the downward facing dog position, draw your right knee forward to the left elbow and place your right thigh on the backs of your upper arms. Keep your elbows bent and pinned in by your ribs; shift your weight forward, engage your core and lift your legs up (with your right leg out to your side and your left leg straight back). Hold for a few breaths and switch sides. Consider how you can keep yourself from being mastered by anything— the need to perform, to get into a certain posture, the need for a certain relationship, role or professional title. What things may not be beneficial in your life right now? Pause and commune with Jesus.

SCRIPTURE:

"I have the right to do anything," you say—but not everything is beneficial. "I have the right to do anything"—but I will not be mastered by anything. (1 Corinthians 6:12)

PRAYER:

Lord, remove anything from my life that is not beneficial. Please help me to identify these areas and not be mastered by any unhealthy thought, action or relationship. I remember *1 Corinthians 10:13: No temptation has overtaken you except what is common to mankind. And God is faithful; he will not let you be tempted beyond what you can bear. But when you are tempted, he will also provide a way out so that you can endure it.* Thank you Lord. I know you will provide a way out of the temptations I face. I acknowledge my temptations here on the mat so that you may help me to endure and overcome them. Amen.

∽

Day 157
EKA PADA KOUNDINYASANA 2 – HURDLERS 2, ONE-LEGGED SAGE POSE 2

To do the hurdlers 2 pose, from a wide legged low lunge with your right leg forward, draw your right arm under your right leg with your fingers forward and your elbows pinned in by your ribs and bent at a 90–degree angle. With your upper right thigh on your upper arm, extend your right leg up and out to your side as your back left leg extends up and your gaze is toward the right. Hold for a few breaths and switch sides. Simply drawing your knee to your elbow and back again a few times is great prep work for this challenging asana. Pondering hurdlers, reflect on how you leap into action in life. What sorts of journeys have you been compelled to take? What has been revealed to you on these journeys, and how have your travels allowed you to see things from a higher perspective? What leap may be next in your life? Share it with Jesus.

SCRIPTURE:
The LORD God is my strength, and he will make my feet like hinds' feet, and he will make me to walk upon mine high places. To the chief singer on my stringed instruments. (Habakkuk 3:19)

PRAYER:
Sovereign Lord, who makes my feet like hinds feet, I am eager to go on the journeys you have planned for me. Holy One, who gives deer and hinds the ability to see in dim lighting, may it be so with me as I practice here in this dimly lit space. Please enable me to spring up and radiate your light in dark places. I rejoice in *Psalm 18:33 He makes my feet like the feet of a deer; he causes me to stand on the heights.* I leap in my practice on the mat, for my trust is in you. Amen.

༺ঔ

Day 158
PARIVRTTA SURYA YANTRASANA – COMPASS POSE

To do the compass pose, start seated with your legs out in front of you and bring your right leg up with your left hand as you thread your right hand under your right leg until your right fingers touch the floor. Gaze up and keep your chin down; work both legs to be straight as you deepen into this advanced hamstring stretch. Hold a few breaths and reverse sides. The compass pose acts as a reminder that no matter how lost or turned around you may get in life, like the Prodigal Son (see Luke 15), the Lord will welcome you back. How have you gotten turned around? In what ways do you need to return to God at this stage with your behaviors and actions? Commune with Jesus.

SCRIPTURE:

So now I have sworn not to be angry with you, never to rebuke you again. Though the mountains be shaken and the hills be removed, yet my unfailing love for you will not be shaken nor my covenant of peace be removed," says the LORD, who has compassion on you. (Isaiah 54:9-10)

PRAYER:

Lord, I come to be internally and externally positioned and directed in you. Thank you for the ways you turn me around from sin and lead me beside quiet and true living waters. Please forgive me for the times I have acted stiff-necked and frustrated when I have been unable to perform a certain yoga pose, or when the events of my life have kept me from seeing clearly. In the midst of emotion, you draw me back as I confess my sin. Please wrap me once again in your mercy. As recorded in the Psalms, Exodus, Nehemiah and Jonah, you are a "compassionate and gracious God, slow to anger, abounding in love and faithfulness." Praise to you, Eternal Compass. Amen.

༄

Day 159
ASTAVAKRASANA – EIGHT-ANGLE, EIGHT-LIMBED STAFF POSE

To do the eight-angle pose, start in a seated position with your legs extended; draw your right leg up and work it behind your right shoulder while keeping your back straight. When you have the leg positioned there, begin to work your left leg up, hands firmly rooted by your sides with your fingers forward. Wrap your left leg around the right and shift your weight forward to balance on your hands. Hold a few breaths and switch sides. As you reflect on the number eight while you're in the eight-angle pose, note how it is shaped like the infinity sign. Consider how there are seven days in a week, and the eighth day marks the first day of a new week. Additionally, it was on the eighth day that circumcision took place in traditional Jewish custom. Circumcision was a physical marker of being God's chosen. How do you feel marked as 'chosen' and sealed in Spirit? Meditate on *Revelation 14:1: Then I looked, and there before me was the Lamb, standing on Mount Zion, and with him 144,000 who had his name and his Father's name written on their foreheads.*

SCRIPTURE:

You must give me the firstborn of your sons. Do the same with your cattle and your sheep. Let them stay with their mothers for seven days, but give them to me on the eighth day. (Exodus 22:29-30)
On the eighth day they must bring them for their cleansing to the priest at the entrance to the tent of meeting, before the LORD. (Leviticus 14:23)

PRAYER:

Father, thank you for Your Son Jesus, and for placing Your Spirit in me as a deposit for what is to come. Thank you for sacred rites, such as circumcision of the heart and for calling and anointing me. I understand that *'what counts is a new creation' (Galatians 6:15)* and muse *Luke 9:27-29: Truly I tell you, some who are standing here will not taste death before they see the kingdom of God. About eight days after Jesus said this, he took Peter, John and James with him and went up onto a mountain to pray. As he was praying, the appearance of his face changed, and his clothes became as bright as a flash of lightning.* Jesus, your wonders amaze me! Thank you for the symbolic nature of the number eight; may you lift me in light here on the mat. Amen.

∽

Day 160
MAYURASANA – PEACOCK POSE

To do the peacock pose, start kneeling, lean forward and press your palms on the floor with your fingers turned back toward your torso. With your elbows pressed against your abs, walk your feet back to a low plank position. Gaze ahead of you and draw your chest forward as your chin comes to rest softly to the mat; extend one leg up and then the other. An option is to lift your chin off the mat, and another is to position your legs in the lotus pose. The peacock position strengthens your wrists and forearms and tones your abdominal muscles. In the natural world, the peacock sheds its feathers every year and grows new brighter ones. Similarly, every time you try this posture, you will increase your ability to hold it; and every time you read God's word and apply it, you further shed unwholesome habits and develop righteous ones. How has the Lord's grace enabled you to act in new ways? Commune with Jesus about any bad habits you may be ready to give up and any good ones you could develop.

SCRIPTURE:

For his anger lasts only a moment, but his favor lasts a lifetime; weeping may stay for the night, but rejoicing comes in the morning. (Psalm 30:5)

PRAYER:

Lord, here on the mat, I repent of my sin to you—my faults, mistakes, inadequacy, lack of reliance on your Spirit and my hidden sins. I weep inwardly; your Holy Spirit convicts me, Lord. I remember *Psalm 40:13: Be pleased, to save me Lord*. Help me to act in a new way that aligns with truth, knowledge and love. Let your mercy reign in me as I confess my sins; refresh me in your light. I hear the command of *Isaiah 51:9: Awake, awake, arm of the Lord, clothe yourself with strength!* Just as the peacock sheds old feathers and grows new ones each year, let me shed my sins and put on your garment of salvation and holy strength here on the mat. Amen.

༄

Day 161
TOLASANA – SCALE POSE

To do the scale pose, start seated with your legs crossed. Place your hands by your sides with your fingers forward, and press downward with your hands to lift up your body. You can also keep your legs extended and work to elevate yourself. This posture strengthens your arms and wrists. What walls have you had to scale in your life? How has God helped you stand up to adversity and overcome obstacles? Commune with Jesus about any walls you may need to scale at this time.

SCRIPTURE:

With your help I can advance against a troop; with my God I can scale a wall. (2 Samuel 22:30)

PRAYER:

Lord, thank you for enabling me to scale walls. Please help me to overcome any obstacles that come my way. I hear Job's cry in *Job 6:2: If only my anguish could be weighed and all my misery be placed on the scales!* I remember the full story of Job and am amazed at how you returned to him a double portion of what he had owned and lost. Father, your scales reveal justice, love and blessing. I remember this as I aim to position myself in the scale pose. Victorious I AM, thank you for constantly strengthening and guiding me to rise above opposition. Amen.

∽

Day 162
UTTHITA PADMASANA – ELEVATED LOTUS POSE

To do the elevated lotus pose, start seated in lotus with your hands down by your sides and your fingers forward, and lift your body up. Hold for a few breaths, then switch the cross of your legs and repeat. If lotus legs are not accessible to you at this time, focus on your scale pose. Both positions strengthen your wrists and arm muscles while bringing fresh blood flow to the hands. As you aim to elevate your body, think about the tasks for which you use your hands—daily chores, work tasks, activities with your family, and so on. How do you keep your hands active? In the midst of your activity, how can you stay present with the Lord? Reflect on *Proverbs 31:17: She sets about her work vigorously; her arms are strong for her tasks.* Commune with Jesus.

SCRIPTURE:

Sow your seed in the morning, and at evening let your hands not be idle, for you do not know which will succeed, whether this or that, or whether both will do equally well. (Ecclesiastes 11:6)

PRAYER:

Father, I come to the mat to develop stamina and energy to do the tasks you have designed for me. Help me to strengthen my hands and body. Jesus, I reflect on the activities you did with your hands—washed feet, healed bodies, broke bread, overturned tables, wrote in the sand, and so many more. I also reflect on the activities you refrained from doing—using a sword, casting a stone, striking someone. I desire to be like you, Jesus. I hear *Proverbs 14:23: All hard work brings a profit, but mere talk leads only to poverty*. I come to work hard on the mat so that I may build the stamina to do the tasks you have called me to do. Amen.

༄

Day 163
LOLASANA – PENDANT POSE

To do the pendant pose start seated with your legs up and core engaged, draw your hands down to the mat, cross your feet and then lift your seat up. Let your arms support your weight. An advanced option is to swing your legs under your seat into the downward facing dog position or into an arm balance. The word 'Lola' in Sanskrit translates to fickle, swinging back and forth like a pendant hanging on a necklace or an earring. Consider the areas in your life where you are fickle. Do you routinely change directions and/or act indecisively? How can you ask the Lord for wisdom to discern what is best, and then swing into action when the situation calls for it? Share your responses with Jesus.

SCRIPTURE:

The end of a matter is better than its beginning, and patience is better than pride. Do not be quickly provoked in your spirit, for anger resides in the lap of fools. (Ecclesiastes 7:8-9)

PRAYER:

Father, I thank you for your steadiness, love and patience. I apologize for every time I have let me emotions get out of control and have waivered back and forth instead of consistently following your Spirit. Quiet me in your love and help me to be patient in my practice on the mat, in life and with others. I hear *Isaiah 35:3-4: Strengthen the feeble hands, steady the knees that give way; say to those with fearful hearts, "Be strong, do not fear; your God will come."* Thank you for coming to me and drawing me into your arms. Let me swing in love for you. Amen.

෨

Day 164
BHUJAPIDASANA – SHOULDER PRESSING POSE

To do the shoulder pressing pose, start squatting with your feet about shoulder width apart and your knees wide with your hands on the mat. Walk them back so that the 'Ls' of your hands hug your ankles. Lift your gluts and work your thighs to press the upper outside of your arms as you engage your core and shift your weight forward onto your hands; lift your feet as one foot wraps around the other. Work to straighten your arms. Try out this advanced asana and reflect on what you feel dedicated to in your life right now. Where may you need to cultivate a spirit of dedication—be it to your work, in your family life, with your health, or in your service to others? What are you putting on your shoulders? *Deuteronomy 33:12: About Benjamin he said: "Let the beloved of the LORD rest secure in him, for he shields him all day long, and the one the LORD loves rests between his shoulders."* Pause and meditate on this verse.

SCRIPTURE:
Engrave the names of the sons of Israel on the two stones the way a gem cutter engraves a seal. Then mount the stones in gold filigree settings and fasten them on the shoulder pieces of the ephod as memorial stones for the sons of Israel. Aaron is to bear the names on his shoulders as a memorial before the LORD. (Exodus 28:11-12)

PRAYER:
Lord, like Benjamin's blessing, please let your love rest between my shoulders. Let my work in the shoulder pressing pose act as a physical expression of a memorial, like Aaron wore, for all your sons and daughters. Through this practice, guide me in fostering a spirit of dedication where it is needed in my life. Help

me to press into you, Jesus, as I focus on taking your yoke upon my shoulders. I remember the prophetic words of *Isaiah 9:6: For to us a child is born, to us a son is given, and the government will be on his shoulders,* and *Isaiah 22:22: I will place on his shoulder the key to the house of David; what he opens no one can shut, and what he shuts no one can open.* Holy One of righteous shoulders, I press into your Spirit. Amen.

৩১৯

Day 165
TITTIBHASANA – FIREFLY POSE

To do the firefly pose start in a squat, then tip your pelvis forward until it is about knee high. Bring your arms down to the mat and place them behind your heels, fingers forward, with back thighs hugging your upper arms. Gaze forward and work to straighten your arms as your legs straighten and lift up. You may be able to hold this posture for only a second when you first try it, just like a firefly that lights up for a moment in the night sky and returns to darkness. Mastering difficult postures like the firefly requires focus and trust. It is like learning how to ride a bike; it is daunting at first, yet once you achieve balance, joy comes and lights up your face, and it seems so easy, as though you've been doing it forever. Are there any yoga poses that you have learned how to do that you first thought were not possible? Reflect on *Mark 9:23: Everything is possible for those who believe.* Consider how God has given you a spirit to stick with things and see them through to completion. How does He direct your energies on the mat and in life, and encourage you through glimpses of His light? Share your responses with Jesus.

SCRIPTURE:

However, as it is written: "What no eye has seen, what no ear has heard, and what no human mind has conceived"—— the things God has prepared for those who love him. (1 Corinthians 2:9)

PRAYER:

Father, I cannot fully understand the wondrous things you have in store for me. I trust that they are good, for you are good! In your Word is Life and Light. When I catch a glimpse of it, help me to apprehend it. Lord, I come to glow in body, mind and spirit—united, committed and submitted to you. I commune *Mark 9:24: I do believe; help me overcome my unbelief.* Yes, Lord, all things are possible through you, even things I cannot conceive or imagine. No one could ever recall and recount all the things you have planned for those who love you! I joyfully explore your indwelling presence and remember *Luke 11:35-36: See to it, then, that the light within you is not darkness. Therefore, if your whole body is full of light, and no part of it dark, it will be just as full of light as when a lamp shines its light on you.* Whether I am balancing on my hands or seated on the mat, you Lord, I praise. Let your eternal light shine through me. Amen.

∽

Day 166
CRADLE POSE

To do the cradle pose, start seated, hug one of your shins toward your chest, wrap your arms around it and move it slowly side to side. This movement is a gentle hip opener that may also be done reclining on your back. Just as the Levite woman placed baby Moses in a basket and set it adrift in the Nile, trusting the Lord to cradle him, as you do the cradle pose, reflect on what thing in your life—an item, a habit or activity—you have had to give up reluctantly, but you knew it needed to be done. How did your trust in God grow through that experience, and what was the result? What may you need to give up or set down in your life now? Listen for the Lord's voice as He speaks to your heart.

SCRIPTURE:
Now a man of the tribe of Levi married a Levite woman, and she became pregnant and gave birth to a son. When she saw that he was a fine child, she hid him for three months. But when she could hide him no longer, she got a papyrus basket for him and coated it with tar and pitch. Then she placed the child in it and put it among the reeds along the bank of the Nile. His sister stood at a distance to see what would happen to him. (Exodus 2:1-4)

PRAYER:
Lord, I come to my mat to surrender to your holy, pleasing and perfect will. Help me align my habits, activities and behaviors with your truth, and let go of

anything that does not serve you. I remember the story of Moses in *Exodus 2:6, 10: She opened it and saw the baby. He was crying, and she felt sorry for him. "This is one of the Hebrew babies," she said. When the child grew older, she took him to Pharaoh's daughter and he became her son. She named him Moses, saying, "I drew him out of the water."* Like Pharaoh's daughter, teach me to have enough compassion to pick up and cradle anything you desire me to comfort and protect. Thank you for the opportunity to be with you here on the mat. Cradle me in your love. Amen.

∽

Day 167
EKA PADA RAJAKAPOTASANA – HALF KING PIGEON POSE

To do the half king pigeon pose from downward facing dog, draw your right leg forward and set your right knee down by your right wrist while your right shin works to be parallel to the front of the mat. With your hips down and square, lift up your chest, and for a restorative option, walk your hands forward until your forehead makes contact with the mat, your fists or a block. If you feel any discomfort, roll over to your back keeping your knees up and feet down, then draw your right leg towards your chest with your right knee splaying out and your right ankle resting on your left thigh. Wrap your arms around the back of your left thigh and draw it into your chest. You may hold for several minutes and then switch sides. This is a deep hip opener that may cause a lot of emotions to spring up. Have you poured out your heart to the Lord with tears recently? When was the last time you let down the floodgates of your emotions? Practicing yoga can sometimes make you feel like you are wrestling with God. You may feel the Lord challenging you in a wondrous way that leaves you limp yet empowered. Reflect on *Romans 12:12: Be joyful in hope, patient in affliction, faithful in prayer.* Commune with Jesus about this verse and about any emotions you're wrestling with on a regular basis.

SCRIPTURE:
So Jacob was left alone, and a man wrestled with him until daybreak. When the man saw that he could not overpower him, he touched the socket of Jacob's hip so that

his hip was wrenched as he wrestled with the man. So Jacob called the place Peniel, saying, "It is because I saw God face to face, and yet my life was spared." The sun rose above him as he passed Peniel, and he was limping because of his hip. (Genesis 32:24-25, 30-31)

PRAYER:

Lord, I come to focus on you through physical engagement and cathartic emotion. Thank you for being an active God who is willing to wrestle with me and refine me through it. I remember *James 5:7: Be patient, then, brothers and sisters, until the Lord's coming. See how the farmer waits for the land to yield its valuable crop, patiently waiting for the autumn and spring rains.* Father, here I am to cultivate patience, to demonstrate faithfulness and to have joyful hope in you. Please guide me through any emotions that come up one the mat. Amen.

୬

Day 168
RAJAKAPOTASANA – KING PIGEON POSE

The word 'kapota' means pigeon or dove in Sanskrit. To do the king pigeon pose from downward facing dog, draw your right knee to your right wrist and lower your legs to the mat; your chest lifts, the back of your knee bends and your left arm reaches around for your back left foot. Your elbow fastens around your foot and your right hand goes back to interlace with your left one. Another option is to reach both arms back and over your head to your foot or hook the back of your foot with a strap as you work your hands further back. Keep your elbows by your ears if you choose this option. Remember to reverse sides. This is an advanced posture that opens your hips and chest. As you open your heart and hips, visualize a dove descending on your heart. Reflect on what baptism means to you. Have you been baptized? If so, do you remember anything about your experience? Perhaps more recently you have renewed your baptismal vows with a holy water cross on your forehead. Commune with Jesus about these experiences.

SCRIPTURE:

As soon as Jesus was baptized, he went up out of the water. At that moment heaven was opened, and he saw the Spirit of God descending like a dove and lighting on him. (Matthew 3:16)

PRAYER:

Lord of living water, thank you for baptism. I remember that it was a dove that brought Noah a twig, thus revealing that there was dry land, and I recall those precious words of *Isaiah 53:2: He grew up before him like a tender shoot, and like a root out of dry ground. He had no beauty or majesty to attract us to him, nothing in his appearance that we should desire him.* Jesus, fulfiller of prophesies, I come in meekness, tenderly reaching into the king pigeon pose. Spirit, descend on me like a dove and fill my entire inner being. Let this practice be a reminder of my baptism in You. Amen.

༄

Day 169
ARDHA BHEKASANA – HALF FROG POSE

To get into the half frog pose, lie on your belly with your hands by your shoulders and press down into the mat as your arms straighten and your chest lifts. Then bend your right leg and reach your right arm around to clasp the inside of your foot. Work your elbow toward the ceiling and your fingers around your toes with the palm of your hand pressing gently onto the top of your foot. Reverse sides. Frogs go through three stages of development—from egg to tadpole to fully formed amphibian. What types of transformation have you experienced? Have you felt transformed by God? Commune with Jesus about any ways your faith has been developing.

SCRIPTURE:

And we all, who with unveiled faces contemplate the Lord's glory, are being transformed into his image with ever-increasing glory, which comes from the Lord, who is the Spirit. (2 Corinthians 3:18)

PRAYER:

Lord, thank you for being a transformative God. I delight in the words of *Philippians 3:21: Who [Christ], by the power that enables him to bring everything under his control, will transform our lowly bodies so that they will be like his glorious body.* Here on the mat, mold my body, mind and heart to be like yours. Amen.

༄

Day 170
HANUMANASANA – SPLITS, MONKEY POSE

To do the monkey pose, start in a low lunge with your right leg forward with your back straight and your knee down on the mat. Ease your right leg forward and your left leg backward as you breathe deeply. Keep your hands on the mat, or as an option, you can place them on blocks by your sides. If your groin makes contact with the mat and your hips and shoulders are square to the front, feel free to reach your arms up and gently arch your back. You can also bend forward reaching your arms toward the foot of your extended forward leg. Reverse sides. The monkey pose stimulates your hamstrings, groin and abdominal organs. Working on your splits, reflect on the temple curtain that separated the Holy of Holies, where only the high priest could enter, from the rest of the temple where the people worshipped. What does the temple curtain symbolize to you? Do you talk to the Lord privately, or do you prefer to go through a priest or minister by engaging in activities such as counseling and confession? How can you further develop a more personal relationship with the Lord? Share your responses with Jesus.

SCRIPTURE:

And when Jesus had cried out again in a loud voice, he gave up his spirit. At that moment the curtain of the temple was torn in two from top to bottom. The earth shook, the rocks split and the tombs broke open. The bodies of many holy people who had died were raised to life. (Matthew 27:50-51)

PRAYER:

Lord, thank you for the way you care for me intimately and personally. Let my relationship with you be strengthened here on the mat. I remember *Isaiah 48:21:*

They did not thirst when he led them through the deserts; he made water flow for them from the rock; he split the rock and water gushed out. Father, who splits rocks and gives water, I part my legs in the splits pose in gratitude of this holy power. Help me to tap into your living waters flowing within me. Amen.

༄

Day 171
SETU BANDHA SARVANGASANA – BRIDGE POSE

To do the bridge pose, lie on your back with your knees pulled up until they're just over your ankles, with your feet hip width apart and your hands on the mat by your sides. Lift your hips lift up, draw your shoulders together and interlace your hands behind your back. In the bridge pose, reflect on Eli's conversation with Samuel. Eli told Samuel to answer the Lord whenever he heard God call Samuel's name. Samuel heard his name called three times in the middle of the night, so he got up and ran to Eli because he thought Eli was calling him. But it was the Lord! Here, Eli acted as a bridge; he taught Samuel how to commune with the Lord. Ponder who has served as a bridge in your life. Consider how Jesus acts as a bridge between our heavenly Father and us. Finally, take note of any ways you serve as a bridge for others. Commune with Jesus as you ponder these things.

SCRIPTURE:
So Eli told Samuel, "Go and lie down, and if he calls you, say, 'Speak, Lord, for your servant is listening.'" (1 Samuel 3:9)

PRAYER:
Lord, here I am to be a bridge and a passerby. I breathe Paul's holy words of *2 Corinthians 4:16: If our outer man is perishing, our inner man is renewed day by day.* Lord, your servant is here to listen to you and to be an arch for others to be blessed by Your holy light. As I do the bridge pose, let it be an expression of gratitude to those who have taught me in truth and guided me on the path of faith. Jesus, bridge to our Father; direct me in light, knowledge and love. Amen.

༄

Day 172
PURVOTTANASANA – UPWARD FACING PLANK, INCLINED PLANE

To do the upward facing plank pose, start seated with your legs extended out and your arms by your sides. Lift your hips and chest, and gaze upward. Your shoulders draw together and away from ears, arms stay active, thighs inner rotate, gluts soften and toes point downward. As you look up in this asana reflect on your spirit of hope and how the Lord is the Savior of all people. How do you labor and strive in hope of the living God and honestly note your hopes—from a concert ticket to a baby, from a promotion to a date? Commune with Jesus.

SCRIPTURE:
That is why we labor and strive, because we have put our hope in the living God, who is the Savior of all people, and especially of those who believe. (1 Timothy 4:10)

PRAYER:
Living God, Savior of all, especially those who believe, I marvel and praise your holy essence. I labor, stretch and exercise on this mat for my hope is you. I commune *Romans 15:13 (MSG): Oh! May the God of green hope fill you up with joy, fill you up with peace, so that your believing lives, filled with the life-giving energy of the Holy Spirit, will brim over with hope!* Brimming with hope, I say Amen.

❧

Day 173
USTRASANA – CAMEL POSE

For the camel pose, start kneeling with knees hip width apart, hands to your low back, fingers down, elbows and shoulders draw together and hips over your knees. Heart lifts, throat opens and gaze draws back. If your eyes meet the back wall, feel free to reach for heels with your hands. Hold several breaths and slowly come back up. Read today's scripture, Acts 28:27, and note that the original Greek word for calloused is *pachyno*, meaning to make fat, callused as if from fat. Camel pose helps physically prevents *pachyno* by opening your heart—enhancing circulation. How do you open your heart to the Lord and to others? In what ways can you listen and look with a willing spirit? Are you open to change in your perceptions or plans, and to new ways of thinking without judging or assuming you already know what is best? Take a moment to commune with Jesus.

SCRIPTURE:

For this people's heart has become calloused; they hardly hear with their ears, and they have closed their eyes. Otherwise they might see with their eyes, hear with their ears, understand with their hearts and turn, and I would heal them. (Acts 28:27)

PRAYER:

Sovereign Lord, I trust in you and open my heart to you that I may enter your rest. Through the camel pose I physically express my willing spirit and pray that you would remove any callousness from my heart. Let me be pliable in your holy hands. *Proverbs 3:5-6: Trust in the LORD with all your heart and lean not on your own understanding; in all your ways acknowledge Him, and He will make your paths straight.* As I place my heart in your hands, I pray that you would purify, strengthen and enlighten it. Amen.

❧

Day 174
LAGHU VAJRASANA – LITTLE THUNDERBOLT POSE

To do the little thunderbolt pose, start by standing on your shins, hands to your lower back, heart lifted and your gaze facing back; your hands come down to your heels and walk up your calves until the crown of your head reaches the mat. This pose may or may not be accessible for you at this time, so feel free to focus on the camel pose as an alternative option. Practice by practice you will deepen your postures. Each practice presents the opportunity to observe the subtle changes happening in your own body. What small physical changes have you noticed in yours? Have there been any changes in your character or persona since you started practicing yoga? What are the subtle ways the Lord is shaping you in your life right now? Commune with Jesus.

SCRIPTURE:

Little by little I will drive them out before you, until you have increased enough to take possession of the land. (Exodus 23:30)

PRAYER:

Lord, as I tend to my spirit, little by little I grow closer to you. I aim to stretch my body slightly further in this yoga practice than I have done previously. While doing so, please let my heart and mind be further opened to your will and way. I remember Paul's final charge to Timothy in *1 Timothy 6:11: But you, man of God, flee from all this, and pursue righteousness, godliness, faith, love, endurance and gentleness.* As the crown of my head works back in the little thunderbolt pose, drive out anything in my life that is not serving you. Lifting my heart to pursue righteousness, godliness, faith, love, endurance and gentleness here on the mat, I say Amen.

⁂

Day 175
KAPOTANASANA – PIGEON POSE

To do the pigeon pose, start by standing on your knees with your hands at your lower back and heart lifted. Draw your head down and back until crown of your head touches to mat. With your hands by your head, fingers pointing to your toes, work the crown of your head toward your feet, then interlace your fingers together behind your head, bringing your forearms down to the mat with your elbows hugging your ears. Note that this is an extremely advanced asana; respect your body and only go as far as you are able to do comfortably. As you work on the pigeon pose, reflect on how you give part of what you earn (your 'harvest') to others. Without judging yourself, note how much of your income do you share with those who are less fortunate. As you commune with Jesus, ponder all the ways your actions show a deep care for others.

SCRIPTURE:

Do not go over your vineyard a second time or pick up the grapes that have fallen. Leave them for the poor and the foreigner. I am the LORD your God. (Leviticus 19:10)

PRAYER:

Lord, I come to thank you for the harvest you have given me, and for the blessing of being able to sow, reap and give. Please forgive me for the way I have not been generous with my talent and treasure. Help me to recognize opportunities like Boaz did in *Ruth 2:15-16: As she got up to glean, Boaz gave orders to his men, "Let her gather among the sheaves and don't reprimand her. Even pull out some stalks for her from the bundles and leave them for her to pick up, and don't rebuke her."* Let the pigeon pose, a big heart opener, teach me how to act that way on and off the mat. Give me the insight needed to identify the Ruths and Naomis in my life. In your holy Name, I say Amen.

༄

Day 176
CHAKRASANA, URDHVA DHANURASANA – WHEEL, UPWARD FACING BOW POSE

To do the wheel pose, start on your back with your feet on the floor by your gluts and hips apart, knees up; finger kiss your shoulders, pointing them toward your feet; place your palms on the mat and elbows in and up, then rise up. The wheel pose is an expansive heart opener that strengthens your legs, arms and spine. Even though it takes lots of energy to do this pose, it stimulates fresh energy as well. There is great symbolism concerning the wheel in Ezekiel's vision of the 'living creatures' described in the books of Daniel and Revelation. What sorts of visions have you experienced? Close your eyes and commune with the Lord about any current visions you have on your mind. Doing so, open your heart to the Lord so that He may expand your vision, enable you to clearly interpret signs and respond to them with truth and courage as He wills it.

SCRIPTURE:

Rise up; this matter is in your hands. We will support you, so take courage and do it. (Ezra 10:4)

PRAYER:

Lord, my vision and light, I take courage in you. I open my heart and mind to fresh revelation from your Spirit. Please reveal anything new you desire me to see, acknowledge or interpret during this practice. Taking the position of a wheel, encircled in your light, I move for you. *Matthew 14:27: But Jesus immediately said to them:"Take courage! It is I. Don't be afraid."*Holy Lord, your whirlwind of love shields me from any attacks or fears—my courage is in you. Let my movement express my gratitude. Amen.

౭ᵔ౨

Day 177
MATSYASANA – FISH POSE

To do the fish pose, start lying down on your back with your arms by your sides, palms down and hands almost under your gluts. Lift up your upper body so that you're resting on your forearms, then lift your chest, open your throat and gaze backwards; your head may kiss the mat as your shoulders draw down and back. Keep your legs straight and engaged. As an optional pose, you can raise them up and draw your hands together in the prayer position at your heart or directly out, parallel to your legs. Another challenging variation is to do this pose with your legs in the lotus position, which means your knees and the crown of your head are the only points touching the mat. The fish pose stretches and opens your chest, throat and belly. Traditionally, this asana is thought to be a curer of all diseases in yoga. How has the Lord cured you physically? How about emotionally and spiritually? How might you currently need healing? Share your responses with Jesus.

SCRIPTURE:
At that very time Jesus cured many who had diseases, sicknesses and evil spirits, and gave sight to many who were blind. (Luke 7:21)

PRAYER:
Lord, I thank you for curing me from sickness and for revitalizing and strengthening me on your living, active and enduring Word. I remember *Mark 6:41: Taking the five loaves and the two fish and looking up to heaven, he gave thanks and broke the loaves. Then he gave them to his disciples to distribute to the people. He also divided the two fish among them all.* Grand miracle enabler, who fed five thousand with these

five loaves and two fish, I look up towards the heavens to give thanks to you, and I open myself to be a fisher of men and women for you. Please use me as a means to nourish others on your holy words, and in doing so, may your blessings multiply. Alleluia. Amen.

⁓

Day 178
HALASANA – PLOW POSE

To do the plow pose, start by lying on your back, then raise your feet up 90 degrees keeping your legs straight; lift your hips with your hands supporting your lower back. Your legs go up, back and over your head so that your toes touch the mat behind you. If they do, feel free to interlace your hands and extend them long on the mat. The plow pose is a restorative inversion that opens your back and shoulders. *Hosea 10:11-12: Ephraim is a trained heifer that loves to thresh; so I will put a yoke on her fair neck. I will drive Ephraim, Judah must plow, and Jacob must break up the ground. Sow righteousness for yourselves, reap the fruit of unfailing love, and break up your unplowed ground; for it is time to seek the LORD, until he comes and showers his righteousness on you.* Reflecting on this scripture, think about how you see your work as a spiritual act. Review your daily tasks, and think about how you might make them even more of an extension of God's Spirit within you. Commune with Jesus.

SCRIPTURE:
He told them, "The harvest is plentiful, but the workers are few. Ask the Lord of the harvest, therefore, to send out workers into his harvest field." (Luke 2:10)

PRAYER:
Lord, I come to be your harvester and to sow in Spirit. I remember *John 4:35-38: Don't you have a saying, 'It's still four months until harvest'? I tell you, open your eyes and look at the fields! They are ripe for harvest. Even now the one who reaps draws a wage and harvests a crop for eternal life, so that the sower and the reaper may be glad together. Thus the saying 'One sows and another reaps' is true. I sent you to reap what you have not worked for. Others have done the hard work, and you have reaped the benefits*

of their labor. Such powerful, passionate, holy words to posture on my heart as I move into the plow pose. I understand that I did not do the work to receive your grace, Lord—I simply opened my heart. Jesus, thank you for your work and your Word—I trust in you. Make me a tool for others to reap the fruits of your Spirit. Thank you for planting your holy seed as a deposit in me. Your Kingdom come, Amen.

෧෨

Day 179
SARVANGASANA – SHOULDER STAND POSE

To do the shoulder stand pose, start in the plow pose and raise your legs so that they are straight up in the air. Keep the back of your head pressed against the mat and fix your gaze upward. This neutralizes the body and calms the nervous system while releasing the muscles of the neck and shoulders. The shoulder stand is referred to as the queen of postures. While you're in the shoulder stand, ponder your current positions in life and what the Lord may be positioning you to do. Do you accept your roles in life? How can you use them to stand up for yourself, for others and the Lord? Share your responses with Jesus.

SCRIPTURE:
For if you remain silent at this time, relief and deliverance for the Jews will arise from another place, but you and your father's family will perish. And who knows but that you have come to your royal position for such a time as this?" (Esther 4:14)

PRAYER:
Sovereign Lord, thank you for drawing me to the mat that you may heal and enlighten my body and spirit. I reflect on the positions I hold in life and thank you for bringing me into them. Let me use them for your goodness. I remember Queen Esther in *Esther 7:3: Then Queen Esther answered, "If I have found favor with you, Your Majesty, and if it pleases you, grant me my life—this is my petition. And spare my people—this is my request."* Lord, teach me how to pray and petition for the people you have called me to love and care for, starting with myself. Please help me to understand why you have called me to this time and place. Strengthen my inner

spirit in the shoulder stand pose and in each asana I do. I desire to stand for you forever and always. Amen.

෮ல

Day 180
SHOULDER STAND POSE VARIATIONS

Start on your back and draw your legs straight up with your hands on your lower back. Aim for a straight line from your shoulders to your toe tips. One option from here is urdhva padmasana. For this position, draw your legs into the lotus position (or simply crossed); lower your knees in toward your shoulders and back up again, then reverse the cross of your legs. Another option from the shoulder stand is urdhva baddha konasana. For this pose, the tops of your feet are together and your knees are wide. Still others include eagle legs, splits, tree, or one knee pressing into the top of your forehead with that leg's foot gracing your extended leg's thigh. The shoulder stand can be playtime—discovering what is good and fitting for your practice. How do you explore in the larger arena of your life? Do you let the Lord lead you into new places, environments and positions? How comfortable are you with change, and how have you reacted to any recent changes in your life? Share your responses with Jesus.

SCRIPTURE:
Send some men to explore the land of Canaan, which I am giving to the Israelites. From each ancestral tribe send one of its leaders. (Numbers 13:2)

PRAYER:
Lord, I come to the mat to explore your presence in my inmost being and the various ways I can use my limbs to praise Your Holy Name. I desire to learn about your creation through my body here on the mat. Thank you for your intimate presence in each cell and sinew of my being. I embrace *Psalm 139:14: Your works are wonderful, I know that full well,* and aim to live out the words Solomon shared in *Ecclesiastes 1:13: I applied my mind to study and to explore by wisdom all that is done under the heavens.* Father, guide me. Amen.

෮ல

Day 181
KARNAPIDASANA – EAR PINNING, DEAF MAN'S POSE

The ear pinning pose is a posture to do once you have developed a strong foundation in the plow pose. To do the ear pinning pose, lie on your back and draw your legs over your head while keeping space between your chest and chin. Lower your knees toward your forehead, then down to hug your ears, closing off external noise. Ponder how you can close off external noise around you, such as honking horns, TV shows, ungodly conversations, and anything else that might distract you from hearing the Lord. How about the internal voice that is making a shopping list, remembering an email, craving to buy something, critiquing others and judging your own thoughts? Become quiet in body and mind and listen for Jesus.

SCRIPTURE:
Sacrifice and offering you did not desire—but my ears you have pierced [opened]. (Psalm 40:6)

PRAYER:
Father, thank you for opening my ears to hear your holy voice, and for telling me you love me. Continue to quiet me here on the mat and forgive me for the distractions I have given in to in the past. I hear *Psalm 40:8: I desire to do your will, O my God; your law is within my heart.* Thank you for placing your law in my heart, Lord. I am here to turn my attention away from the noises around me and in my mind and to listen to you with all my being. Amen.

ᖆᖇ

Day 182
MUKTA HASTA SIRSANA – TRIPOD HEADSTAND

To do the tripod headstand, start from a yogi squat position; place your hands shoulder width apart on the mat, fan your fingers wide and draw the top of your head down an equal distance in front of your hands keeping your elbows in line with your wrists. Next, place your knees on the backsides of your elbows and lift one leg straight up, then extend the other leg to meet it. This asana shifts your perspective. It is grounded in three points, thus creating a solid foundation to invert. Think of the will of the Father at the crown of your head, the words of the Son in your right hand, and the way of Spirit in your left. Reflect on *Deuteronomy 11:16: Be careful, or you will be enticed to turn away and worship other gods and bow down to them.* What are the idols in your life—the things that draw you away from your firm foundation in the Lord? Think about how you can place the Lord first in the various areas of your life—your eating habits, fitness routines, family life, social relationships, work, and finances. Take a moment and draw in His presence.

SCRIPTURE:
Nevertheless, God's solid foundation stands firm, sealed with this inscription: "The Lord knows those who are his," and, "Everyone who confesses the name of the Lord must turn away from wickedness." (2 Timothy 2:19)

PRAYER:
Lord, I come to the mat to lay down anything I have not fully surrendered to you and to draw your presence into each facet of my life. Please forgive me for anything that has been an idol. Father, help me to turn away, refocus and recommit wholly to you. I hear *1 Samuel 19:20-21: "Do not be afraid," Samuel replied. "You have done all this evil; yet do not turn away from the LORD, but serve the LORD with all your heart. Do not turn away after useless idols. They can do you no good, nor can they rescue you, because they are useless.* I turn to you with all my heart, body, mind and spirit here on the mat. Enliven my perspective in your will, word and way. Amen.

ଙ୬

Day 183
SALAMBA SIRSASANA – SUPPORTED HEADSTAND

To do a supported headstand from the downward facing dog pose, draw your forearms to the mat, interlace your hands and place the crown of your head down between your hands. Work your feet towards your head and then lift them straight up into the air. Please note, most of your weight should be supported by your forearms, not your head, and your elbows should only be six to eight inches apart. The headstand tends to heat the body and stimulate the nervous system, and it tones the neck muscles as well. In traditional yoga the headstand is thought of as the 'king' of poses—which makes it the perfect position in which to praise the King of kings! How has the Lord shifted your vision and/or given you a new perspective recently? In what ways may you need one now? Commune with Jesus.

SCRIPTURE:
They will make war against the Lamb, but the Lamb will overcome them because he is Lord of lords and King of kings--and with him will be his called, chosen and faithful followers. (Revelation 17:14)

PRAYER:
Sovereign Lord, in love, I surrender my-'self' to your divine Self. In whatever way is needed, turn me upside down. Jesus, I remember when you overturned the tables in the temple, as described in *Luke 19:46: 'My house will be a house of prayer'; but you have made it 'a den of robbers.'* As I invert my body here on the mat, remove anything from my head or heart that is not grounded in Truth, and realign me in Spirit. Here to keep my body a temple of prayer, I say Amen.

☙

Day 184
VRSCHIKASANA – SCORPION POSE

This is an advanced posture that may best be first practiced against the wall. To do the scorpion pose, start by placing your hands down shoulder width apart about a foot and half away from the wall and walk your feet in. Then kick your legs up to the wall, tuck your feet under and move them down as far as it is accessible for you to do comfortably. Your gaze is on your fingertips. If this pose is beyond your practice—that is okay! It is fun to become aware of different yoga possibilities. Have there been any yoga moves you did not feel were possible when you first tried them, and now they are accessible for you? How has God made things that seemed impossible at some point in your life, possible? Reflect on as many examples as come to mind. Share with Jesus anything that may seem impossible for you now.

SCRIPTURE:

Jesus looked at them and said, "With man this is impossible, but with God all things are possible." (Matthew 19:26)

PRAYER:

Father, all things are possible with you. I rejoice in *Mark 10:27: Jesus looked at them and said, "With man this is impossible, but not with God; all things are possible with God,"* and *Luke 18:27 Jesus replied, "What is impossible with man is possible with God."* Lord, thank you for your never-ending and everlasting possibilities. Teach me how to tap into this truth on the mat and in life. Amen.

❧

Day 185
PINCHA MAYURASANA – FOREARM STAND, FEATHERED PEACOCK POSE

To do the forearm stand, begin in a forearm plank with your elbows under the shoulders. You may want to start against a wall with your fingers an inch away from it. Walk your legs forward toward the wall; lift one leg up, then the other. Keep your ribs knit and your core and legs engaged. There is softness to this pose—as you walk your legs in, it should feel as if they lift themselves off the mat. This pose is all about less effort, more grace. The feathered peacock is a posture to work on while reflecting on how the Lord sees beauty in you even if you feel more like a sheep grounded on all fours then a feathered peacock. (Remember—the Lord loves sheep!) Read *Song of Solomon 5:2: Listen! My beloved is knocking: "Open to me, my sister, my darling, my dove, my flawless one."* Can you imagine yourself as the beloved? Can you fathom the Lord speaking these tender, loving words to you? Commune with Jesus.

SCRIPTURE:

Even while you sleep among the sheep pens, the wings of my dove are sheathed with silver, its feathers with shining gold. (Psalm 68:13)

PRAYER:

Lord, to be your beloved is such an indescribable and wondrous gift. I come to soar into the heavens with you; whether I balance on my forearms or not, my trust is in you. Align me in the positions you have designed for my body, mind and spirit to take today. I remember *Psalm 91:4: He will cover you with his feathers, and under his wings you will find refuge; his faithfulness will be your shield and rampart.* Glorious King, please cover me with your feathers and embrace me under your holy wings. Amen.

෨෨

Day 186
ADHO MUKHA VRKSASANA – HANDSTAND

To do the handstand pose, start in the downward facing dog pose with your hands planted shoulder width apart. Bring one leg in about 12 inches and bend the knee of that leg; extend the other leg straight out and softly spring the extended leg up with the other following it. You may want to start by practicing this pose against a wall, and if so, place your hands an inch or two away from the wall then follow the same steps. The handstand pose strengthens your arms and improves your sense of balance. As you turn your body upside down, reflect on *1 Corinthians 1:28: God chose the lowly things of this world and the despised things—and the things that are not—to nullify the things that are.* What are the lowly, despised and things that are not? Share your response with Jesus.

SCRIPTURE:

You turn things upside down, as if the potter were thought to be like the clay! Shall what is formed say to the one who formed it, "You did not make me"? Can the pot say to the potter, "You know nothing"? (Isaiah 29:16)

PRAYER:

Great Potter, your way is infinitely higher than mine; what may I say? Thank you for positioning your presence within me through your Spirit so that I may know your light intimately. As I seek to flip myself over here on the mat, may it be representative of my intention to see things from your holy perspective. Whatever physical position I take, let me remember that you chose the lowly things of this world. I hear *Proverbs 24:21: Fear God, dear child—respect your leaders; don't be defiant or mutinous. Without warning your life can turn upside down, and who knows how or when it might happen?* Lord, I hold fast to you with utmost reverence, and as I shake and wobble in my yoga practice and in my life, please sustain me—for you are my strength and my life. Amen.

❧

Day 187
UTTANASANA – STANDING FORWARD FOLD

To do the standing forward fold pose, start standing and hinge at your hips, lead with your heart, and bend your torso forward and down. Bring the crown of your head down to the floor while maintaining a straight back; keep your hands down by your sides and your feet together or hip width apart. Finally, bring your forehead to your shins as your legs straighten. This posture is often done repeatedly throughout a practice session. Each fold offers you the opportunity let go of any thoughts that entangle your mind and keep you from the truth; thus, the standing forward fold is a wonderful pose for renewing your mind. What hinders you in your faith? What sin entangles you? Get clear about anything you seem to be grappling with, and reflect on who in your life is among your "cloud of witnesses"? In other words, who affirms, enlightens and blesses you in faith? Share your responses with Jesus.

SCRIPTURE:

Therefore, since we are surrounded by such a great cloud of witnesses, let us throw off everything that hinders and the sin that so easily entangles. (Hebrews 12:1)

PRAYER:

Righteous Father, I come to my mat to throw off all entangling thoughts. As your child, I focus all my attention and energy on you. I thank you for surrounding me with a cloud of witnesses in this space and in life. I remember *Hebrews 12:10: But God disciplines us for our good, in order that we may share in his holiness.* Father, I bow my head in obedience; please discipline me as your righteousness sees fit. Amen.

∽

Day 188
RAGDOLL POSE

To do the ragdoll pose, start in a forward fold with your feet hip width apart, then grab opposite elbows with your hands and softly sway side to side. Enjoy the movement of this pose—bending and straightening your legs, rolling your neck side-to-side, reversing your grip and direction, and so on. This is a position of bowed reverence and gentle motion. Think of when you were first called into relationship with the Lord and the various ways the Lord has used you without special training, titles or certifications by worldly standards. How have you served the Lord and others humbly yet confidently? How might He be calling you to serve now? Commune with Jesus.

SCRIPTURE:

Brothers and sisters, think of what you were when you were called. Not many of you were wise by human standards; not many were influential; not many were of noble birth. (1 Corinthians 1:26)

PRAYER:

Lord, thank you for calling me to be your vessel even though my resumé lacks credentials. I do not feel like the 'right' candidate, yet through reading your Word, I understand you have a history of using misfits—those who stumble, who stammer, who are weak and who are poor. Thank you for choosing the ones the world does not see. I thank you for choosing me! Help me to listen, for *'my spirit is willing though my flesh is weak' (Mark 14:38)*. I hear *Zephaniah 2:3: Seek the Lord, all you humble of the earth, who have observed his law; seek justice, seek humility*. Yes, I seek you wholeheartedly, remembering *Zephaniah 3:12: I will leave as a remnant in your midst a people humble and lowly, who shall take refuge in the name of the Lord: the remnant of Israel*. Let me be a remnant of grace and a refugee in you. Amen.

ꙮ

Day 189
PADANGUSTASANA

To do the padangustasana pose, start in a forward fold and wrap your two peace fingers, index and middle fingers around your big (great) toes. Inhale as you straighten your back and exhale as you melt your forehead to your shins. Hold for a few breaths. As you do this pose, ponder how you lead a quiet life. How do you sow peace with your hands through your work and activities in life? Read *1 Corinthians 4:12: We work hard with our own hands. When we are cursed, we bless; when we are persecuted, we endure it*. Reflect on how you may or may not live out this verse and commune with Jesus.

SCRIPTURE:
And to make it your ambition to lead a quiet life: You should mind your own business and work with your hands (1 Thessalonians 4:11)

PRAYER:
Lord, I come to put my hands to work and to sow in peace with my fingers. Please help me to cultivate peacefulness on and off the mat and to lead a quiet life. I remember *Proverbs 31:13: She selects wool and flax and works with eager hands*. Yes, I have an eagerness to put my hands to work for you. Help me to be like a wife of noble character to you. May I live out the words of *1 Thessalonians 5:12: Acknowledge those who work hard among you, who care for you in the Lord and who admonish you*. Sealing all my work in peace, I say Amen.

ꙮ

Day 190
PADAHASTASANA – HANDS-TO-FEET POSE

To do the hands-to-feet pose, start in a forward fold, then lift your feet and draw the palms of your hands to the bottoms of your feet until your wrists kiss your toes. Bend your knees as much as you need to then aim to straighten your legs. This asana brings fresh blood to your wrists and hands. It is a venerable position because your hands normally catch you from falling, and here you express physical trust in the Lord's hands to save you first. Do you let Jesus wash your feet? Consider the areas of your life, and whether in each one you say "not my will, but your will be done, Lord." Where in your life may you still be holding on to control and thus need to surrender? Share your responses with Jesus.

SCRIPTURE:

"No," said Peter, "you shall never wash my feet." Jesus answered, "Unless I wash you, you have no part with me." (John 13:8)

PRAYER:

Lord, here postured in complete surrender, may my feet be washed in You. Holy One, forgive me for the ways I have tried to hold on to control. Letting go, Jesus, I remember the command you gave the disciples in *John 13:14: Now that I, your Lord and Teacher, have washed your feet, you also should wash one another's feet.* Yes, let me wash the feet of others. Let me do little gestures of kindness and care as a way of revealing your great love and grace. Amen.

◦◦

Day 191
BALASANA – CHILD'S POSE

The child's pose is often the first posture taken in class, thus marking the beginning of one's yoga practice. The traditional pose is done with your knees and feet together, your forehead on the mat, and your arms down by your torso. A common variation is the wide-legged balasana, in which your knees spread wide, big toes touch and arms extend out in front of you. In what ways do you experience life like a little child? How do you keep a child-like sense of wonder, openness, curiosity and creativity in your practice and life? How can you explore scriptures, ask questions and believe with eagerness and an open heart? Commune with Jesus.

SCRIPTURE:

And he said: "Truly I tell you, unless you change and become like little children, you will never enter the kingdom of heaven. Therefore, whoever takes the lowly position of this child is the greatest in the kingdom of heaven." (Matthew 18:3-4)

PRAYER:

Lord, I come to you like a little child remembering *Psalm 139:13-14: For you created my inmost being; you knit me together in my mother's womb. I praise you because I am fearfully and wonderfully made.* Father, thank you! I am excited to engage with you on the mat—exploring new poses with childlike wonder—and if I lose sight of my breath, returning to the child's pose to reconnect. As I try to balance and reach, I am open and vulnerable to falling; yet, I trust you will lift, lead and instruct me in the way I show go. Jesus, I hear *John 14:4: You already know the way.* Alleluia! Amen.

৩৬

Day 192
THREAD-THE-NEEDLE

Thread-the-needle is an arm variation that may be taken from different asanas including the tabletop and the half pigeon pose. To do thread-the-needle from the tabletop position, your right arm reaches up and comes down under your left arm, palm up. Your right shoulder opens, right cheek draws to the mat, left arm reaches forward and hips move back as your hamstrings meet your calves. Another variation is for the left leg to go out to the side, and to take a half-bind around your back using your left arm. Hold for a few breaths and reverse sides. Tread-the-needle opens your upper back and stretches your shoulders. As you do this pose, reflect on the areas in your life where you may be rich and where you may be poor. Read Mark 10:25, today's scripture, and note what it signifies to you.

SCRIPTURE:

It is easier for a camel to go through the eye of a needle than for a rich man to enter the kingdom of God. (Mark 10:25)

PRAYER:

Jesus, I come to the mat to take the lowest position, and I thank you for teaching me how to serve—for you came to earth to serve. Steady my step on your path. Father, I commune *Psalm 25:17: The troubles of my heart have multiplied; free me from my anguish.* Save me, for my trust is in you. Acknowledging *Psalm 40:17: Yet I am poor and needy; may the Lord think of me,* I say Amen.

❦

Day 193
ARDHA KURMASANA – HALF TORTOISE POSE AND KURMASANA – TORTOISE POSE

To do the half tortoise pose, start in the child's pose with your knees together and extend your arms above your head; draw your hands into the prayer position and form a cross with your thumbs. To do the full tortoise pose, start in a seated position with your legs spread wide apart. Keeping a gentle bend in your knees, fold forward with a flat back; as your chest lowers, slide your arms under your upper legs, palms down. You must act slowly and steadily like a tortoise to get into this asana's full expression. How do you exemplify patience in your practice—carefully getting into and coming out of postures? How do you find contentment in the journey and not fret when others do things differently or achieve different results from you both on and off the mat? Commune with Jesus.

SCRIPTURE:

Be still before the LORD and wait patiently for him; do not fret when people succeed in their ways, when they carry out their wicked schemes. (Psalm 37:7)

PRAYER:

Lord, I come to listen for your voice and to be patient in this practice, for I know you will answer my prayers when the time is right according to you. I understand that I can accomplish or achieve nothing in particular on the mat. This practice simply requires me to be attentive to your Spirit. I hear *Proverbs 14:29: Whoever is patient has great understanding, but one who is quick-tempered displays folly*, and *Proverbs 15:18: A hot-tempered person stirs up conflict, but the one who is patient calms a quarrel*. I come to cultivate patience and be a calming force to those around me. Breathing with ease and steadiness, I say Amen.

◌

Day 194
SASANGASANA – RABBIT POSE

To do the rabbit pose, start in the child's pose with your knees together, then lift your hips up and arch your back; draw your hands to your heels and forehead to your knees as the crown of your head kisses the mat. The rabbit pose supports your circulatory system, thyroid gland and hormone levels. Binding your forehead to your knees marks discipline; being in a position with your head down marks submission. How has the Lord disciplined you and restored you after you have sinned? Reflect on *Psalm 147:3: He heals the brokenhearted and binds up their wounds*. Commune with Jesus about any ways you may feel brokenhearted, and any wounds that need binding.

SCRIPTURE:
I have surely heard Ephraim's moaning: 'You disciplined me like an unruly calf, and I have been disciplined. Restore me, and I will return, because you are the LORD my God.' (Jeremiah 31:18)

PRAYER:
Lord, in so many ways I am like an unruly calf in need of your discipline. Thank you for doing so, for I know it is a mark of love. Repenting in broken heartedness, please bind up my wounds. Praise to you Lord, *'who forgives all our sins and heals all our diseases' (Psalm 103)*. Restore me as I return to you here on the mat; crown me in your compassion as my head gently presses on the mat in the rabbit pose. I have done nothing to deserve this blessing, yet I

know your unfailing love surrounds me and surpasses all my understanding. I give all praise to you! Amen.

᭡

Day 195
UTTANA SHISHOSANA – EXTENDED PUPPY POSE

To do the puppy pose, start from the tabletop position with your hips over your knees and knees on the mat hip width apart; stretch your arms out in front of you shoulder width apart and fold downward to rest your forehead on the mat. Positioning your forehead on the mat is thought to hone your sense of intuition. The extended puppy pose is very similar to the melting heart pose, anahastasana, in which your chin is resting on the mat. As you maintain the melting heart pose, ponder how you keep a soft heart. Both of these postures are thought to be soothing and grounding. Commune with Jesus about any new things the Lord has been doing in your life and any area that may feel like a 'wasteland'.

SCRIPTURE:

See, I am doing a new thing! Now it springs up; do you not perceive it? I am making a way in the desert and streams in the wasteland. (Isaiah 43:19)

PRAYER:

Lord, thank you for constantly doing new things in my life and for always making a way through the deserts for me. My heart melts in your loving embrace, and like a puppy, I am so curious about what you are going to do next in my life. Guide me with your wisdom and intuition. Father, I hear *Isaiah 48:6: From now on I will tell you of new things, of hidden things unknown to you. They are created now, and not long ago; you have not heard of them before today. So you cannot say, 'Yes, I knew of them.'* I am here to discover these new things, Lord; let your word and your presence fall afresh on me. Amen.

᭡

Day 196
MAKARASANA – CROCODILE POSE

The crocodile pose is a restorative posture. Lay on your belly with your arms up, upper arms on the mat, forearms bent, and your hands positioned under on your jaw, with your index finger and thumb behind the ear and the other fingers forward on your cheek. Another option is to keep your head down with your arms folded on the mat above your head. Sampson had taken a Nazarite vow because he had been set apart to God from birth. God's power resided in him and enabled him to do great and mighty things as recorded in Judges. How have you consecrated yourself to the Lord and vowed to walk in His ways? In what ways have you felt His power resting on you, giving you strength? Commune with Jesus.

SCRIPTURE:
Finding a fresh jawbone of a donkey, he grabbed it and struck down a thousand men. (Judges 15:15)

PRAYER:
Lord, I come to declare my faith in you, and show it symbolically here on the mat as Sampson did with his hair and actions. I consecrate myself to you. Let your holy power rest on me and in me, for I trust in your deliverance. I marvel at how you displayed your supernatural strength in Sampson. I ponder *Judges 16:12: Delilah took new ropes and tied him with them. Then, with men hidden in the room, she called to him, "Samson, the Philistines are upon you!" But he snapped the ropes off his arms as if they were threads.* Even when his hair was cut, you did a mighty act through Sampson, *Judges 16:30: Samson said, "Let me die with the Philistines!" Then he pushed with all his might, and down came the temple on the rulers and all the people in it. Thus he killed many more when he died than while he lived.* Dedicated as your vessel, Father, give me the daily strength I need to live out your will for me. Amen.

෩

Day 197
PASCHIMOTTANASANA – INTENSE WEST STRETCH, SEATED FORWARD BEND

To do the seated forward bend, start in a seated position with your legs extended straight out in front of you; then lift your hands above your head and fold forward with a flat back. As you inhale, lengthen through the crown of your head, and as you exhale, melt your heart closer to your legs. This is a humble, restorative pose. It is also an active stretch, in that each breath enables you to deepen in the pose. Reflect on what the act of bowing signifies. How does your physical positioning express devotion? Do you actively seek to deepen your relationship with the Lord? In your yoga practice today, bow and rise continuously for a minute or two, then silently commune with the Lord.

SCRIPTURE:
Then Abraham rose and bowed down before the people of the land. (Genesis 23:7)
Again Abraham bowed down before the people of the land. (Genesis 23:12)
Then the man bowed down and worshiped the LORD. (Genesis 24:26)

PRAYER:
Lord, I bow in reverence to your Holy Name. I come to the mat to actively surrender to you and to praise you. I remember *Philippians 2:10-11: That at the name of Jesus every knee should bow, in heaven and on earth and under the earth, and every tongue acknowledge that Jesus Christ is Lord, to the glory of God the Father.* Jesus, I bow forward acknowledging your truth, grace and faithfulness. Lead me on this journey. Amen.

ରୟ

Day 198
APANASANA – SEED POSE

To do the seed pose, lie on your back and hug your knees into your chest with you arms wrapped around your shins. Gently rock side-to-side and forward and back like a seed that is being worked into the ground. Imagine that you are physically planting yourself in God's truth. Like a kernel of wheat fallen to the ground, have you fallen to your knees, repented, and felt your sins die as a result? In what areas of your life have you laid down any selfish ambitions or vain conceits and surrendered to the Lord? Read *Hosea 10:12: Sow righteousness for yourselves, reap the fruit of unfailing love, and break up your unplowed ground; for it is time to seek the LORD, until he comes and showers his righteousness on you.* Commune with Jesus about seeds, sowing and reaping.

SCRIPTURE:

Very truly I tell you, unless a kernel of wheat falls to the ground and dies, it remains only a single seed. But if it dies, it produces many seeds. (John 12:24)

PRAYER:

Lord, I come to die to sin and to experience aliveness in your Spirit. I am here to lay down selfishness to serve in selflessness. I seek your word, surrender to your will, and deeply desire to sow good seeds in others' lives as you have done in mine. *2 Corinthians 9:10: Now he who supplies seed to the sower and bread for food will also supply and increase your store of seed and will enlarge the harvest of your righteousness.* Guide me in sowing seeds of love, harvesting faith and serving bread that will last. Amen.

৩৶

Day 199
SUPTA BADDHA KONASANA – RECLINING BOUND ANGLE POSE

To do the reclining bound angle, lie on your back, draw the bottoms of your feet together and spread your knees wide. Option to bring your right hand to your heart and left hand to your belly. Doing so, feel your heartbeat and belly rise and fall with each breath. The reclining bound angle is a grounding, opening and restoring pose. How do you cast your anxieties on the Lord? What requests have you expressed recently, and have you done so with thanksgiving? Listen quietly for what the Spirit may be urging you to pray for now.

Do not be anxious about anything, but in every situation, by prayer and petition, with thanksgiving, present your requests to God. (Philippians 4:6)

PRAYER:

Lord, I am so grateful for your holy presence. I rejoice in *Romans 8:38-39: For I am convinced that neither death nor life, neither angels nor demons, neither the present nor the future, nor any powers, neither height nor depth, nor anything else in all creation, will be able to separate us from the love of God that is in Christ Jesus our Lord.* What an amazing blessing! Nothing may separate me from you. Resting in this truth, I say Amen.

⁓

Day 200
ANANDA BALASANA – HAPPY BABY POSE

To do the happy baby pose, lie on your back and bring your legs up. Grab the insides of your feet and pull your knees and tailbone down toward the mat. You may choose to rock side to side. While you're in the happy baby pose, ponder how babies have such tender hearts. Rest in the image of Jesus lying in the manager, or think of what it's like to hold a baby in your arms. Think of their innocence and how their birth brings good news to a family. Commune with Jesus about the wonder of infants.

SCRIPTURE:

But when the chief priests and the scribes saw the wonderful things that he did, and the children crying out in the temple, "Hosanna to the Son of David!" they were indignant, and they said to him, "Do you hear what these are saying?" And Jesus said to them, "Yes; have you never read, 'Out of the mouth of infants and nursing babies you have prepared praise'?" (Matthew 21:15-16 ESV)

PRAYER:

Lord, I remember *Psalm 8:2: Through the praise of children and infants you have established a stronghold against your enemies, to silence the foe and the avenger.* I come like a happy baby with curiosity and openness to hear your word. Like an infant, provide me with the spiritual milk I need to grow and develop in faith and understanding. Heavenly Father, I am reliant on your saving hand; cradle me in your loving arms. Amen.

༄

Day 201
SUPTA MATSYENDRASANA – SUPINE TWIST POSE

To do the supine twist, start by lying on your back and draw your right knee into your chest. Reach your right arm out to your right side and gaze to the right. Keep your right shoulder down and draw your right knee across your body. It may or may not reach the mat on the left side. Only draw it down as far as you are able to do so while keeping your right shoulder down on the mat. You can also do this asana with a straight leg. Hold for a few breaths and reverse sides. The supine twist is a renewing and rejuvenating pose. It also has a cleansing effect and is considered a therapeutic pose for your back. As you practice this twist, reflect on how the Lord, the great I AM, sends you to be His messenger in various situations. How has the Lord drawn you to certain roles and/or places to learn something specific or to contribute in a particular way? Interestingly, I AM comes from the Hebrew word *Hayah*, which means *to be* or simply *be*. As you deepen your twist, ponder how you relate to the Lord as the 'I AM'. Who are you? Whose are you? Share your responses with Jesus.

SCRIPTURE:
Moses said to God, "Suppose I go to the Israelites and say to them, 'The God of your fathers has sent me to you,' and they ask me, 'What is his name?' Then what shall I tell them?" God said to Moses, "I AM WHO I AM. This is what you are to say to the Israelites: 'I AM has sent me to you.'" (Exodus 3:13-14)

PRAYER:
I AM, I come to further understand your majestic nature and to be with you. Jesus, I take heart in *John 8:12: I am the light of the world. Whoever follows me will never walk in darkness, but will have the light of life.* Rinse me of any darkness as I

twist here on the mat, and fill me with light that I might truly live in you. Lord, I want to go where you send me, acknowledging *John 8:58: "Very truly I tell you,"* *Jesus answered, "before Abraham was born, I am!"* I AM, renew my perspective and rejuvenate my heart through these asanas so that I may confidently live, breath and *be* where you want me to be. Amen.

୧

Day 202
VIPARITA KARANI – LEGS-UP-THE-WALL POSE

To do the legs-up-the-wall pose, start in a seated position with your side body against a wall. Swing the leg that is closest to the wall up and let the other leg follow it. Your legs may stay together or be spread wide. Your gluts are as close to the wall as possible. (You may want to place a cushion under your lower back.) Walls were built around cities during Biblical times as a form of protection and symbolized strength, prosperity and peace. Without walls, cities could be captured easily. In what ways can you put up walls to protect you from falling into temptation? How have you repaired broken walls in relationships? Commune with Jesus about what walls may need building or rebuilding in your life.

SCRIPTURE:
Your people will rebuild the ancient ruins and will rise up the age-old foundations; you will be called Repairer of Broken Walls, Restorer of Streets with Dwellings. (Isaiah 58:12)

PRAYER:
Lord, thank you for providing me the strength needed to rebuild walls and for restoring me time and again with your indwelling Spirit. I remember Rahab, who, because she lived close to the wall of Jericho, housed and protected Joshua's men, and in return, *Joshua 6:25: But Joshua spared Rahab the prostitute, with her family and all who belonged to her.* Father, help me to have the wisdom and confidence in you to act as Rahab did—knowing what walls to protect and what doors to open. Guard and protect me within the walls of your love. Amen.

୧

Day 203
SAVASANA – CORPSE POSE

Traditionally, the corpse pose is the final resting posture and done with your feet directed towards the front of the room. It may be perceived as the most important and challenging pose because it requires you to completely let go. To do the corpse pose, lie on your back, rest your arms at your sides, and let your feet naturally splay open. Close your eyes and breathe naturally. Reflect on *Luke 9:23-24: Then he said to them all:"Whoever wants to be my disciple must deny themselves and take up their cross daily and follow me. For whoever wants to save their life will lose it, but whoever loses their life for me will save it."* How might you need to let go and die to certain things and relationships in your life? Commune with Jesus about dying to 'self' and taking up your cross.

SCRIPTURE:
For to me, to live is Christ and to die is gain. (Philippians 1:21)

PRAYER:
Lord, I come to die to sin and to live in you. Please still me in your presence. I recite *Romans 8:10: But if Christ is in you, your body is dead because of sin, yet your spirit is alive because of righteousness.* Thank you for making me alive by your holy grace and righteousness. I place myself in the corpse pose acknowledging *1 Samuel 2:6: The LORD brings death and makes alive; he brings down to the grave and rises up.* Lord, I accept your holy cycles of death and rebirth. Dying to fleshly desires here on the mat, bring me life in your Spirit. Amen.

෨෮

Day 204
GARBHASANA – FETAL POSE

Before you come up to a seated position for a final prayer or gesture in a class, typically you are asked to roll to one side. It is generally done with your knees gently bent and your lower arm acting like a pillow—it marks rebirth. How do you feel embraced by the Lord and reborn in Christ? Meditate on *John 3:6-8: Flesh gives birth to flesh, but the Spirit gives birth to spirit. You should not be surprised at my say-ing, 'You must be born again.' The wind blows wherever it pleases. You hear its sound, but you cannot tell where it comes from or where it is going. So it is with everyone born of the Spirit.*

SCRIPTURE:

His left hand is under my head, his right arm embraces me. (Song of Solomon 8:3)

PRAYER:

Lord, thank you for your intimate embrace, and for death and rebirth. I rejoice in *1 Peter 1:23: For you have been born again, not of perishable seed, but of imperishable, through the living and enduring word of God.* What an indescribable glorious gift! As I am embraced in Your arms and reborn of Spirit, I live, move and breathe in the fullness of Life on the mat. Amen.

∽

Day 205
THE MAT

Practicing yoga is most often done on a mat. Jesus healed many from a mat. Reflect on your yoga practice on the mat. What does it do for you and in you? How have you experienced healing in physical, emotional and/or spiritual sense by the Lord? Share with Jesus any ways may you need to feel healed today.

SCRIPTURE:

I tell you, get up, take your mat and go home. (Mark 2:11)

PRAYER:

Lord, thank you for meeting me on the mat. I remember *John 5:8: Get up! Pick up your mat and walk.* Let my yoga practice propel me to get up, go forth and walk more closely in your way. I hear *Acts 9:34: Peter said to him, "Jesus Christ heals you. Get up and roll up your mat."* As you will it, help me to bless others in such a powerful way. As I roll up my mat at the end of the practice, I acknowledge your blessings and move boldly in Spirit, restored and redeemed. Amen.

∽

Day 206
BLOCKS

Blocks are props often used in yoga. They may be used to help stabilize you in poses like the triangle or half moon pose. To experience this steadying factor, rest your lowered hand on the block in these asanas. It essentially brings the floor closer to you. Blocks can also be used to elevate your heart in postures such as the reclining bound angle by placing the block under your upper back. Additionally, they can help with alignment and spacing, such as keeping the right amount of distance between your hands in the forearm stand. Like a yoga block, who supports your faith journey and conversely, whose spiritual journeys do you bless? Commune with Jesus about what types of support you may need now.

SCRIPTURE:
Because the gracious hand of my God was on me, the king granted my request. (Nehemiah 2:8)

PRAYER:
Sovereign Lord, thank you for the tools and people you have used to build, establish, support and strengthen me in faith. May your gracious hand rest on me as I trust in you. You called Nehemiah to rebuild the walls of Jerusalem; what walls are you calling me to rebuild? I listen for your response as I move on the mat. I rejoice in the glorious nature of *John 2:19: Jesus answered them, "Destroy this temple, and I will raise it again in three days."* Meditating on this verse and its wondrous truth, I say Amen.

༄

Day 207
STRAPS

Straps are used to help foster correct alignment and to deepen poses into full expressions. One asana that is really benefitted by using a strap is the reclining big toe pose, or supta padangusthasana. To do this pose, lie on your back, draw your right leg up to your chest, place a strap around the arch of your foot and then straighten your right leg while lifting it up. Keep your hips down and work your right leg towards your chest. Next, with your left hip remaining down, draw your right leg out to your right side. Hold for a few breaths and reverse sides. This posture stretches your hips, thighs, hamstrings, groin, and calves. It strengthens the knees. Using a strap to enhance your stretches, reflect on the tools and resources that have helped to further connect you with the Lord. Which ones have you been utilizing in life? Commune with Jesus about what tools or resources may be helpful to you now.

SCRIPTURE:
He is the one who comes after me, the straps of whose sandals I am not worthy to untie. (John 1:27)

PRAYER:
Jesus, I am unworthy to untie your sandal straps, and I am wonderfully struck by the straps of your love wrapped around me. Heavenly Father, I come to humbly thank you for the tools and resources you have blessed me with in my yoga practice and in life. I delight in *Isaiah 5:26-27: He lifts up a banner for the distant nations, he whistles for those at the ends of the earth. Here they come, swiftly and speedily! Not one of them grows tired or stumbles, not one slumbers or sleeps; not a belt is loosened at the waist, not a sandal strap is broken.* Provider of strong straps, fasten me in Your light and align me in truth as I deepen in poses. Amen.

෴

Day 208
BOLSTERS

Bolsters are cushions that can be placed below your seat to provide you with a softer base to pray and meditate. Similarly, what helps you to be still and listen to God? Have you felt the Lord fight for you at various time in your life, and if so, how? Ponder any recent quarrels or disagreements you have experienced. Commune with Jesus about whatever you may be battling internally or externally.

SCRIPTURE:

The LORD will fight for you; you need only to be still. (Exodus 14:14)

PRAYER:

Lord, I to come to be still and dwell in your holy peace both inwardly and outwardly. I surrender any battle within me to your will because the victory is yours. Father, please remove any sinful desire of my heart. As I surrender to you, I focus my heart entirely on your light and my mind wholly on your truth. Thank you fighting for me. I remember *Isaiah 54:17: "No weapon forged against you will prevail, and you will refute every tongue that accuses you. This is the heritage of the servants of the LORD, and this is their vindication from me," declares the LORD.* Almighty Protector, I am stilled in your all-surpassing power, love and grace. Glory to you in the Highest! Amen.

∽

Day 209
BLANKETS

Blankets are used in restorative yoga postures such as the legs-up-the-wall pose or for the final relaxation time. When do you use blankets? Think about the last time you covered someone you love with a blanket to keep them warm, and how the Lord has covered you with love and warmed your spirits. Commune with Jesus about any 'blankets' you feel in need of in your life today.

SCRIPTURE:

When it snows, she has no fear for her household; for all of them are clothed in scarlet. She makes coverings for her bed; she is clothed in fine linen and purple. (Proverbs 31:21-22)

PRAYER:

Lord, you are my comforter. Using a blanket during the restorative parts of this practice, I feel you wrap me in love and clothe me in salvation. I muse *Jeremiah 8:18: You who are my Comforter in sorrow, my heart is faint within me.* I am utterly unworthy of your wondrous grace lavishly given; my heart faints with joy. I proclaim *2 Corinthians 4:7: I am greatly encouraged; in all our troubles my joy knows no bounds.* Finally, *Psalm 119:50, 52: My comfort in my suffering is this: Your promise preserves my life.* Amen.

༄

Day 210
SURYA NAMASKAR A – SUN SALUTATION A

Sun As are typically done in the beginning of yoga class to warm the body, generating internal heat. Start in the equal standing pose; inhale draw your arms overhead to the upward salute pose, then exhale as you fold forward. Inhale as you lift up halfway, then exhale as you place your hands on the mat, step back and move from the high to the low plank. Inhale upward facing dog or cobra, exhale downward facing dog. Inhale step forward, exhale forward fold. Inhale upward salute, exhale begin again. There are many variations of this routine. Please choose a movement pattern that is energizing to you. What are the first things you do when you get up in the morning? How do you draw in the Lord's presence at the beginning of your day and as you start each new activity? What 'warm-ups' might be good to add into your daily practices? Commune with Jesus.

SCRIPTURE:

Because you are his sons, God sent the Spirit of his Son into our hearts, the Spirit who calls out, "Abba, Father." (Galatians 4:6)

PRAYER:

Abba, thank you for heating me throughout my entire being with your internal light and for refining me with your holy fire. I am here to fan the flame of your love starting by synchronizing my breath to your Spirit in Sun A Salutations. I remember *Hebrews 2:10: In bringing many sons and daughters to glory, it was fitting that God, for whom and through whom everything exists, should make the pioneer of their salvation perfect through what he suffered,* and *Hebrews 5:8-9: He learned obedience from what he suffered and, once made perfect, he became the source of eternal salvation for all who obey him.* Jesus, illuminator, path and Word of the Living Father, Abba, lead me in each breath and movement as I take up my cross to follow you. In reverence, I start this practice by musing the words of *Hebrews 10:14: for by one sacrifice he has made perfect forever those who are being made holy.* Amen.

༄

Day 211
SURYA NAMASKAR B – SUN SALUTATION B

From the forward fold inhale into the chair pose, exhale hands through heart center forward fold; inhale halfway lift; exhale plant hands, step back and move high to low plank. Inhale upward facing dog; exhale downward facing dog; inhale right leg forward warrior 1; exhale hand to mat; step back and continue the series—alternating left and right foot coming forward. Many variations of Sun Bs exist. The key is matching your breath with the movement. Generally speaking, when you move forward or up, you inhale, and when you move down or back, you exhale. Reflect on your faith path. When did you receive Christ? How has Jesus walked with you, and how have you grown spiritually? How do you keep in step with the Spirit and in step with your breath? Neither is easy to do; they both require attention, concentration and awareness. In what ways could you further develop a focused, committed, harmonious spirit through your breathing? Commune with Jesus.

SCRIPTURE:

Surely then you will count my steps but not keep track of my sin. (Job 14:16)

PRAYER:

Compassionate Lord, I breathe in Spirit and breathe out lifting your Name on high. I come to keep in step with your mighty love. Jesus, with faith in you, I meditate on *John 14:12: I tell you the truth, anyone who has faith in me will do what I have been doing. He will do even greater things than these, because I am going to the Father.* What a glorious truth! Help me awaken to the full meaning of these holy words here on the mat. Amen.

༄

Day 212
MANDALA

A mandala is a sacred circle expressed by performing a series of poses in a full circle (360 degrees) on the mat. It is thought to balance your brain by shifting your perspective as you move and face different ways. Listen to Jesus' holy words, "for the Father is greater than I." Ponder its meaning and reflect on the ways your perspective has shifted recently about a person, activity or belief. Read *Romans 7:10: I found that the very commandment that was intended to bring life actually brought death.* What examples of this can you think of in your life? Commune with Jesus.

SCRIPTURE:

You heard me say, 'I am going away and I am coming back to you.' If you loved me, you would be glad that I am going to the Father, for the Father is greater than I. (John 14:28)

PRAYER:

Jesus, I marvel at your holy ways. Thank you for going to the Father. You constantly draw my views into greater congruency with Truth and reveal new things to me. As I turn around and back again on the mat, attune my body, mind and heart to your holy perspective. Father, I note *Joshua 6:15-16: On the seventh day, they got up at daybreak and marched around the city seven times in the same manner, except that on that day they circled the city seven times. The seventh time around, when the priests sounded the trumpet blast, Joshua commanded the army, "Shout! For the LORD has given you the city!"* This Biblical account is so sweet—through their obedience to your command by encircling the city, you brought them victory. I circle here on the mat, for my victory is in you! Amen.

❧

Day 213
VINYASA

Vinyasa is actually a two-part word: *Vi* means 'in a special way' and *nyasa* means 'to place'. Essentially, vinyasa is posturing your body, heart and spirit in a special way by synchronizing your movement to your breath. It may be cued inhale pose A, exhale pose B. The movement becomes like a dance as you move up, down and around your mat in various positions. Think about how you position your body, mind and heart in a special way as you practice yoga, and likewise, how you do so in life. Taking a moment to feel the Lord's holy energy within you, reflect on where the Lord may be calling you to go to now.

SCRIPTURE:

But you will receive power when the Holy Spirit comes on you; and you will be my witnesses in Jerusalem, and in all Judea and Samaria, and to the ends of the earth. (Acts 1:8)

PRAYER:

Lord, thank you for placing your Spirit in me in a special way—packed with holy power, grace and light. I hear Paul's words in *Acts 20:22: And now, compelled by the Spirit, I am going to Jerusalem, not knowing what will happen to me there.* Like Paul, let me be compelled to listen and move at the impulse of your Spirit. Journey with me, Jesus, here on the mat; teach me where you desire me to go. Keep me in step with your Spirit and let me be a witness for you. Posturing myself in a sacred way with this breath, I say Amen.

෴

Day 214
EQUANIMITY

What you do on the right side of your body in yoga, you also should do on the left. This fosters equanimity. How do you practice equanimity on the mat, as well as, off the mat in your daily life? Do you strive for balance between receiving blessing and extending blessing? How does the Lord provide you with directional truth and inner harmony? Commune with Jesus.

SCRIPTURE:

Whether you turn to the right or to the left, your ears will hear a voice behind you, saying, "This is the way; walk in it." (Isaiah 30:21)

PRAYER:

Lord, I come to create equanimity in my body, mind and spirit and heed *1 Peter 1:17: Since you call on a Father who judges each person's work impartially, live out your time as foreigners here in reverent fear.* Help me to demonstrate this reverent fear and fairness in my interactions and to keep non-judgmental thoughts in my mind. Aiming for equipoise, I remember *James 2:3-4: If you show special attention to the man wearing fine clothes and say, "Here's a good seat for you," but say to the poor man, "You stand there" or "Sit on the floor by my feet," have you not discriminated among yourselves and become judges with evil thoughts?* Guide me in a spirit of equal care— to the right and to the left, to the rich and to the poor, to men and to women. This is my sacred intention. Amen.

༄

Day 215
COMING INTO A CERTAIN POSITION

The word 'come' is often used as a directive in classes, such as 'come to a seated position' or 'come up to a standing position.' What positions have you 'come into' in your practice recently, and in your life? How have you experienced the Lord asking you to come and follow Him? Read *Matthew 9:9: As Jesus went on from there, he saw a man named Matthew sitting at the tax collector's booth. "Follow me," he told him, and Matthew got up and followed him.* Commune with Jesus.

SCRIPTURE:

"Come, follow me," Jesus said, "and I will make you fishers of men." (Matthew 4:19)

PRAYER:

Lord, I thank you for calling me according to your purpose. Let your power be displayed, your Name proclaimed, and your way be glorified in my being. Help me to be ever attentive to your voice. I hear *Mark 3:13: Jesus went up a mountain, called those whom he wanted, and they came to him.* Jesus, I come to you. Please receive me in eternal love and grace. Amen.

༄

Day 216
CORRECTIONS AND ENHANCEMENTS

Teachers often give verbal cues and/or physical adjustments to further align and enhance your poses, thereby enabling you to more readily receive the benefit of their instruction. How do you feel when you are adjusted on the mat? Are you comfortable with someone touching you? How do react when you receive verbal refinement directions both on and off the mat? In what ways are you experiencing 'corrections of disciple' in your faith and in life? Commune with Jesus.

SCRIPTURE:
For these commands are a lamp, this teaching is a light, and the corrections of discipline are the way to life. (Proverbs 6:23)

PRAYER:
True Vine and Gardener—Great I AM, I thank you for pruning me both physically and spiritually. Draw me into alignment with your Spirit in this practice. Your commands are a lamp, your teachings a light and your corrections a way to life. Fasten me to them and forgive me for the ways I have struggled to keep them. I am emboldened by *2 Timothy 2:15: Do your best to present yourself to God as one approved, a worker who does not need to be ashamed and who correctly handles the word of truth*, and rejoice in *John 15:16: You did not choose me, but I chose you and appointed you so that you might go and bear fruit—fruit that will last—and so that whatever you ask in my name the Father will give you.* A mighty truth! Aiming to bear fruit that will last, I pay careful attention to the corrections and enhancements extended toward me both on and off the mat. Amen.

෧෨

Day 217
BEING EARNEST

To acknowledge your limitations is an important aspect of yoga. Certain bodies can do certain moves and others cannot, and that is okay! How have you acknowledged your own body's limitations? It is also important to be honest about

times when you do not to listen to instructions and do your own thing, not because of a physical limitation, but because you didn't like the teachers direction
or weren't carefully listening. How have you felt rebuked and disciplined both on
and off the mat? Commune with Jesus.

SCRIPTURE:

Those whom I love I rebuke and discipline. So be earnest and repent. (Revelation 3:19)

PRAYER:

Lord, may this practice be a time when I am earnest and repentant. You know
my errors, limitations and sin. I expose them to you here. Please forgive
me. I thank you for your mercy that never fails. I recognize *Proverbs 3:11-12:
My son, do not despise the Lord's discipline and do not resent his rebuke, because the
Lord disciplines those he loves, as a father the son he delights in.* This message is so
important it's repeated in *Hebrews 12:6: The Lord disciplines those he loves.* I am
open to discipline and rebuke so that I may be more fruitful. Guide me in
your truth. Amen.

∽

Day 218
HANDLING TRANSITIONS

In yoga there are many transitions—flowing from one breath, one movement
to holding postures for several breaths, to doing different series of postures.
How do you handle transitions? What transitions in your practice do you find
challenging, and what transitions in life have you found challenging? How open
are you to change? Are you able to shift gears smoothly and easily when circumstances change? Commune with Jesus about any transitions currently occurring
in your life.

SCRIPTURE:

*Jesus said, "Do not hold on to me, for I have not yet ascended to the Father. Go instead to
my brothers and tell them, 'I am ascending to my Father and your Father, to my God and
your God.'"* (John 20:17)

PRAYER:

Jesus, thank you for ascending to our Father. Please prepare my heart, body, mind and spirit for all the transitions that I will face on this mat and in my life. Father, I remember the story in the Old Testament of when Rebekah was a young woman; she had given Abraham's servant some water, and the very next day she left her family and went to marry Jacob whom she had never met—a big transition! *Genesis 24:58: So they called Rebekah and asked her, "Will you go with this man?" "I will go," she said.* Help me to have the same poise and confidence that Rebekah showed when your Spirit calls me to transition from one thing to the next. In your holy Name, I say Amen.

ᴖ

Day 219
FACING

Cues in yoga are often given to direct which way the instructor wants you to face, such as 'face the side wall' or 'face down on the mat.' Which direction you face is important. Reflect on *Genesis 19:17, 26: Do not look back. But Lot's wife looked back, and she became a pillar of salt,* and *Joshua 7:10: The LORD said to Joshua, "Stand up! What are you doing down on your face?"* Have you received direction in your life about where 'to face' physically as well as spiritually? From decisions to people, or from challenges to opportunities, what are you facing now? Commune with Jesus.

SCRIPTURE:

The LORD turn his face toward you and give you peace. (Numbers 6:26)

PRAYER:

Lord, thank you for turning your face to me and giving me peace. Help me to heed your commands about where I should face and how I should act. Guide me in promptly and obediently responding to your voice. I remember *2 Chronicles 20:18: Jehoshaphat bowed down with his face to the ground, and all the people of Judah and Jerusalem fell down in worship before the LORD.* Yes, Lord, I start this practice with my face bowed down in reverence awaiting and listening for which direction you want me to face. Thank you for your guidance. Amen.

ᴖ

Day 220
FACIAL EXPRESSION

Many beautiful refinement cues in yoga have to do with your face, such as to soften your neck, jaw, the muscles around your eyes and forehead. Your face should have a gentle, soft expression during your practice. Often in the midst of an activity, such a yoga practice, you can forget what expression is on your face. Take note, is your face relaxed? When you feel connected to the Lord, you cannot help but glow! Has anyone ever commented on your face when you felt refreshed in the Spirit? What have you noticed about the faces of others who are filled with faith? Read *Psalm 34:4-5: I sought the LORD, and he answered me; he delivered me from all my fears. Those who look to him are radiant; their faces are never covered with shame.* Touch your face and commune with Jesus.

SCRIPTURE:
When Moses came down from Mount Sinai with the two tablets of the covenant law in his hands, he was not aware that his face was radiant because he had spoken with the LORD. (Exodus 34:29)

PRAYER:
Lord, thank you for refreshing tired faces, for softening expressions with your gentleness, and for calming them with your grace. I rejoice in *Hebrews 1:3: The Son is the radiance of God's glory and the exact representation of his be-ing, sustaining all things by his powerful word. After he had provided purification for sins, he sat down at the right hand of the Majesty in heaven.* Thank you for drawing me to you, Lord. Let my face radiate your love. I remember *Acts 6:15: All who were sitting in the Sanhedrin looked intently at Stephen, and they saw that his face was like the face of an angel.* As you did with Stephen, keep me illuminated with your holy glow here on the mat and off it wherever I may go. Amen.

Day 221
FOCUSING THE GAZE — PART 1

A central yoga term is dristi, which means gaze. Generally speaking, it means having a relaxed and soft focus, a place to direct your energy to flow. Where your gaze goes, your attention follows. Are you aware of your gaze during your practice? How about at home or when you're out in public? What captures your eyes? Where have you found your eyes wandering recently—maybe at another person, a particular website or a certain part of your own body? How can you keep drawing your eyes back to the Lord? Reflect on *John 8:7-11: When they kept on questioning him, he straightened up and said to them, "Let any one of you who is without sin be the first to throw a stone at her." Again he stooped down and wrote on the ground. At this, those who heard began to go away one at a time, the older ones first, until only Jesus was left, with the woman still standing there. Jesus straightened up and asked her, "Woman, where are they? Has no one condemned you?" "No one, sir," she said. "Then neither do I condemn you," Jesus declared. "Go now and leave your life of sin."* Commune with Jesus about these verses and your gaze.

SCRIPTURE:
Let your eyes look straight ahead, fix your gaze directly before you. (Proverbs 4:25)

PRAYER:
Sovereign Lord, I come to focus my eyes on you—on your word, will and way. I turn inward to see what you are teaching me from the inside out, remembering *Matthew 7:3: Why do you look at the speck of sawdust in your brother's eye and pay no attention to the plank in your own eye?* Help me see the plank in my eye and the truths you so deeply desire to reveal to me. Keep redirecting my gaze back to the straight and narrow path of Life. Amen.

◌

Day 222
FOCUSING THE GAZE — PART 2

Your gaze in yoga embodies the physical positioning of your eyes and the internal positioning of your heart and mind. Reflect on how you have sensed or experienced the Lord's presence within you; how have you set the presence of the Lord in the forefront of your heart and mind? Meditate on *Genesis 13:14-17: The LORD said to Abram after Lot had parted from him,"Lift up your eyes from where you are and look north and south, east and west. All the land that you see I will give to you and your offspring forever. I will make your offspring like the dust of the earth, so that if anyone could count the dust, then your offspring could be counted. Go, walk through the length and breadth of the land, for I am giving it to you."*

SCRIPTURE:

David said about him,"I saw the Lord always before me. Because he is at my right hand, I will not be shaken." (Acts 2:25)

PRAYER:

Lord, I come to seek your face—to place my eyes, attention and focus where you desire. As I set my gaze beyond my extended fingers, out and upward in love, I feel your Spirit well up inside me and radiate out light. Intimate Lord, I rejoice upon remembering the only one in the Bible who gives you a personal name: a woman named Hagar. *Genesis 13:16: She gave this name to the LORD who spoke to her:"You are the God who sees me," for she said,"I have now seen the One who sees me."* Here I am on a small mat, and there are billions of people you have to attend to, yet right here, right now, you see me, just like you saw Hagar. Thank you for being a God who sees me. Living Father, help me to realize this truth in a fresh way as I direct my gaze to you. Amen.

◌◌

Day 223
KEEPING A NARROW STANCE

The full expression of many standing postures is with a heel-to-heel or heel-to-arch alignment of your feet. This is challenging to do. The modification is always to take a wider stance. Similarly, with faith it is much harder to stay on the straight and narrow path. It is much easier to broaden your approach, values and pursuits. Ironically, it is much easier to fall when you take a narrow stance, yet how much greater the reward! How do you keep on the narrow path in your yoga practice? How about in your life and in your faith? Share your responses with Jesus.

SCRIPTURE:

Enter through the narrow gate. For wide is the gate and broad is the road that leads to destruction, and many enter through it. But small is the gate and narrow the road that leads to life, and only a few find it. (Matthew 7:13-14)

PRAYER:

Jesus, thank you for knocking on my heart. I open the small gate and come to stay on your narrow path. Lord, I start by aligning my feet, as your Word says in *Hebrews 12:13: Make level paths for your feet, so that the lame may not be disabled, but rather healed.* Doing so, I rejoice in *Job 4:4: Your words have supported those who stumbled; you have strengthened faltering knees.* Keep me strong and stable in your love and light. Amen.

℘

Day 224
BLADING

'Blade your foot down' is a yoga cue given for you to further ground the outside edge of your back foot. This cue is typically offered in standing poses to enhance your stability and direct your energy upward. What actions and activities provide you with a sense of stability and strength—physically, emotionally and spiritually? Conversely, what reminds you of your fragility? Share your responses with Jesus.

SCRIPTURE:

Slash to the right, you sword, then to the left, wherever your blade is turned. I too will strike my hands together, and my wrath will subside. I the LORD have spoken. (Ezekiel 21:16-17)

PRAYER:

Lord, as I blade my back foot down, anchoring myself securely on the mat, I remember your almighty touch that secures, protects and enables me to grow. At the same time, I'm aware that my fragility is like a blade of grass, as your Word says in *Psalm 103:15-16: The life of mortals is like grass, they flourish like a flower of the field; the wind blows over it and it is gone, and its place remembers it no more.* Holy One, thank you for your salvation! I hear *Hosea 14:5-6: I will be like the dew to Israel; he will blossom like a lily. Like a cedar of Lebanon he will send down his roots; his young shoots will grow.* Green with hope like a blade of grass, let me flourish and grow for You. Amen.

6∿9

Day 225
MICRO-BENDING

Micro-bend is a term used to remind you not to lock your joints, such as your knees in poses like the triangle. The micro-bend allows you to strengthen while keeping your energy channels open. Although it is one of the smallest movements, it is also one of the most important because by not locking your joints, you protect them from injury. What are some of the seemingly small things in your life that bring you closer to the Lord? Is there anything in your life that seems insignificant to you but that really matters to God? Commune with Jesus about the small but important things.

SCRIPTURE:

Again he said, "What shall we say the kingdom of God is like, or what parable shall we use to describe it? It is like a mustard seed, which is the smallest of all seeds on earth. Yet when planted, it grows and becomes the largest of all garden plants, with such big branches that the birds can perch in its shade." (Mark 4:30-32)

PRAYER:

Lord, I am amazed at all the little ways you show your love for me. I marvel at *Matthew 17:20: Truly I tell you, if you have faith as small as a mustard seed, you can say to this mountain, 'Move from here to there,' and it will move. Nothing will be impossible for you.* I come to grow in faith and position myself in a way that's conducive for your living waters to flow in me. Jesus, lead me in your light, one micro-bend at a time. Amen.

6∿9

Day 226
INTERNAL ROTATION

Internal rotation is a common cue in yoga practice that means to engage your muscles toward the midline of your body. Examples include inner rotating your back thigh in the warrior 1 pose and your forearms in the downward facing dog. Come to a seated position with your legs extended, inwardly rotate your thighs and read *Romans 8:23: Not only so, but we ourselves, who have the firstfruits of the Spirit, groan inwardly as we wait eagerly for our adoption to sonship, the redemption of our bodies.* What are some ways you groan inwardly within your spirit? Next, soften your legs and read *Romans 2:29: No, a person is a Jew who is one inwardly; and circumcision is circumcision of the heart, by the Spirit, not by the written code. Such a person's praise is not from other people, but from God.* Are you a Jew by the Spirit, circumcised of the heart? Commune with Jesus about your internal rotation.

SCRIPTURE:

Of David. Praise the LORD, my soul; all my inmost being, praise his holy name. (Psalm 103:1)

PRAYER:

Lord, I am here to praise you with my inmost being. As I inwardly rotate my muscles to the midline of my body, I do so to focus on your inner presence. Hugging to your truth, I want to engage my whole physical and spiritual being. I remember *2 Corinthians 4:16: Therefore we do not lose heart. Though outwardly we are wasting away, yet inwardly we are being renewed day by day.* Yes, Lord, you renew me in each internal engagement I do. Glory to you in the highest! Amen.

༄

Day 227
EXTERNAL ROTATION

External rotation is a cue that directs you to engage the muscles away from the midline of the body; it is an opening motion. Examples of external rotation include your back leg in the warrior 2 pose and your upper arms in the downward facing dog. From a seated pose, extend your legs in front of you and rotate them externally. Read *Nehemiah 1:3-4: They said to me, "Those who survived the exile and are back in the province are in great trouble and disgrace. The wall of Jerusalem is broken down, and its gates have been burned with fire." When I heard these things, I sat down and wept. For some days I mourned and fasted and prayed before the God of heaven.* Take a moment to reflect on what makes you stop and pray for others. When and what triggers you to ask for counsel? Commune with Jesus about any news you may have heard recently that is weighing heavily on your heart.

SCRIPTURE:

Hezekiah received the letter from the messengers and read it. Then he went up to the temple of the LORD and spread it out before the LORD. And Hezekiah prayed to the LORD: "LORD, the God of Israel, enthroned between the cherubim, you alone are God over all the kingdoms of the earth. You have made heaven and earth. Give ear, LORD, and hear; open your eyes, LORD, and see; listen to the words Sennacherib has sent to ridicule the living God. (2 Kings 19:14-16)

PRAYER:

Lord, I come before you and remember the news I have heard about people who are in pain, and who are lonely, poor and oppressed—news that has saddened me. Please teach me how to compassionately respond to such news. Every time I externally rotate my limbs, I do so to physically signify lifting up before you in prayer those grieving, troubled, lowly and meek. I remember how you responded to Hezekiah in *2 Kings 20:5: Go back and tell Hezekiah, the ruler of my people, 'This is what the LORD, the God of your father David, says: I have heard your prayer and seen your tears; I will heal you.'* Lord, I trust you will heal those I lift up in prayer to you. In gratitude for your care, love and grace, I say Amen.

∽

Day 228
EXPLORING ARM VARIATIONS

There is a plethora of arm variations for each asana. To explore a few, start in the crescent lunge pose with your left leg forward; stretch your right hand forward and your left arm back keeping your arms even with your shoulders; hold for a few breaths, then lower your left arm to the backside of your right leg, then your left arm lifts up. Hold for a few more breaths then reverse sides. Next, come into the chair position and sweep one arm forward and the other back, then reverse. As you do this motion, keep your palms up and gaze at your back palm. Third movement, sweep both arms back, palms face down, and draw your chest to your thighs, then stretch your arms in front of you with palms facing up. These suggestions are simply to get you thinking about different ways to move. Thinking about the various ways you have moved your arms on the mat, reflect on Jesus telling the crippled man to reach out his hand—to take action and move it, and by doing so in faith, it was healed. Opening your hands physically shows a readiness to give and receive. How has the Lord called you to take action? How may you have experienced healing through the opening of your hands? What miracles have happened with your hands? Gaze at your hands and reflect on how the Lord might want you to use your hands for His glory.

SCRIPTURE:
He looked around at them all, and then said to the man, "Stretch out your hand." He did so, and his hand was completely restored. (Luke 6:10)

PRAYER:
Lord, thank you telling me to stretch out my hands so that you may heal me. Help me to open my hands and heart to receive your expansive love, and then to share it. I hear *Acts 4:29-30: "Now, Lord, consider their threats and enable your servants to speak your word with great boldness. Stretch out your hand to heal and perform signs and wonders through the name of your holy servant Jesus." After they prayed, the place where they were meeting was shaken. And they were all filled with the Holy Spirit and spoke the word of God boldly.* As I move my hands on the mat and physically shake while holding challenging postures, let it all be done as a prayer to you, Lord. May I actively treat my body as your temple and be willing for my hands to be your hands here on earth. Father, I offer up my arms and my entire being to serve you and perform wonders. Amen.

෨෮

Day 229
EXPLORING THE THREE INTERNAL LOCKS: BANDHAS

The three internal locks are the root (mula) lock, the core (uddiyana) lock and the throat (jalandhara) lock. These internal energy locks tone the muscles engaged by sustained contraction. They also serve to heighten your sense of focus and stimulate internal heat. Can you feel yourself locked and engaged in the Spirit in your yoga practice? Read *Hebrews 4:12: For the word of God is alive and active. Sharper than any double-edged sword, it penetrates even to dividing soul and spirit, joints and marrow; it judges the thoughts and attitudes of the heart*, and *Galatians 3:22: But Scripture has locked up everything under the control of sin, so that what was promised, being given through faith in Jesus Christ, might be given to those who believe.* Commune with Jesus about these verses and internal locks.

SCRIPTURE:
Then he said to me, "Son of man, eat this scroll I am giving you and fill your stomach with it." So I ate it, and it tasted as sweet as honey in my mouth. (Ezekiel 3:3)

PRAYER:
Sovereign Lord, thank you for locking up everything within me that had been under the control of sin, freeing me in your mighty grace and sealing me in your truth. Your words are alive and active inside me—thank you! I remember *Revelation 10:9-10: So I went to the angel and asked him to give me the little scroll. He said to me, "Take it and eat it. It will turn your stomach sour, but in your mouth it will be as sweet as honey. I took the little scroll from the angel's hand and ate it. It tasted as sweet as honey in my mouth, but when I had eaten it, my stomach turned sour.* As I engage the base of my torso, belly and jaw during this practice, please seal these areas in Spirit. Your words are sweet but at the same time packed with indescribable power. Thank you, for your indwelling energy. Here to kindle it, I say Amen.

෴

Day 230
ROOT LOCK – MULA BANDHA

The root lock is activated when you engage your bottom torso muscles as if you had to hold the urge to go to the bathroom. When you go back and forth between engaging and disengaging your pelvic floor, you are essentially doing what are known as Kegel exercises. This movement strengthens your pelvic floor. By activating your root lock, your may feel energy rise up inside you. As you try out this lock, reflect on how are you like a spring enclosed, a sealed fountain. Close your eyes and picture yourself as the Lord's beloved. Now release the lock and ponder how the Lord has impregnated you with an idea, a vision or holy truth.

SCRIPTURE:

You are a garden locked up, my sister, my bride; you are a spring enclosed, a sealed fountain. (Song of Solomon 4:12)

PRAYER:

Lord, I thank you for the gift of pregnancy and new life, thoughts, ideas and visions. As I engage mula bandha on the mat, I marvel at recreation, intimacy and sexuality. Father, I remember Hagar in *Genesis 16:11: The angel of the LORD also said to her, "You are now pregnant and you will give birth to a son,"* and Rachel in *Genesis 30:5-6: She became pregnant and bore him a son. Then Rachel said, "God has vindicated me; he has listened to my plea and given me a son."* I also remember Mary in *Matthew 1:18: His mother Mary was pledged to be married to Joseph, but before they came together, she was found to be pregnant through the Holy Spirit.* Lord, who impregnates and opens wombs, I am fascinated by your intimate workings. Impregnate me with your Spirit and seal me in a fountain of living waters here on the mat. Amen.

༄

Day 231
CORE LOCK – UDDIYANA BANDHA

Lifting your belly up and in engages your core lock. This belly engagement can really help your practice because your belly is the central hub of your physical strength. Place your hands on your belly, breathe deeply into that space and reflect on *John 7:38 (KJV): He that believeth on me, as the scripture hath said, out of his belly shall flow rivers of living water.* Can you feel living water and the flame of the Lord lit within you by engaging your core? What do you hunger for and crave? What nourishes you and gives you strength, stamina and energy? Share your responses with Jesus.

SCRIPTURE:
The spirit of man is the candle of the LORD, searching all the inward parts of the belly. (Proverbs 20:27 KJV)

PRAYER:
Lord, as I lift my belly in and up, I do so to tap into your living essence and presence within me. What an amazing gift! I remember *Leviticus 1:9: You are to wash the internal organs and the legs with water, and the priest is to burn all of it on the altar. It is a burnt offering, a food offering, an aroma pleasing to the LORD.* Lord, wash and strengthen my inner organs and core through your living waters, and set them alight with your holy fire in the depths of my being. Jesus, thank you for bringing a new covenant, a covenant that cleanses with grace. Remembering *Proverbs 18:20: From the fruit of their mouth a person's stomach is filled; with the harvest of their lips they are satisfied,* I say Amen.

༄

Day 232
THROAT LOCK – JALANDHARA BANDHA

It is done by slightly lowering the chin while raising your sternum and collarbones and bringing your tongue to your mouth's palate. While doing this lock, settle your gaze on the tip of your nose. Reflect on how you have been responding to the needs of those around you—spouse/significant other, friends, children, parents, boss, etc. How have you responded to those in need in your community and around the world? Ponder how the Lord may use you now.

SCRIPTURE:

A friend of mine on a journey has come to me, and I have no food to offer him.' And suppose the one inside answers, 'Don't bother me. The door is already locked, and my children and I are in bed. I can't get up and give you anything.' I tell you, even though he will not get up and give you the bread because of friendship, yet because of your shameless audacity he will surely get up and give you as much as you need. (Luke 11:6-8)

PRAYER:

Lord, I thank you for your responsiveness and patience with me. Please forgive me for the ways I have been inattentive to the needs of those around me, those I do care about yet sometimes neglect to demonstrate it through my actions. Guide me in being alert and compassionate. I remember *1 Corinthians 9:8-10: For it is written in the Law of Moses: "Do not muzzle an ox while it is treading out the grain." Is it about oxen that God is concerned? Surely he says this for us, doesn't he? Yes, this was written for us, because whoever plows and threshes should be able to do so in the hope of sharing in the harvest.* Let the engagement of my throat lock physically embody my hope in your harvest. Focused on cultivating true offerings, I say Amen.

❧

Day 233
LINES OF ENERGY

Yoga aims to help your energy flow by lengthening and straightening your natural lines such as the one from your tailbone to the crown of your head. In classes you may hear cues such as slightly tuck your tailbone, lift your belly up and in, draw your shoulders down and back, lengthen through the crown of your head, keep your chin neutral, maintain heel-to-heel alignment and/ or reach evenly through your fingertips. These cues all have to do with your body's alignment, enabling your energy to flow. How do you physically position yourself to hear God's word? How do you align yourself emotionally as well as spiritually? Commune with Jesus about lines of energy—straight and narrow paths in the Spirit.

SCRIPTURE:

For God's Word is solid to the core; everything he makes is sound inside and out. He loves it when everything fits, when his world is in plumb-line true. Earth is drenched in God's affectionate satisfaction.
(Psalm 33:4 MSG)

PRAYER:

Lord, I am here to make straight paths for you with my body and being. I hear *Isaiah 28:17: I will make justice the measuring line and righteousness the plumb line.* Please let your holy energy of justice and righteousness alignment in your might truth. I remember your conversation with Amos in *Amos 7:7-8: This is what he showed me: The Lord was standing by a wall that had been built true to plumb, with a plumb line in his hand. And the LORD asked me, "What do you see, Amos?" "A plumb line," I replied. Then the Lord said, "Look, I am setting a plumb line among my people Israel."* Righteous Father, I trust you to make me plumb as you will it. Focused on radiating your light through my fingers, toes, heart and crown of my head, I say Amen.

৩৩

Day 234
SPINAL ALIGNMENT

Most asanas, such as warriors, planks and forward folds, are done with a straight back. In other words, with a neutral spine. Of course there are exceptions, such as the wheel or camel pose, yet generally, you want to elongate the back, and cues are frequently given to lengthen it. How has God given you reminders that direct you on the path of life? Commune with Jesus about any areas or ways you may currently need to be pruned.

SCRIPTURE:

I am the true vine, and my Father is the gardener. He cuts off every branch in me that bears no fruit, while every branch that does bear fruit he prunes so that it will be even more fruitful. You are already clean because of the word I have spoken to you. (John 15:1-3)

PRAYER:

Lord, thank you for tending to me with your Word. Please prune me, for it is my desire to remain in you and do your will. I hear *Proverbs 3:6: In all your ways submit to him, and he will make your paths straight*. I submit to you and straighten my back in forward folds, planks and warriors to physically express my desire to stay on your straight and narrow path. Amen.

٭

Day 235
DRAWING

Throughout a yoga practice, you are continuously aligning your body in the asanas. You make adjustments, such as drawing your left hip forward or drawing right foot closer to your left. This sort of action can be a physical reminder to draw into the Lord. Do you draw near to God at all times—when you are sick and when you are healthy? When you are in need and when you have plenty? When do you feel closest to the Lord, and how do you draw near to Him daily? Share your responses with Jesus.

SCRIPTURE:

Come near to God and he will come near to you. (James 4:8)

PRAYER:

Father, I come to my mat to draw near you in reverence, for I know you understand what is happening in my life even before I do, and you have perceived my thoughts and heart accordingly. Lord, may your Spirit cleanse me from the inside out. Jesus, I reflect on your words spoken in *Luke 8:48 (KJV): Daughter, be of good comfort: your faith hath made you whole; go in peace.* I hear you speak these words to me and feel them enter my being. Drawing closer to you, I move my body as an act of praise and peace. Amen.

٭

Day 236
LOWERING

To lower is a common cue. Examples of lowering include lowering your shoulders down and back in a standing position, or lowering your head down towards to the mat in a forward fold. Like the man on the mat in Luke 5, Saul's friends also showed they cared in *Acts 9:25: But his followers took him by night and lowered him in a basket through an opening in the wall.* How you been lowered or humbled in an act of care? Reflect on any times when you have leaned down to attend to someone. Commune with Jesus about how you lift others up and lower yourself in humility.

SCRIPTURE:
When they could not find a way to do this because of the crowd, they went up on the roof and lowered him on his mat through the tiles into the middle of the crowd, right in front of Jesus. (Luke 5:19)

PRAYER:
Lord, thank you for your divine protection, care and love. As I lower my limbs to deepen into the poses, may that action physically express *John 3:30: He must become greater; I must become less.* I come to practice with humility and meekness. Please give me the courage and creativity I need to break a hole in any ceiling when needed. Lowering in love, I say Amen.

෨

Day 237
KNEELING

Kneeling is a posture often used as a transition in yoga, and it is not to be taken lightly. Kneeling is a posturing for prayer. Think of times when you kneel—maybe in church or by your bedside. It is often perceived as uncomfortable. *Ephesians 3:13-14: I ask you, therefore, not to be discouraged because of my sufferings for you, which are your glory. For this reason I kneel before the Father.* How hard or easy is it for you to stay in a kneeling position? How is the Lord growing you through uncomfortable positions both on the mat and in life? As you kneel and bow before Him, quietly listen for His voice.

SCRIPTURE:

Come, let us bow down in worship, let us kneel before the LORD our Maker. (Psalm 95:6)

PRAYER:

Lord, kneeling, I come to you, acknowledging *Romans 14:11: It is written: 'As surely as I live,' says the Lord, 'every knee will bow before me; every tongue will acknowledge God.'* Bowing my knees in love, light and wholehearted gratitude your holy presence, I say Amen.

∾

Day 238
SOFTENING

A common cue is to soften or relax in a pose. For example, you may be asked to soften the grip of your toes in a balance pose or the muscles of your neck and face in the runner's lunge. Softening is the opposite of engaging and gripping. You cannot deepen a stretch of a particular area with the associated muscle contracted. Ponder the openness of your muscles in yoga and your sense of openness in life. Do you demonstrate gentleness, softness and flexibility both on and off the mat? Commune with Jesus.

SCRIPTURE:

You care for the land and water it; you enrich it abundantly. The streams of God are filled with water to provide the people with grain, for so you have ordained it. You drench its furrows and level its ridges; you soften it with showers and bless its crops. You crown the year with your bounty, and your carts overflow with abundance. (Psalm 65:9-11)

PRAYER:

Rock and Redeemer, strong and stable, soft and compassionate, I thank you for your expansive presence and muse *Philippians 2:1-2: Therefore if you have any encouragement from being united with Christ, if any comfort from his love, if any common sharing in the Spirit, if any tenderness and compassion, then make my joy complete by being like-minded, having the same love, being one in spirit and of one mind.* Let me be like-minded—tender and compassionate. Provide me with the softness in heart and body I need to experience the fullness of the asanas, and more importantly, your presence. Amen.

◌

Day 239
FLEXING

During yoga classes there are times when your muscles are flexed. By engaging your muscles, you build strength. Flexing the muscle that opposes the area you're looking to stretch helps advance your positioning in the pose. For example, when you activate your quadriceps in a wide-legged forward fold, your hamstrings soften—deepening the stretch along the backsides of your legs. Think about how your various muscle groups work together and how it feels to be fully engaged physically. Reflect on *Ecclesiastes 9:10: Whatever your hand finds to do, do it with all your might.* How do you exemplify this sort of passion? Commune with Jesus about how you engage on the mat and in life.

SCRIPTURE:
Serve wholeheartedly, as if you were serving the Lord, not people. (Ephesians 6:7)

PRAYER:
Lord, with all my *'passion, prayer, muscle and intelligence' (Luke 10:27 MSG)*, I come to love you and others as myself. May I work with all my might on and off the mat, serving others unreservedly in you. I hear *Colossians 3:23-24: Whatever you do, work at it with all your heart, as working for the Lord, not for human masters, since you know that you will receive an inheritance from the Lord as a reward. It is the Lord Christ you are serving.* This is my focus; alert, engaged and ready for action, I say Amen.

◌

Day 240
BINDING

A bind is an advanced option that brings your hands together. It is typically done by positioning one arm around your back and the other arm through one or both of your legs. A half bind, in which you wrap one arm around, is often more accessible. Binds help you lift your heart and draw your energy upwards. How can you bind the Lord's words on your fingers? How can you feel bound in His love and light? Conversely, what binds are constricting you now? Lift your heart and commune with Jesus.

SCRIPTURE:

Bind them on your fingers; write them on the tablet of your heart. (Proverbs 7:3)

PRAYER:

Lord, I thank you for sealing me in your love. I come to bind your words on my fingers and forehead and seal them on my heart, remembering *Deuteronomy 6:8: Tie them as symbols on your hands and bind them on your foreheads.* Let it be so, Holy Lord. Like Sampson in Judges 16:12 help me to snap out of any restricting binds, and fasten me in faith here on the mat. Amen.

༝

Day 241
RISING UP

In yoga, you rise up again and again. Think about moving from a forward fold to mountain pose or low plank to upward facing dog. Likewise, your life is full of rising up moments—physically, emotionally and spiritually. How have you recently 'risen up'? Commune with Jesus.

SCRIPTURE:

As he spoke, the Spirit came into me and raised me to my feet, and I heard him speaking to me. (Ezekiel 2:2)

PRAYER:

Righteous Father, I lift my heart, spirit and soul to you. Thank you for strengthening my step. I transition all my energy to listening to your voice, remembering *Daniel 8:18: While he was speaking to me, I was in a deep sleep, with my face to the ground. Then he touched me and raised me to my feet.* Here to rise up and ascend in your light, I say Amen.

∽

Day 242
STANDING FIRM

In standing poses you are often asked to balance your weight through the four corners of your feet to help stabilize and ground you. Likewise, the love of the Father, grace of the Son, presence of the Spirit, and fellowship of other believers are four spiritual pillars that can help you stand firm in faith. There may be times in yoga, as in life, when you need to be like Shadrach, Meshach and Abednego in Daniel 3 and refuse to bow down and worship an idol. How do you stand in truth in the face of worldly pressure? What 'idols' have been getting in your way recently—whether in terms of a relationship, food, money, control? How do you embody a 'but if not, I am still going to stay faithful' spirit? Commune with Jesus about any idols you may be struggling with in your life.

SCRIPTURE:

If it be so, our God whom we serve is able to deliver us from the burning fiery furnace, and he will deliver us out of thine hand, O king. But if not, be it known unto you, O king, that we will not serve your gods, nor worship the golden image which thou hast set up. (Daniel 3: 17-18 KJV)

PRAYER:

Lord, thank you for calling me to stand firm in the faith and for being faithful. Help me to be like Shadrach, Meshach and Abednego, and let nothing move me from loving and trusting in you first and foremost. Please forgive me for any idols I have let get in my way. Draw me back to your holy ways. I rejoice in *Isaiah 43:2: When you pass through the waters, I will be with you; and when you pass through the rivers, they will not sweep over you. When you walk through the fire, you will not be burned; the flames will not set you ablaze.* Father, glory to you! My trust is in your saving grace. Amen.

༄

Day 243
TAKING STEPS

Practices are often filled with moments of stepping forward or back on the mat. Likewise, life is full of steps. Pondering the simple motion of a step, think about how you make each one sacred—full of Spirit. Reflect on any big steps forward you have taken in life recently and how the Holy Spirit played a role. Conversely, note any ways you have felt the Spirit tell you to move away or step back from something. Commune with Jesus about these experiences and any current steps you are considering taking in your life.

SCRIPTURE:
Since we live by the Spirit, let us keep in step with the Spirit. (Galatians 5:25)

PRAYER:
Lord, I come to keep in step with your Spirit. Attuning my spirit to you, I remember *Galatians 6:4: Each one should test his own actions.* Let this time be a time to examine my moves and ensure they are in grounded in truth. Focused on stepping prayerfully with attention, alertness and dedication to you, I say Amen.

༄

Day 244
SETTLING

At the beginning of a class there is often some time allotted to settle on your mat, and there may be times throughout the practice that you are asked to settle in a pose. Settling is cued to enable you to receive the full benefits of that particular asana or the practice at large. Reflecting on settling and finding stillness, read *Psalm 23:2: He leads me beside quiet waters* and *Lamentations 3:26: It is good to wait quietly for the salvation of the LORD*. How have you experienced this in your life? How may you still need to settle down in your practice and life at large? Commune with Jesus.

SCRIPTURE:

The priests, the Levites, the gatekeepers, the musicians and the temple servants, along with certain of the people and the rest of the Israelites, settled in their own towns. (Nehemiah 7:73)

PRAYER:

Lord, I come to settle in your presence. Still me in your love, and please forgive me for times when I have wasted moments fiddling and adjusting. Restore me by your living waters. United with those around me, may we *'live peaceful and quiet lives in all godliness and holiness' (1 Timothy 2:2)*. Guide me in doing so here on the mat and in life. Amen.

෨෮

Day 245
SEALING YOUR LIPS

Sealing your lips is cued to return you to controlled breathing through your nose after a cooling exhale through your mouth, 'om' or amen. This helps you focus on listening internally versus externally. With your mouth gently shut, read *Psalm 141:3: Set a guard over my mouth, LORD; keep watch over the door of my lips*. How are you mindful and astute of your speech and actions? Three times in *Song of Solomon (2:7, 3:5, 8:4)* it is written: *Daughters of Jerusalem, I charge you: Do not arouse or awaken love until it so desires*. Commune with Jesus about what this means to you.

SCRIPTURE:

He said, "What pledge should I give you?" "Your seal and its cord, and the staff in your hand," she answered. So he gave them to her and slept with her, and she became pregnant by him. (Genesis 38:18)

PRAYER:

Lord, I come to speak and move only when your Spirit compels me to act. Please place a guard over my mouth and a seal over my heart so I do not arouse love until it so desires. I muse *Song of Solomon 2:14, 16: Show me your face, let me hear your voice; for your voice is sweet, and your face is lovely. My beloved is mine and I am his.* Surrendered in your unconditional, everlasting love, I rejoice in your Name and pulse of love. Amen.

৶

Day 246
SMILING

There are moments when you need to be reminded to smile and express joy in the midst of intense focus and effort in your practice. Read *Proverbs 17:22: A cheerful heart is good medicine, but a crushed spirit dries up the bones.* Reflect on when you smile and what causes you to smile. A grateful heart often spurs sincere smiles. Note of what you're grateful for in this present moment. Finding a smile, commune with Jesus.

SCRIPTURE:

A cheerful heart brings a smile to your face; a sad heart makes it hard to get through the day. (Proverbs 15:13 MSG)

PRAYER:

Lord, I am grateful for your holy presence—it cheers my heart, spirit, life and inner being. Here to manifest joy, please forgive me for the times I have lost sight of doing so. I acknowledge *Ephesians 6:5 (MSG): Don't just do what you have to do to get by, but work heartily, as Christ's servants doing what God wants you to do. And work with a smile on your face, always keeping in mind that no matter who happens to be giving the orders, you're really serving God.* Yes Lord, let me not just go through the motions on the mat or in life, but rather, let me move exuberantly, for it is you I am really serving! Smiling, I say Amen.

৶

Day 247
CELEBRATING

As recorded in the gospel of John, the first recorded miracle Jesus did was turn water into wine at a wedding, a time of celebration. In yoga, as in life, there are moments of celebration, such as when you do a challenging pose for the first time or when you graduate from a certain program. Identify moments of celebration in your yoga practice as well as ones you've recently encountered in life. How do you draw the Lord into your celebratory moments? Commune with Jesus.

SCRIPTURE:

Jesus said to the servants, "Fill the jars with water"; so they filled them to the brim. Then he told them, "Now draw some out and take it to the master of the banquet." They did so, and the master of the banquet tasted the water that had been turned into wine. He did not realize where it had come from, though the servants who had drawn the water knew. Then he called the bridegroom aside and said, "Everyone brings out the choice wine first and then the cheaper wine after the guests have had too much to drink; but you have saved the best till now." What Jesus did here in Cana of Galilee was the first of the signs through which he revealed his glory; and his disciples believed in him. (John 2:7-11)

PRAYER:

Jesus, when you turned water into wine, you performed a beautiful miracle and acknowledged a wedding as a time of celebration. You still do. Celebrating you presence, I hear *Exodus 12:14: This is a day you are to commemorate; for the generations to come you shall celebrate it as a festival to the LORD—a lasting ordinance*, and *Exodus 12:47: The whole community of Israel must celebrate it.* Let my movement be a dance of gratitude for each miracle I encounter. Amen.

∾

Day 248
EXPERIENCING SADNESS

Yoga classes can be cathartic. They offer a safe space to display godly sorrow and engage in repentance. Reflect on any cathartic moments you have experienced on the mat and any ways you have recently experienced godly sorrow. Read *Psalm 40:12: For troubles without number surround me; my sins have overtaken me, and I cannot see. They are more than the hairs of my head, and my heart fails within me.* Ponder how you can relate to this verse.

SCRIPTURE:

Godly sorrow brings repentance that leads to salvation and leaves no regret, but worldly sorrow brings death. (2 Corinthians 7:10)

PRAYER:

Lord, thank you for allowing me to come to you when I am worn out, broken down, tired, weak and sinful. Thank you for forgiving the guilt of my sin and purifying me from the inside out. I come to repent of my mistakes, inadequacies, broken relationships and hidden sins. I remember *2 Corinthians 7:11: See what this godly sorrow has produced in you: what earnestness, what eagerness to clear yourselves, what indignation, what alarm, what longing, what concern, what readiness to see justice done.* Here to express godly sorrow, I say Amen.

൭൨

Day 249
CRYING

Physically stretching on the mat can unearth deep emotions, and at times, move you to tears. Have you cried in a practice? When was the last time you really cried, and why? Read and ponder the following two verses. *Ecclesiastes 7:2: It is better to go to a house of mourning than to go to a house of feasting,* and *James 4:9: Grieve, mourn and wail. Change your laughter to mourning and your joy to gloom.*

SCRIPTURE:

As a pregnant woman about to give birth writhes and cries out in her pain, so were we in your presence, LORD. (Isaiah 26:17)

PRAYER:

Lord, thank you for tears and for times of mourning that draw me closer to you. I remember *John 11:35: Jesus wept.* I say it again, Jesus wept. And again, Jesus wept. Father, I weep for I understand I do not deserve this very moment, yet breath upon breath you continuously bless me—showering me with love, grace, hope and light. Please stir any emotions in me that need to be stirred and released. Amen.

༄

Day 250
REPENTING

Your practice may provide you space to repent, humble yourself and admit the guilt of your sin. Purifying you in one way or another, your time on the mat may be used to cry out to the Lord, share any missteps and ask for forgiveness. How do you repent? Reflect on *Ezekiel 18:32: Repent and live!* Take a few moments in repentance.

SCRIPTURE:

"The time has come," he said. "The kingdom of God has come near. Repent and believe the good news!" (Mark 1:15)

PRAYER:

Father, I offer this time up in repentance—admitting my mistakes, inadequacies and blindness. Gracious and Compassionate One, please turn to me, hear me, and forgive me for the guilt of my sin. I hear *Isaiah 30:15: This is what the Sovereign LORD, the Holy One of Israel, says: In repentance and rest is your salvation, in quietness and trust is your strength.* In humility and woe, I share my errors. Quieted in your love and grace, I turn my unwavering attention to the words of *Matthew 3:2: Repent, for the kingdom of heaven has come near.* In reverential awe, I say Amen.

༄

Day 251
SEEKING

In yoga class you may be asked to seek to straighten your leg or seek to raise your arm higher. As you seek to advance or align in poses, reflect on how you seek to align yourself with God's will. Meditate on *Psalm 27:8: My heart says of you, "Seek his face!" Your face, LORD, I will seek.*

SCRIPTURE:
But if from there you seek the LORD your God, you will find him if you seek him with all your heart and with all your soul. (Deuteronomy 4:29)

PRAYER:
Lord, I come to seek your face. Physically and spiritually reaching for you, I remember *1 Chronicles 22:19: Now devote your heart and soul to seeking the LORD your God. Begin to build the sanctuary of the LORD God, so that you may bring the ark of the covenant of the LORD and the sacred articles belonging to God into the temple that will be built for the Name of the LORD.* I build a sanctuary here with my body, treating it as your temple and seeking you with all my heart and soul. I muse *Hebrews 3:6: But Christ is faithful as a son over God's house. And we are his house, if we hold on to our courage and the hope of which we boast.* With my courage and confidence in you and rest knowing I will find you when I seek you with all my heart. Your Kingdom come, Amen.

❦

Day 252
REFRAINING FROM POSES

There might be some postures you cannot hold for more than a few seconds, and others you cannot do at all and that is okay! How are you comfortable with your current abilities in your practice and in your daily life? Reflect on *1 Corinthians 9:22: To the weak I became weak, to win the weak. I have become all things to all people so that by all possible means I might save some.* How are you weak? How are you strong? How can you 'become all things' to others? Commune with Jesus.

SCRIPTURE:

If I must boast, I will boast of the things that show my weakness. (2 Corinthians 11:30)

PRAYER:

Lord, I thank you for providing me with weakness so that I may place my trust in your strength. I hear *2 Corinthians 12:9: My power is made perfect in your weakness. That is why, for Christ's sake, I delight in weaknesses, in insults, in hardships, in persecutions, in difficulties. For when I am weak, then I am strong.* Father, help me to understand and appreciate this glorious blessing and like Paul, help me to 'become all things' to those around me. Amen.

∾

Day 253
JUDGING

It is just as easy to fall into the trap of judging in yoga spaces as it is in life. Take a moment to consider the judgments you find yourself making about others—from the type of yoga they do or do not practice to the type of church they do or do not attend. Likewise, it is tempting to judge others about how they spend their money or free time, what they wear, or what they choose to talk about in public. What causes you to have judgmental thoughts? Meditate on *Matthew 7:2: For in the same way you judge others, you will be judged, and with the measure you use, it will be measured to you.*

SCRIPTURE:

Stop judging by mere appearances, but instead judge correctly. (John 7:24)

PRAYER:

Lord, I want to be merciful and compassionate to those around me. I am here to develop a spirit of acceptance and to learn to see others as you see them. I desire to evaluate correctly and not by mere appearances. Please forgive me for the moments I have been critical and have passed judgment; help me to do so no longer. Jesus, I remember *John 8:15: You judge by human standards; I pass judgment on no one.* Help me to do likewise. Amen.

∾

Day 254
BUILDING FAITH

Yoga is a journey, and like any aspect of life, there are times when people just stop practicing for whatever reason. Have you ever veered away from your practice and if so, why? How may you have veered away from your faith at some point in your life? Read the following verses slowly and pause after each one. See if there is any way you are like the Pharisees Jesus is addressing.

> *Woe to you when everyone speaks well of you, for that is how their ancestors treated the false prophets.* (Luke 6:26)
>
> *Woe to you Pharisees, because you give God a tenth of your mint, rue and all other kinds of garden herbs, but you neglect justice and the love of God. You should have practiced the latter without leaving the former undone.* (Luke 11:42)
>
> *Woe to you Pharisees, because you love the most important seats in the synagogues and respectful greetings in the marketplaces.* (Luke 11:43)
>
> *Jesus replied, "And you experts in the law, woe to you, because you load people down with burdens they can hardly carry, and you yourselves will not lift one finger to help them."* (Luke 11:46)
>
> *Woe to you experts in the law, because you have taken away the key to knowledge. You have not entered, and you have hindered those who were entering.* (Luke 11:52)

SCRIPTURE:

The Son of Man will go as it has been decreed. But woe to that man who betrays him! (Luke 22:22)

PRAYER:

Lord, woe to me because in so many ways I am like the Pharisees. Forgive me, for I am a sinner—one who has betrayed your commands and who has focused on rules I cannot follow. Praise You for grace and mercy. I so desperately need it. Guide me in keeping in step with your Spirit. I hear *1 John 3:18: Dear children, let us not love with words or speech but with actions and in truth.* Help me to do so, Father. Amen.

∽

Day 255
LOVING THROUGH ACTION — PART 1

Kriya is a Sanskrit word meaning deed or action. Kriya is a type of yoga that includes personal and spiritual effort. This effort may be thought of as the embodiment of selfless love. How do you live in love? How do you show love to yourself, from the way you talk to yourself to the types of foods you put in your body? How do you show love for your family, from the way you listen to their stories to how you show patience with their attitudes? How about with your neighbors and colleagues? Commune with Jesus about selfless love.

SCRIPTURE:

And so we know and rely on the love God has for us. God is love. Whoever lives in love lives in God, and God in him. (1 John 4:16)

PRAYER:

Lord, I come to you to understand how to live in love and live in you. I come to practice selfless love—to give without expecting anything in return. Here on the mat I want to put in motion the words found in *Luke 10:27: Love the Lord your God with all your heart and with all your soul and with all your strength and with all your mind*; and *love your neighbor as yourself*, and then I want to roll up the mat and live these words in my life. Amen.

༄

Day 256
LOVING THROUGH ACTION — PART 2

Yoga offers a space to physically channel emotions in a positive way. Yoga classes may be themed around love, forgiveness or grace. Think about what has caused you to be angry in the recent past. Has anything caused you to be physically violent, or have you been the victim of violence? Close your eyes and touch the spot that reminds you of any acts of violence and channel peace to that area. Visualize the Lord restoring those tender places in a sacred way. Read *Matthew 26:52: "Put your sword back in its place," Jesus said to him, "for all who draw the sword will die by the sword."* As you draw near to the Lord's presence, may you feel any anger residing in you melt away.

SCRIPTURE:

Then Simon Peter, who had a sword, drew it and struck the high priest's servant, cutting off his right ear. (John 18:10)

But Jesus answered, "No more of this!" And he touched the man's ear and healed him. (Luke 22:51)

PRAYER:

Lord, I come to let your holy peace, which transcends all understanding, wash over me. Thank you for being the great healer who soothes my soul, revitalizes my body and restores my spirit. Forgive me for the times I have not acted in compassion but rather, like Peter with the sword, I have reacted in frustration and anger, and have directed harmful thoughts to others. I remember *Luke 6:35: But love your enemies, do good to them, and lend to them without expecting to get anything back. Then your reward will be great, and you will be children of the Most High, because he is kind to the ungrateful and wicked.* With this intention, I listen to *Matthew 5:44: But I tell you, love your enemies and pray for those who persecute you.* Here I am to extend blessings to those who have wounded me and those who have desired to harm me. Please sweep away any current anger and fill me with your everlasting love from the inside out. Amen.

༄

Day 257
REST AND BLESS

In classes you may be asked to rest in a pose and reflect on what you are grateful for in your life. Take a moment to recognize how your practice has been a blessing, and think of what you are currently grateful for in life. Read *Hebrews 4:11: Let us, therefore, make every effort to enter that rest.* Commune with Jesus about what this transcendent inner peace feels like, and attune to it through any sense of gratitude that may arise in the moment.

SCRIPTURE:

The LORD bless you and keep you; the LORD make his face shine on you and be gracious to you. (Numbers 6:24-25)

PRAYER:

Lord, thank you for blessing me and giving me rest. Here I pause and delight in *Genesis 12:2: I will make you into a great nation, and I will bless you; I will make your name great, and you will be a blessing.* Meditating on this glorious truth, I remember *Hebrews 4:1: Therefore, since the promise of entering his rest still stands, let us be careful that none of you be found to have fallen short of it.* With this sacred intention, I say Amen.

∽

Day 258
FOCUSING WITHIN — PART 1

It is common to have your eyes closed in certain yoga poses such as the child's pose, half pigeon or maybe the tree pose for a balance challenge. Likewise, your eyes are often closed during a prayer. Closing your eyes is a beautiful way to help turn off any potential external distractions and focus entirely on the Lord's presence within you. With eyes closed, reflect on what ways you have been 'blind'. How has the Lord turned your darkness into light and remained faithful to you even when you were unfaithful to Him? Take a moment to commune with Jesus about ways your vision may still be blurry.

SCRIPTURE:

I will lead the blind by ways they have not known, along unfamiliar paths I will guide them; I will turn the darkness into light before them and make the rough places smooth. These are the things I will do; I will not forsake them. (Isaiah 42:16)

PRAYER:

Lord, I close my eyes and breathe deeply in your presence, connecting to you in my innermost being. Thank you for your faithfulness and for letting your light shine in human hearts—in my heart! I remember *Ephesians 5:8: For you were once darkness, but now you are light in the Lord. Live as children of light.* With this as my focus, I meditate on *2 Timothy 2:11-13: Here is a trust-worthy saying: If we died with him, we will also live with him; if we endure, we will also reign with him. If we disown him, he will also disown us; if we are faithless, he remains faithful, for he cannot disown himself.* O how great is your faithfulness. Holy One, please center my vision on you and help me to see you here on the mat. Amen.

๏๛

Day 259
FOCUSING WITHIN — PART 2

Yoga classes provide the opportunity to check in with your body and observe any physical sensations. They also provide space to check in with our mind and note any thoughts, and to examine your spiritual heart and tap into its intentions and impulses. Take a moment to draw your attention away from what is around you and focus on what is happening within you. As you check in with yourself, also seek to recognize how you check out other people—their style, positioning, look, attitude, etc. Identify ways you can move beyond external appearances and focus on internal truths both with yourself and others. Commune with Jesus.

SCRIPTURE:

But the LORD said to Samuel, "Do not consider his appearance or his height, for I have rejected him. The LORD does not look at the things man looks at. Man looks at the outward appearance, but the LORD looks at the heart." (1 Samuel 16:7)

PRAYER:

Lord, thank you for looking inwardly at the thoughts and intentions of my heart. Please cleanse me from the inside out. I am in need of mercy because so often I view what is on the outside—whether I look a certain way, or how others look—and I fail to notice the heart. Father, please forgive me and help me to draw my attention inward. I come to learn how to see others as you see them. I am reminded of *2 Corinthians 4:18: So we fix our eyes not on what is seen, but on what is unseen. For what is seen is temporary, but what is unseen is eternal.* As

I close my eyes at various moments throughout this practice, let it be express my intention to stay fixed and focused on what is unseen—your eternal presence. Amen.

∽

Day 260
ELIMINATING NEGATIVE SELF-TALK

When certain poses are introduced, there might be moments when your instincts tell you that you cannot do them—that you are not strong enough, capable enough or flexible enough. Are you aware of the small talk that takes place in your head? Have you ever said to yourself, I cannot do this pose, lead that group, start my own business, lose twenty pounds, obtain that degree, be in a committed relationship or whatever it is you so desperately want but are convinced you don't have what it takes? Pause and recall the times the Lord equipped you to do something you didn't think you could do. Commune with Jesus about any current negative self-talk taking place in your mind.

SCRIPTURE:
"Before I shaped you in the womb, I knew all about you. Before you saw the light of day, I had holy plans for you: A prophet to the nations—that's what I had in mind for you." But I said, "Hold it, Master God! Look at me. I don't know anything. I'm only a boy!" God told me, "Don't say, 'I'm only a boy.' I'll tell you where to go and you'll go there. I'll tell you what to say and you'll say it. Don't be afraid of a soul. I'll be right there, looking after you." God's Decree. (Jeremiah 1:5-8 MSG)

PRAYER:
Lord, you have blessed me with all I need to live life to the full, for your Spirit is in me. I place my trust in you and the plans you have for me. Lead me through each moment on this mat and in life. My Strength and Salvation, I delight in the words of *Psalm 121:1-4 (MSG): I look up to the*

mountains; does my strength come from mountains? No, my strength comes from God, who made heaven, and earth, and mountains. He won't let you stumble, your Guardian God won't fall asleep. Thank you for your divine protection, encouragement and blessing of confidence. Let me feel it fully and breathe in its truth. Amen.

❦

Day 261
LISTENING TO COMMANDS — PART 1

Physical commands and directives are given in class to keep you in safely aligned positions. Likewise, the Lord gives us commands to protect us out of love. How do His commandments take on meaning in your life? Read *Galatians 5:14: For the entire law is fulfilled in keeping this one command:"Love your neighbor as yourself"* and *John 15:14: You are my friends if you do what I command.* Commune with Jesus.

SCRIPTURE:

Lord, by such things people live; and my spirit finds life in them too. You restored me to health and let me live. (Isaiah 38:16)

PRAYER:

Lord, I come to live out your commands. Jesus, I remember your words from *John 10:10: The thief comes only to steal and kill and destroy; I have come that they may have life, and have it to the full.* Thank you for the fullness of life that you bring! As I continue to get a glimpse of what you are teaching me, I reflect on *John 12:50: I know that his command leads to eternal life. So whatever I say is just what the Father has told me to say,* and *John 15:10, 17: If you keep my commands, you will remain in my love, just as I have kept my Father's commands and remain in his love. And this my command: Love each other.* Guide me in keeping your commands and following your call of love. Amen.

❦

Day 262
LISTENING TO COMMANDS — PART 2

Commands, directives and cues provide structure and a framework for experiencing the fullness of the practice. Similarly, the Lord's directives provide a way, path and direction to live life and have it abundantly; and in doing so, this abundance naturally pours forth from us to others. Think about how following commands has allowed you to experience the fullness poses have to offer in yoga. Likewise, think about how listening to the Lord's commands has spurred a freeing and energizing feeling in you off the mat. Commune with Jesus.

SCRIPTURE:

Jesus gave them this answer: "Very truly I tell you, the Son can do nothing by himself; he can do only what he sees his Father doing, because whatever the Father does the Son also does." (John 5:19)

PRAYER:

Father, I come to my mat to listen to your holy words, to be obedient to your will and to walk in Your ways. Please forgive me for the times I have wandered and tried to do my own thing. Through my yoga practice, I aim to physically express my openness and receptiveness to your instruction here on the mat, remembering *Deuteronomy 5:33: Walk in obedience to all that the LORD your God has commanded you, so that you may live and prosper and prolong your days in the land that you will possess.* I hear *John 8:51: Very truly I tell you, whoever obeys my word will never see death.* What an amazing, awe-inspiring gift! Keep my spirit steadfast in you. Amen.

༄

Day 263
LISTENING TO COMMANDS — PART 3

Yoga classes are filled with direct instructions, such as reach your right leg up, square your hips, soften your shoulders, and so on. How do you respond to directions on your yoga mat? Do you follow exactly what was cued, or do you have the tendency to create and explore your own options? What are your natural inclinations as it relates to rules, obedience and adhering to a set structure? Reflect on this as it relates to your professional endeavors, your home life and your spiritual walk with Jesus.

SCRIPTURE:

The fear of the LORD is the beginning of knowledge, but fools despise wisdom and instruction. (Proverbs 1:7)

PRAYER:

Sovereign Lord, I come to listen to your instructions. Please forgive me for the ways I have not been attentive. I thirst for knowledge in your holy ways, and I hear *Isaiah 51:4: Listen to me, my people; hear me, my nation: Instruction will go out from me; my justice will become a light to the nations.* I take heed and remember *Genesis 26:4-5: I will make your descendants as numerous as the stars in the sky and will give them all these lands, and through your offspring all nations on earth will be blessed, because Abraham obeyed me and did everything I required of him, keeping my commands, my decrees and my instructions.* Father, I am awed by the great blessings in store for those who obey and remain faithful. Help me cultivate a spirit of obedience here on the mat. Waiting for direction in Spirit, I say Amen.

∽

Day 264
LISTENING TO COMMANDS — PART 4

Some directives given in classes are hard to do. It is not easy to keep your back foot bladed down, back leg straight, front knee over your front ankle, hips square, core engaged, arms actively up, shoulders soft, gaze up and chin neutral in the warrior 1 pose. This is just one example of an asana's detailed directions. Often you may desire to keep the commands but your body may physically tell you otherwise. There is a lot to focus on and refine while doing yoga poses. Reflect on *Mark 14:38: Watch and pray so that you will not fall into temptation. The spirit is willing, but the flesh is weak.* How have you experienced the truth of this verse in your body, mind and spirit on the mat and in your daily life? Commune with Jesus.

SCRIPTURE:

If you love me, keep my commands. (John 14:15)

PRAYER:

Lord, my deepest desire is to reflect my love for you in all my words, thoughts and actions. I acknowledge that I often fall short. I can relate to Paul's words in *Romans 7:18: For I know that good itself does not dwell in me, that is, in my sinful nature. For I have the desire to do what is good, but I cannot carry it out.* Please help me to keep your commands and receive your grace. Hem me in here on the mat; harness me in your love and yoke me in your light. Amen.

೦ం

Day 265
TURNING AWAY MOMENTS

Sometimes we turn away by not doing a certain posture on the mat or not even coming to practice a certain day. Likewise, there may be moments when we deny our faith by not sharing its significance or not simply speaking truth or aligning our actions with our faith. How have you turned away? Read *Luke 22:34: I tell you, Peter, before the rooster crows today, you will deny three times that you know me.* How can you relate to Peter? Share your response with Jesus.

SCRIPTURE:

So I rebuked the officials and asked them, "Why is the house of God neglected?" Then I called them together and stationed them at their posts. (Nehemiah 13:11)

PRAYER:

Lord, so often I turn away from you, and I am deeply and truly sorry for each and every time I have done so. Please forgive me. I come to draw near you on the mat, to stand firm in faith and not neglect your holy house. I am here to listen to your rebuke, return to you and heed your instructions. My prayer is *Psalm 27:9: Do not hide your face from me, do not turn your servant away in anger; you have been my helper. Do not reject me or forsake me, God my Savior.* Amen.

೦ం

Day 266
PLANNING

If you practice yoga by yourself or teach a class, you need to establish a class plan including the music, poses, and passages you want to use in it. Even simply attending a class requires schedule planning. How much in life do you try to plan? Do you stick to a set schedule or does too much structure seem restricting to you? Have you ever felt the Lord reveal different plans to you than the ones you intended to follow? Reflect on those types of experiences and what the Lord may be calling you to now.

SCRIPTURE:
"For I know the plans I have for you," declares the LORD, "plans to prosper you and not to harm you, plans to give you hope and a future." (Jeremiah 29:11)

PRAYER:
Lord, thank you for your glorious plans; they are bigger and vaster than I could ever imagine. I am truly grateful for the blessing of your presence that brings hope and confidence beyond understanding. I remember *Romans 8:28: And we know that in all things God works for the good of those who love him, who have been called according to his purpose.* What grand news! I know you have a good plan for this class and every moment in my life. Help me to balance purposeful planning with a spirit of active surrender and openness to your holy, pleasing and perfect will. Amen.

༄

Day 267
FINDING STILLNESS

In yoga there are pauses for exploring stillness. Interestingly, Patañjali, who is thought to have written the Yoga Sutras, only mentions a few things about the asanas in all 196 sutras. One, that asana should embody sukham, meaning ease, and two, sthira, meaning steadiness. Pauses are given to help you cultivate these attributes—moments to relax, become grounded in truth and experience effortless ecstasy. Consider selah, a word used 71 times in the Psalms that means to take a moment and reflect. The Amplified Bible states it more directly, defining Selah as 'pause and think of that'. In Biblically times this word could have been used for the singing of an Amen. It is possible that this Hebrew word comes from *calah*, meaning to hang, as if on a scale. If so, it may signify to weigh the statement preceding the 'Selah' worth or consider it carefully. Reflect on the following verses and commune with Jesus.

> *I cried unto the LORD with my voice, and he heard me out of his holy hill. Selah.* (Psalm 3:4 KJV)
>
> *This is the generation of them that seek him, that seek thy face, O Jacob. Selah.* (Psalm 24:6 KJV)
>
> *I acknowledge my sin unto thee, and mine iniquity have I not hid. I said, I will confess my transgressions unto the LORD; and thou forgavest the iniquity of my sin. Selah.* (Psalm 32:5 KJV)
>
> *Thou art my hiding place; thou shalt preserve me from trouble; thou shalt compass me about with songs of deliverance. Selah.* (Psalm 32:7 KJV)
>
> *The LORD of hosts is with us; the God of Jacob is our refuge. Selah.* (Psalm 46:7 KJV)

SCRIPTURE:

Stand in awe, and sin not: commune with your own heart upon your bed, and be still. Selah. (Psalm 4:4 KJV)

PRAYER:

Lord, I thank you for pauses—moments to rest and reflect, and to find ease and steadiness. I thank you for teaching me in times of stillness. Treasuring and pondering your Spirit dwelling in my heart, I hear *Psalm 48:8: As we have heard, so have we seen in the city of the LORD of hosts, in the city of our God: God will establish it forever. Selah.* Yes Father, may this practice be filled with moments of Selah. Amen.

Day 268
HOLDING POSTURES

Many times throughout a yoga session, you get into a posture and hold it for a few breaths or minutes. How do you soften and deepen into an asana in these moments? Do you find that sometimes you move before being cued because you're already anticipating the next pose, or do you wait, holding still and steady? How about in life? When it comes to waiting in a grocery store checkout line or for the right relationship to come into your life, are you patient? In what ways can you continue to foster a willing spirit, waiting and resting with certainty that joy will come? Commune with Jesus.

SCRIPTURE:
Wait for the LORD; be strong and take heart and wait for the LORD. (Psalm 27:14)

PRAYER:
Lord, I come here to wait for your will, word and way to be revealed. With strength, heart, passion and prayer, I wait. I recite *Psalm 40:1: I waited patiently for the LORD; he turned to me and heard my cry.* Thank you for turning to me and hearing my cries. I muse *Isaiah 64:4: Since ancient times no one has heard, no ear has perceived, no eye has seen any God besides you, who acts on behalf of those who wait for him.* This gives me hope as I wait for you. Amen.

෧෧

Day 269
LYING DOWN

To lie down is a common yoga directive. Taking a moment to lie on your mat, reflect on how you experience this motion as an act of surrender and a prostration of humility. Think about your practice and note whether you frequently go into resting poses preemptively to shy away from challenging asanas, or whether you attempt to stay in 'go mode' for as long as possible, undervaluing the benefit of resting poses. What spurs you to lay yourself down physically, emotionally and spiritually? How do you find harmony between lying down in surrender, and remaining standing in steadfastness? Share your responses with Jesus.

SCRIPTURE:

This is how we know what love is: Jesus Christ laid down his life for us. And we ought to lay down our lives for our brothers and sisters. (1 John 3:16)

PRAYER:

Jesus, your extension of love through the cross amazes me more than words can describe. I hear *John 15:13: Greater love has no one than this: to lay down one's life for one's friends.* Father, here I am to follow Jesus and lay down my life at your feet. I recognize *1 Thessalonians 5:10: He died for us so that, whether we are awake or asleep, we may live together with him.* Risen Holy One, may I live in you and with you. Let every action of laying myself down on the mat express my desire to take the lowest position and place others first like you. Illuminate me through this surrender. Teach me when to stay standing and when to rest. Amen.

⁊⁊

Day 270
TREMBLING

Muscles sometimes shake when you are holding a challenging yoga pose, which at first can seem like weakness, but actually is a good thing. It helps strengthen that area of your body and acts as a reminder to trust in the Lord to will and act in you according to His good purpose. Working out your salvation with fear and trembling happens in a very physical sense on the mat. In what ways is the Lord working in you for good? Commune with Jesus and meditate on *Philippians 1:6: Being confident of this, that he who began a good work in you will carry it on to completion until the day of Christ Jesus.*

SCRIPTURE:

Therefore, my dear friends, as you have always obeyed—not only in my presence, but now much more in my absence—continue to work out your salvation with fear and trembling, for it is God who works in you to will and to act in order to fulfill his good purpose. (Philippians 2:12-13)

PRAYER:

Lord, I am here to work out my salvation with fear and trembling. I trust that your Spirit is working in me for good and that you will carry out this work to completion. Father, strengthen me from the inside out. Let me be active in my faith, not only here on the mat but in each moment of my life. I remember *Nehemiah 2:18: I also told them about the gracious hand of my God on me and what the king had said to me. They replied, "Let us start rebuilding." So they began this good work.* Lord, as I unite with others in faith here on the mat, may we begin a good work together for you. Amen.

ले

Day 271
EXPERIENCING CHALLENGES

Some yoga moves are hard. They challenge you and cause you to sweat. Beyond physical rigor, your practice may be mentally tough and spiritually demanding. How do you welcome Christ by sharing in His suffering? How have you felt intimacy with the Lord through your tears and pain? Is your heart willing and open to being refined and strengthened through painful experiences? Consider how you can hunger and thirst for His wondrous redemptive touch in the midst of pain.

SCRIPTURE:

I want to know Christ—yes, to know the power of his resurrection and participation in his sufferings, becoming like him in his death, and so, somehow, attaining to the resurrection from the dead. (Philippians 3:10-11)

PRAYER:

Jesus, I come to the mat with openness to participate in your suffering. I connect with you through the challenges and hardships that arise in my life. Each experience on the mat draws me closer to you—invigorating my body and emboldening my faith. I recite *Romans 14:8: If we live, we live to the Lord; and if we die, we die to* the Lord. *So, whether we live or die we belong to the Lord*. Father, surrendered in love, I willingly say, 'let your will be done in my life'. Amen.

✧

Day 272
FALLING

Even the most refined yogis fall out of balance and get out of alignment at times. How have you fallen out of alignment in your practice as well as in your faith? Reflect on *Jonah 3:6-10: When Jonah's warning reached the king of Nineveh, he rose from his throne, took off his royal robes, covered himself with sackcloth and sat down in the dust. This is the proclamation he issued in Nineveh:"By the decree of the king and his nobles: Do not let people or animals, herds or flocks, taste anything; do not let them eat or drink. But let people and animals be covered with sackcloth. Let everyone call urgently on God. Let them give up their evil ways and their violence. Who knows? God may yet relent and with compassion turn from his fierce anger so that we will not perish."When God saw what they did and how they turned from their evil ways, he relented and did not bring on them the destruction he had threatened.* In what ways may you currently be stumbling and need to return to the Lord?

SCRIPTURE:
For all have sinned and fall short of the glory of God, and all are justified freely by his grace through the redemption that came by Christ Jesus. (Romans 3:23-24)

PRAYER:
Father, thank you for forgiving me as I repent of my sin right here and now. When I fall or get out of alignment here on the mat, help me to redirect and reposition myself in you. I muse *1 Samuel 12:20:"Do not be afraid," Samuel replied. "You have done all this evil; yet do not turn away from the LORD, but serve the LORD with all your heart."* Lord, I come here to serve you with all my heart, and to lean in and trust in your saving grace, reciting *Psalm 130:4: But with you there is forgiveness, so that we can, with reverence, serve you.* Amen.

✧

Day 273
RETURNING AFTER A BREAK

Have you ever taken an extended break from your practice? If so, what caused it, and what brought you back? How about with your church attendance or a certain personal relationship, job, or other life commitment? Reflect on the Parable of the Prodigal Son in *Luke 15:21-24: The son said to him, 'Father, I have sinned against heaven and against you. I am no longer worthy to be called your son.' But the father said to his servants, 'Quick! Bring the best robe and put it on him. Put a ring on his finger and sandals on his feet. Bring the fattened calf and kill it. Let's have a feast and celebrate. For this son of mine was dead and is alive again; he was lost and is found.' So they began to celebrate,* and muse *Luke 15:7: I tell you that in the same way there will be more rejoicing in heaven over one sinner who repents than over ninety-nine righteous persons who do not need to repent.* Commune with Jesus about how you relate to these verses.

SCRIPTURE:

"Even now," declares the LORD, "return to me with all your heart, with fasting and weeping and mourning." Rend your heart and not your garments. Return to the LORD your God, for he is gracious and compassionate, slow to anger and abounding in love, and he relents from sending calamity. (Joel 2:12-13)

PRAYER:

Lord, I come with my head bowed before you; I apologize for the times I have not clung to your word, and for times when I have gone off and squandered the gifts and talents you have given me on short-term thrills—things that eventually left me heavyhearted. I am utterly ashamed of the ways I have been unfaithful. Holy One, I draw hope in *1 John 1:9: If we confess our sins, he is faithful and just and will forgive us our sins and purify us from all unrighteousness.* Thank you for your relentless love and grace. Here I focus on living *Hebrews 10:22: Let us draw near to God with a sincere heart and with the full assurance that faith brings, having our hearts sprinkled to cleanse us from a guilty conscience and having our bodies washed with pure water.* Amen.

෴

Day 274
SIGN-INS AND AGREEMENTS

Most classes have some sort of a sign-in process. Reflect on how you sign-in to class—not just physically, but emotionally and spiritually, too. How can you 'sign-in' with a spirit of openness toward the experience at hand, and with a sense of clear-minded eagerness to learn and attune to whatever arises? Think of the symbolic significance of writing your name to something, such as on a sign-in sheet, and the commitment it marks. Do you put things in writing to the Lord? 'Sign-in' with Jesus.

SCRIPTURE:

In view of all this, we are making a binding agreement, putting it in writing, and our leaders, our Levites and our priests are affixing their seals to it. (Nehemiah 9:38)

PRAYER:

Lord, 'signing-in' in truth, I take this time on the mat seriously. Sealed in Spirit and bound in love, I listen to your words with reverence, remembering *Deuteronomy 11:18: Fix these words of mine in your hearts and minds; tie them as symbols on your hands and bind them on your foreheads.* Father, align my breath and being with you here on the mat. Keep me loyal, clear-minded, alert and 'signed-in' with what matters. Amen.

ᗞ

Day 275
DEPOSIT

Yoga retreats and programs often require a deposit of money to hold your space. The deposit acts as a pledge that signifies your earnest intention to be a part of that class or program. Reflect on what you have placed a deposit on recently in life, as well as, how has the Lord deposited Spirit in you. Read *Song of Solomon 7:10: I belong to my beloved, and his desire is for me.* Close your eyes, meditate on these words, and commune with Jesus.

SCRIPTURE:

Set his seal of ownership on us, and put his Spirit in our hearts as a deposit, guaranteeing what is to come. (2 Corinthians 1:22)

PRAYER:

Sovereign Lord, I thank you for placing your Spirit in me as a deposit. I belong to you and want whatever you desire for me. Please help me reflect this truth in my actions. I rejoice in *2 Corinthians 5:5: Now the one who has fashioned us for this very purpose is God, who has given us the Spirit as a deposit, guaranteeing what is to come,* and *John 14:16: And I will ask the Father, and he will give you another advocate to help you and be with you forever—the Spirit of truth.* Sealed and deposited in these holy truths, I say Amen.

இ௸

Day 276
SIGNING WAIVERS

Before you practice in a new space, you are often asked to sign a waiver to show your voluntary consent. In life, too, there are many forms to sign. Think about the different contracts you have signed throughout your life. Which ones stand out in your memory as being significant to you? Forms and waivers acknowledge a set of understandings. Likewise, covenants mark commitment in a relationship. In the Bible, covenants are pledges of loyalty. Meditate on *2 Corinthians 3:6: He has made us competent as ministers of a new covenant—not of the letter but of the Spirit; for the letter kills, but the Spirit gives life.* Ponder the various ways the Lord has made you to be a competent minister. Commune with Jesus.

SCRIPTURE:

But I did not want to do anything without your consent, so that any favor you do would not seem forced but would be voluntary. (Philemon 1:14)

PRAYER:

Jesus, thank you for bringing a new covenant of Spirit that gives life—what an incredible, wondrous gift! Please help me to be a faithful minister of it. Where needed, may I receive consent and send waivers with a spirit commitment, faithfulness and authenticity. I come to renew and reaffirm my commitment to you, remembering *Hebrews 8:6, 13: But in fact the ministry Jesus has received is as superior to theirs as the covenant of which he is mediator is superior to the old one, since the new covenant is established on better promises. By calling this covenant "new," he has made the first one obsolete; and what is obsolete and outdated will soon disappear.* Let your covenant be inscribed on the tablet of my heart. Amen.

ᜒ

Day 277
GIVING

Yoga is filled with opportunities to give. Reflect on how you contribute to the classes you attend—with your energy, finances, attitude, breath, talent and friendship to others in the space. Take a few moments to consider your giving choices off the mat, both of your time and treasure. How do you feel about them? Share your responses with Jesus.

SCRIPTURE:
Remember this: Whoever sows sparingly will also reap sparingly, and whoever sows generously will also reap generously. Each of you should give what you have decided in your heart to give, not reluctantly or under compulsion, for God loves a cheerful giver. (2 Corinthians 9:6-7)

PRAYER:
Lord, I thank you for the blessing of being able to give of my time and treasure. Forgive me for the opportunities I've missed to show kindness, offer support, or lost sight of the joy in doing so. Please help me open my heart to care and contribute to the people, ministries, groups and companies you have positioned me to bless. I remember *2 Corinthians 9:8: And God is able to bless you abundantly, so that in all things at all times, having all that you need, you will abound in every good work.* This verse amazes me. Thank you, Father. Amen.

ᜒ

Day 278
SETTING A DEDICATION

Setting an intention or dedication is often an important part of a practice and is typically done at the beginning of a yoga class. It can be an inner resolution or a prayer to extend out for someone or something beyond yourself. Who in your life, or in your community or the world at large, could use some building up? Where is the Lord's healing presence and loving Spirit needed? Commune with Jesus.

SCRIPTURE:
Each of us should please our neighbors for their good, to build them up. (Romans 15:2)

PRAYER:
Father, I dedicate my time on this mat to _____. Remembering *Romans 12:10: Be devoted to one another in love. Honor one another above yourselves*, I come to place the interests of _____ before me and to make this practice be an act of honor to _____. Thank you for neighbors near and far. Help me to care for my neighbor, just as the Samaritan cited in Luke 10 cared for his neighbor. I hear *1 Thessalonians 3:12: May the Lord make your love increase and overflow for each other and for everyone else.* Let these holy words come to life in this yoga space and in my inmost being. Amen.

ॐ

Day 279
UNROLLING

Each time you unroll a mat it is as if you are unrolling a scroll, and your movement on it is like a physical message. As you unroll your mat, take a moment to reflect on the unrolling of the testament scroll and the fulfillment of the Scriptures. Commune with the Lord about the scriptures He desires you to open, read, obey, fulfill and physically embody.

SCRIPTURE:

And the scroll of the prophet Isaiah was handed to him. Unrolling it, he found the place where it is written: "The Spirit of the Lord is on me, because he has anointed me to proclaim good news to the poor. He has sent me to proclaim freedom for the prisoners and recovery of sight for the blind, to set the oppressed free, to proclaim the year of the Lord's favor." (Luke 4:17-19)

PRAYER:

Jesus, fulfiller of Isaiah's holy words, I hear you calling me to go and do likewise—to love your people and bring them the Good News. Father, I join Jesus in reciting *Isaiah 61:1-3: The Spirit of the Sovereign LORD is on me, because the LORD has anointed me to proclaim good news to the poor. He has sent me to bind up the brokenhearted, to proclaim freedom for the captives and release from darkness for the prisoners, to proclaim the year of the LORD's favor and the day of vengeance of our God, to comfort all who mourn, and provide for those who grieve in Zion—to bestow on them a crown of beauty instead of ashes, the oil of joy instead of mourning, and a garment of praise instead of a spirit of despair. They will be called oaks of righteousness, a planting of the LORD for the display of his splendor.* Plant me in your truth for the display of your splendor, oh Lord. Let your living scrolls be expressed here on the mat and inscribed on my heart. Amen.

∽

Day 280
ACKNOWLEDGING INSTRUCTORS — PART 1

Instructors aim to safely guide you through your yoga practice. How do your teachers give clear meaning to what is cued in class? Note the teachers who are blessing you at this juncture your life and in what areas you could use a strong teacher. Commune with Jesus.

SCRIPTURE:

They read from the Book of the Law of God, making it clear and giving the meaning so that the people understood what was being read. (Nehemiah 8:8)

PRAYER:

Lord, thank you for the blessing of teachers. Please equip me with understanding here on the mat. I hear *Ecclesiastes 12:9-10: Not only was the Teacher wise, but he also imparted knowledge to the people. He pondered and searched out and set in order many proverbs. The Teacher searched to find just the right words, and what he wrote was upright and true.* Let this sort of teacher be ever present in my life. Rabboni, help me listen, learn and grow in faith and ability here on the mat and in my daily life. Amen.

༄

Day 281
ACKNOWLEDGING INSTRUCTORS — PART 2

Yoga teachers come in all different shapes, sizes, backgrounds and education levels. Formalized yoga teacher trainings are fairly new to this ancient practice. Before structured programs became the norm, yoga was simply studied and shared from teacher to student over time. Pondering this type of training, reflect on how the Lord has used you without formalized trainings or credentials often esteemed by worldly viewpoints. What role might the Lord be calling you into next, and what may that require of you? Pause and reflect.

SCRIPTURE:

When they saw the courage of Peter and John and realized that they were unschooled, ordinary men, they were astonished and they took note that these men had been with Jesus. (Acts 4:13)

PRAYER:

Lord, I thank you for equipping me with just what I need to do the tasks you have designed for me, even when I do not feel I have what it takes. I remember the words you shared with your servant Moses in *Exodus 4:11-12: The LORD said to him, "Who gave man his mouth? Who makes him deaf or mute? Who gives him sight or makes him blind? Is it not I, the LORD? Now go; I will help you speak and will teach you what to say."* Lord, I am excited about the ways you are going to use me; please help me to see the opportunities and take action when I hear your voice. I muse *1 Chronicles 28:19: "All this," David said, "I have in writing as a result of the LORD's hand* on me, and he enabled me to understand all the details of the plan." Like David, thank you for providing me with the knowledge I need for the tasks you have given me. Thank you for calling me to this practice. Amen.

ᥴᥱ

Day 282
HANDLING NEGATIVITY

Not everyone is a fan of yoga, and not everyone is a fan of Jesus. There are stereotypes of yoga and there are stereotypes of Christianity. Have you encountered any adversity from others pertaining to your practice of yoga? Have you encountered adversity from others because of your faith? Commune with Jesus about any adversities you seem to be facing now.

SCRIPTURE:

When Sanballat heard that we were rebuilding the wall, he became angry and was greatly incensed. He ridiculed the Jews, and in the presence of his associates and the army of Samaria, he said, "What are those feeble Jews doing? Will they restore their wall? Will they offer sacrifices? Will they finish in a day? Can they bring the stones back to life from those heaps of rubble—burned as they are?" Tobiah the Ammonite, who was at his side, said, "What they are building—even a fox climbing up on it would break down their wall of stones!" (Nehemiah 4:1-3)

PRAYER:

Lord, I come to stand firm in my faith and my practice no matter what opposition comes my way. I ponder how Nehemiah handled the opposition; I consider what he proclaimed in *Nehemiah 4:14: After I looked things over, I stood up and said to the nobles, the officials and the rest of the people, "Don't be afraid of them. Remember the Lord, who is great and awesome, and who fights for your families, your sons and your daughters, your wives and your homes."* Father, like Nehemiah, I know you will be with me through any ridiculing, name calling or questioning that comes my way. I remember that the Jews in Nehemiah prayed and then went to work with all their heart in the face of opposition. Let me do likewise, Lord. Amen.

ᥴᥱ

Day 283

Treating All with Fairness

One of the beautiful things about yoga is that it is designed to be fair and accessible to all. In reality, however, there may be an element or two that does not seem fair or accessible to all. Can you recognize any such areas in your practice or in your life? The behavior cited in Nehemiah 5:7, today's scripture, is something done out of fear. Is there any area of your life where you feel you are operating out of fear? Ponder *Proverbs 31:8: Speak up for those who cannot speak for themselves, for the rights of all who are destitute. Speak up and judge fairly; defend the rights of the poor and needy.* How do your actions exemplify this verse? Commune with Jesus.

Scripture:

I told them,"You are charging your own people interest!" So I called together a large meeting to deal with them. (Nehemiah 5:7)

Prayer:

Lord, I come to learn how to demonstrate your justice and speak up for those without a voice. Equip me with the confidence I need to boldly defend the rights of the poor and destitute. Forgive me for the times I have neglected to do so and the times I have operated in fear or favoritism. I remember *Isaiah 58:6-7: Is not this the kind of fasting I have chosen: to loosen the chains of injustice and untie the cords of the yoke, to set the oppressed free and break every yoke? Is it not to share your food with the hungry and to provide the poor wanderer with shelter—when you see the naked, to clothe them, and not to turn away from your own flesh and blood,* and *Deuteronomy 16:19-20: Do not pervert justice or show partiality. Do not accept a bribe, for a bribe blinds the eyes of the wise and twists the words of the innocent. Follow justice and justice alone.* Yes, help me to follow justice and welcome and bless all in fairness and faith. Amen.

◌◌

Day 284
ELIMINATING GOSSIP

Gossip may happen in any environment including the yoga space and it hurts. Read *Proverbs 18:8: The words of a gossip are like choice morsels; they go down to the inmost parts.* Have you ever felt someone gossip about you? Reflect on any such experiences and any conversations in which you've heard another person gossip. Note if you took a stand against it and commune with Jesus.

SCRIPTURE:

I sent him this reply:"Nothing like what you are saying is happening; you are just making it up out of your head." (Nehemiah 6:8)

PRAYER:

Father, I come to learn how to be truthful, loving, kind and gentle in all my speech. Gossip hurts. Help me to take a stand against it. Please forgive me for the times I have neglected to do so and for the words I have spoken that were not grounded in your truth. I recognize *James 4:1:What causes fights and quarrels among you? Don't they come from your desires that battle within you?* Guide me in awareness of this truth every time I think of quarrelling. I muse Paul's words to the church of Corinth in *2 Corinthians 12:20: For I am afraid that when I come I may not find you as I want you to be, and you may not find me as you want me to be. I fear that there may be discord, jealousy, fits of rage, selfish ambition, slander, gossip, arrogance and disorder.* Humble me before I go into any space; examine my heart and enable me to speak truth where discord, jealousy or gossip may be present. Amen.

❦

Day 285
TIMES TO PRACTICE

It is often considered beneficial to practice yoga early in the morning to center your body, mind and spirit in a healthy and holy way. Plus, it kick-starts your metabolism by stimulating blood flow to all your limbs and organs. Other recommended times include before meals, at dusk or at bedtime.

When do you typically practice? Do you naturally weave in pauses, moments to reconnect with what is good and true, into your day? Commune with Jesus the structuring of your day.

SCRIPTURE:

LORD, be gracious to us; we long for you. Be our strength every morning, our salvation in time of distress. (Isaiah 33:2)

PRAYER:

Lord, I commune *Psalm 143:8: Let the morning bring me word of your unfailing love, for I have put my trust in you.* Holy One, illumine my practice, whether it is in the morning, noon or night. Help me structure my time in accordance with your divine will. Pausing and reflecting on your goodness, I say Amen.

ᄋᄼᓕ

Day 286
PRACTICING ON AN EMPTY STOMACH

It is recommended to practice yoga when your stomach is not digesting food to receive its full cleansing benefits. This is especially helpful when doing twists, which 'rinse' your internal organs through compression and release, as well as when doing inversions, which reverse the blood flow in your body. Doing yoga on an empty stomach is a spiritual discipline. Like a fast, it reminds you that "man does not eat of bread alone, but of the word of God." The feeling of being physically hungry provides space to focus on the Lord's provision. Note how you feel when you refrain from eating before doing yoga or taking communion. Reflect also on any spiritual disciplines you have taken on as it relates to food. Commune with Jesus.

SCRIPTURE:

[The Israelites Confess Their Sins] On the twenty-fourth day of the same month, the Israelites gathered together, fasting and wearing sackcloth and putting dust on their heads. (Nehemiah 9:1)

He humbled you, causing you to hunger and then feeding you with manna, which neither you nor your ancestors had known, to teach you that man does not live on bread alone but on every word that comes from the mouth of the LORD. (Deuteronomy 8:3)

PRAYER:
Lord, I come to my mat with an empty stomach and a heart that hungers and thirsts for your holy righteousness and light. Please fill me with Spirit. I read *Matthew 6:17-18: But when you fast, put oil on your head and wash your face, so that it will not be obvious to others that you are fasting, but only to your Father, who is unseen; and your Father, who sees what is done in secret, will reward you.* No matter what sensations I experience in my stomach, muscles or being during this practice, let me remember to keep a soft expression on my face and joyful heart. Amen.

༄

Day 287
DRINKING WATER

If there is one item on the side of a yoga mat, it is often a water bottle. How does the Lord show you His provision through water? Statistics show that around one billion people on the planet do not have access to clean drinking water. It is a great blessing to have safe drinking water. Reflect on your daily water consumption and how your body's nourished by water. *Psalm 62:1: Oh God, you are my God, for you my soul is thirsting.* Are you thirsty for the Lord? What is your current state; are you parched and dried up or overflowing abundantly like a natural spring? Share your responses with Jesus.

SCRIPTURE:
They will neither hunger nor thirst, nor will the desert heat or the sun beat down on them. He who has compassion on them will guide them and lead them beside springs of water. (Isaiah 49:10)

PRAYER:

Lord, thank you for providing me with physical and spiritual water. Teach me how to share water with those who are thirsty. Tapping into your springs of living water flowing in me, I remember *John 4:13-14: Everyone who drinks this water will be thirsty again, but whoever drinks the water I give them will never thirst. Indeed, the water I give them will become in them a spring of water welling up to eternal life.* Thank you for this great blessing and for always filling my cup. Lord, help me point others to your living streams. Amen.

∞

Day 288
HEALTHY EATING

The practice of yoga does not simply consist of your time on the mat. All elements of your life make up your practice. Mindful eating is a part of yoga and can be a spiritual act. Reflect on *Luke 22:19-20: And he took bread, gave thanks and broke it, and gave it to them, saying, "This is my body given for you; do this in remembrance of me." In the same way, after the supper he took the cup, saying, "This cup is the new covenant in my blood, which is poured out for you."* Each meal is an opportunity to give thanks and treat your body as God's temple. Note how your yoga practice has shaped your eating habits and what sorts of healthy eating habits are you cultivating. Commune with Jesus about your food choices and how they reflect your faith.

SCRIPTURE:

They said to him, "John's disciples often fast and pray, and so do the disciples of the Pharisees, but yours go on eating and drinking." Jesus answered, "Can you make the friends of the bridegroom fast while he is with them? But the time will come when the bridegroom will be taken from them; in those days they will fast." (Luke 5:34-35)

PRAYER:

Lord, I marvel at all the ways you nourish me. Help me make good, disciplined eating choices so that I may receive the full benefits of the practice.

I remember Daniel could have eaten the king's food but *'resolved not to defile himself with the royal food and wine, and he asked the chief official for permission not to defile himself this way.' (Daniel 1:8)* Daniel asked for vegetables and water for himself and his companions, and *'at the end of the ten days they looked healthier and better nourished than any of the young men who ate the royal food.' (Daniel 1:15)* Like Daniel, help me to make wholesome choices and treat my body as your sacred temple. Amen.

ᕽ

Day 289
PURIFYING — PART 1

In yoga, you sweat. Some yogis choose to practice in 105-degree heat—stimulating lots of sweat! Sweating has a detoxifying and purifying effect on the body. How does it make you feel? Does sweating feel cleansing to you, or do you perceive it as dirty? Note, how you react to the internal heat that leads to sweat and how you respond to physical labor and exercise. Share your responses with Jesus.

SCRIPTURE:
By the sweat of your brow you will eat your food until you return to the ground, since from it you were taken; for dust you are and to dust you will return. (Genesis 3:19)

PRAYER:
Lord, I come to sweat—*'to work out my salvation with fear and trembling' (Philippians 2:12)*. Jesus, I remember how you agonized in prayer in the Garden of Gethsemane, knowing that soon you would be enduring the pain of the cross. *Luke 22:44: And being in anguish, he prayed more earnestly, and his sweat was like drops of blood falling to the ground*. I cannot begin to comprehend the pain you felt; it is beyond my comprehension. Righteous King, please heat my body, mind and spirit with your holy light. I am ready and willing to sweat for you! Amen.

ᕽ

Day 290
PURIFYING — PART 2

The cleansing benefits of yoga are not only experienced through sweat but also through the breath. Deep, full breathing while stretching brings rich oxygenated blood to your limbs and organs. Each asana offers unique strengthening, healing and centering qualities that support your major systems including your respiratory, circulatory and lymph systems. How has yoga seemed purifying to you? As is written in today's scripture passage, Titus 1:15, can you see the purity in all things? Reflect on *James 3:17: But the wisdom that comes from heaven is first of all pure; then peace-loving, considerate, submissive, full of mercy and good fruit, impartial and sincere.* Which of these attributes could you further develop at this time? Commune with Jesus.

SCRIPTURE:
To the pure, all things are pure but to those who are corrupted and do not believe, nothing is pure. In fact, both their minds and consciences are corrupted. (Titus 1:15)

PRAYER:
Lord, I come to understand the purity of all things you have created and to be guided in your pure wisdom that comes from the heavens. Cleanse me here on the mat in all my thoughts, actions, words and ways. I acknowledge *Psalm 19:9: The fear of the LORD is pure, enduring forever* and *Proverbs 16:2: All a person's ways seem pure to them, but motives are weighed by the LORD.* I come before you in reverence, remembering *1 John 3:3: All who have this hope in him purify themselves, just as he is pure.* Let me purify myself here and honor your wisdom from heaven. I lift up *Psalm 104:34: May my meditation be pleasing to him, as I rejoice in the LORD.* Amen.

୬

Day 291
GROWING

Good yoga classes stimulate growth. This could be growth in faith, flexibility or inner strength. How are you growing through your practice, both in a physical, as well as, spiritual sense? What developments have you noticed in others?

Commune with Jesus about the environments and relationships that are stimulating you to grow and develop in your daily life.

SCRIPTURE:

Then the church throughout Judea, Galilee and Samaria enjoyed a time of peace and was strengthened. Living in the fear of the Lord and encouraged by the Holy Spirit, it increased in numbers. (Acts 9:31)

PRAYER:

Lord, in reverential fear and encouraged by your Spirit, I come to grow in holy truth. Thank you for all the people and environments that have supported my development and the ways you have grown those near to me. I remember *Acts 14:27: On arriving there, they gathered the church together and reported all that God had done through them and how he had opened a door of faith to the Gentiles.* Likewise, I come to gather with others, rejoice in your presence and grow in faith. Use me as your vessel. Amen.

౿

Day 292
IDENTIFYING INTERMARRIAGE AND KEEPING YOUR FOCUS STEADY

In yoga, as in life, there are moments where one must be careful not to intermarry with practices that do not align with the Lord. Consider *1 Kings 11:4: As Solomon grew old, his wives turned his heart after other gods, and his heart was not fully devoted to the LORD his God, as the heart of David his father had been.* Where do you find yourself tempted to intermarry with worldly ways? What benefit does intermarrying offer and in what ways does it cause pain, confusion or loss? Commune with Jesus.

SCRIPTURE:

They were from nations about which the LORD had told the Israelites, "You must not intermarry with them, because they will surely turn your hearts after their gods." Nevertheless, Solomon held fast to them in love. (1 Kings 11:2)

PRAYER:

Lord, I come to hold fast to your commands and keep your decrees. Please forgive me for the ways I have intermarried and taken on worldly practices that do not align with your truth. Realign me in your light and yoke me in faith and love. I remember *2 Corinthians 6:14: Do not be yoked with unbelievers.* Bring into my life those who delight in your salvation and walk in your ways so that I may not wander from your holy path. In Spirit-filled steadfastness, I say Amen.

∽

Day 293
GETTING REST — PART 1

Rest is an important element of yoga. Read *Exodus 31:15: For six days work is to be done, but the seventh day is a day of sabbath rest, holy to the LORD.* Reflect on your Sabbath day. How comfortable are you with taking time to rest on the mat and in life? If your life seems out of balance, how might you draw into a healthier alignment between rest and activity? Commune with Jesus.

SCRIPTURE:

By the seventh day God had finished the work he had been doing; so on the seventh day he rested from all his work. Then God blessed the seventh day and made it holy, because on it he rested from all the work of creating that he had done. (Genesis 2:2-3)

PRAYER:

Lord, thank you for calling me to rest in your presence. I muse *Psalm 91:1: He who dwells in the shelter of the Most High will rest in the shadow of the Almighty*, and hear *Exodus 20:11: For in six days the LORD made the heavens and the earth, the sea, and all that is in them, but he rested on the seventh day. Therefore the LORD blessed the Sabbath day and made it holy.* Lord, thank you for blessing me when I am still and attuned to your voice. Jesus, healer on the Sabbath, guide me in knowing when to be active and when to be quiet; when to engage and when to restrain; when to move and when to be still. Firm in faith and resting in grace, I say Amen.

∽

Day 294
GETTING REST — PART 2

Yoga nidra is a conscious awareness while in a deep state of sleep. It is often evoked in the corpse pose and is a practice done to arouse a profound experience with God. Abiding in stillness, something new may arise. How do you connect with the Lord while resting? Commune with Jesus about sleeping, openness and listening.

SCRIPTURE:

I slept but my heart was awake. (Song of Solomon 5:2)

PRAYER:

Lord, thank you for speaking to me in times of rest and times of activity. I meditate on Peter's experience recorded in *Acts 11:5-7: I was in the city of Joppa praying, and in a trance I saw a vision. I saw something like a large sheet being let down from heaven by its four corners, and it came down to where I was. I looked into it and saw four-footed animals of the earth, wild beasts, reptiles and birds. Then I heard a voice telling me, 'Get up, Peter. Kill and eat.' I replied, 'Surely not, Lord! Nothing impure or unclean has ever entered my mouth.' The voice spoke from heaven a second time, 'Do not call anything impure that God has made clean.'* As you did with Peter, reveal your truth to me as I sit and meditate, and pray and listen. Remove any spiritual blindness and instruct me in your ways. Your servant is ready and alert. Amen.

‿❧

Day 295
HUMBLING — PART 1

All yogis have asanas that are 'works-in-progress'. There are moments in yoga where instead of striving or straining to get into the posture, it is best to bow your head and simply rest with the Lord. What have you learned about humility from your time on the mat? Read *1 Samuel 24:17: "You are more righteous than I,"* he said. *"You have treated me well, but I have treated you badly."* How have you acknowledged your limitations, mistakes and/or weaknesses to others? Who is humble in your life? Commune with Jesus about humility in your practice and in your life.

SCRIPTURE:

For all those who exalt themselves will be humbled, and those who humble themselves will be exalted. (Luke 18:14)

PRAYER:

Father, I acknowledge my limitations, mistakes and weaknesses. Forgive me for my errors and ignorant ways. Guide me in your mighty strength and holy light. I understand *Acts 17:25: He is not served by human hands, as if he needed anything. Rather, he himself gives everyone life and breath and everything else.* I offer myself up to listen and love, remembering *Luke 14:10-11: When you are invited, take the lowest place, so that when your host comes, he will say to you, 'Friend, move up to a better place.' Then you will be honored in the presence of all the other guests. For all those who exalt themselves will be humbled, and those who humble themselves will be exalted.* Help me to always choose to be humble and take the lowly position. Amen.

༄

Day 296
HUMBLING — PART 2

Yoga is done without shoes or any necessary equipment. It is an activity where all are accepted, none are rejected and all are thought of as equal. Take a moment to consider how you demonstrate humility in your practice and in your life. Reflect on your latest purchases and why you purchased them. Also note the material things you have been craving and why you desire them. Commune with Jesus about any worldly cravings present to you and their perhaps significance or insignificance.

SCRIPTURE:

For you know the grace of our Lord Jesus Christ, that though he was rich, yet for your sake he became poor, so that you through his poverty might become rich. (2 Corinthians 8:9)

PRAYER:

Father, the real position I desire is to be your child. Jesus, thank you for role-modeling how to take the lowly position. Lord, who blesses me with richness in so many ways, everything I have is yours; I lay it at your feet. Your grace and love are more than enough for me. Help me to use the treasures and talents you have entrusted to me to glorify you through them. Amen.

∽

Day 297
SUBMITTING

Sometimes in yoga class you may notice others in a challenging or new pose and doubt you will be able to do it. By following the cues, however, you find yourself in the position. Likewise, in life, how have you found yourself in a less-than-favorable situation yet through submission, felt God raise you up and enable you? Reflect on the ways in which you are submissive both to the Lord and to others, such as your parents, spouse, and authority figures. Commune with Jesus about submission.

SCRIPTURE:

Abraham took the wood for the burnt offering and placed it on his son Isaac, and he himself carried the fire and the knife. As the two of them went on together, Isaac spoke up and said to his father Abraham, "Father?" "Yes, my son?" Abraham replied. "The fire and wood are here," Isaac said, "but where is the lamb for the burnt offering?" Abraham answered, "God himself will provide the lamb for the burnt offering, my son." And the two of them went on together. (Genesis 22:6-8)

PRAYER:

Lord, I trust you will get me into the positions and places you desire of me, even if your ways seem uncomfortable or I cannot see the big picture of your plan. I remember that as Abraham lifted the knife over Isaac, you called to him and placed a ram in the thicket as a substitute sacrifice. *Genesis 22:14: So Abraham called that place The LORD Will Provide. And to this day it is said, "On the mountain of the LORD it will be provided."* You provided for Abraham and I have faith that you will provide for me too. Lord, like Isaac, I am ready to submit. I come to you in the mountain pose and express 'The Lord Will Provide'. Thank you, Father, for all the amazing ways you teach me. Amen.

෯

Day 298
SURRENDERING

Each exhale may act as a moment of surrender in yoga. There is a softening that happens when you exhale. It helps you deepen into a stretch. Take a slow, steady exhale and reflect on how you actively surrender to the Lord. *Matthew 9:29: Then he touched their eyes and said, "According to your faith let it be done to you."* Consider the areas of your life where you need to hear Jesus say, "According to your faith, let it be done to you."

SCRIPTURE:
Father, if you are willing, take this cup from me; yet not my will, but yours be done. (Luke 22:42)

PRAYER:
Father, I come to follow Jesus' example saying "not my will but yours be done." I aim to manifest my faith and trust in you through the asanas. With this sacred intention, I exhale Amen.

෯

Day 299
REFRESHING OTHERS – PART 1

One of the big appeals of teaching yoga is the opportunity it provides to refresh others. Even if you are not a teacher, you can refresh others by having an uplifting presence. Additionally, most yoga spaces offer special classes that support philanthropic causes, thus providing you with another way to bless others. Think about how you refresh others through your practice, as well as, in life.

Commune with Jesus about how you might further be a breath of fresh air to those around you.

SCRIPTURE:

A generous person will prosper; whoever refreshes others will be refreshed. (Proverbs 11:25)

PRAYER:

Lord, I come not only to be refreshed in your word, but also to refresh others. Guide me in supporting this space that refreshes me by giving back. I remember *2 Thessalonians 3:13: And as for you, brothers and sisters, never tire of doing what is good,* and *Galatians 6:9: Let us not become weary in doing good, for at the proper time we will reap a harvest if we do not give up.* Father, please help me to continue to do good on and off the mat. Amen.

ᖪᕫ

Day 300
REFRESHING OTHERS — PART 2

Introducing yourself to those practicing next to you is a way of acknowledging them. This sort of simple acknowledgment of others is an important part of yoga. Seeing the sacredness in all people and things is one of the beautiful lessons your practice may reveal. Reflect on *Luke 14:12-14: Then Jesus said to his host, "When you give a luncheon or dinner, do not invite your friends, your brothers or relatives, or your rich neighbors; if you do, they may invite you back and so you will be repaid. But when you give a banquet, invite the poor, the crippled, the lame, the blind, and you will be blessed. Although they cannot repay you, you will be repaid at the resurrection of the righteous."* Whether someone is poor, disabled, blind, imprisoned or simply a stranger in a physical or spiritual way, how do you acknowledge, recognize and invite them? Right now, identify one way you can refresh those around you. Share it with Jesus.

SCRIPTURE:

Then the King will say to those on his right, 'Come, you who are blessed by my Father; take your inheritance, the kingdom prepared for you since the creation of the world. For I was hungry and you gave me something to eat, I was thirsty and you gave me something to drink, I was a stranger and you invited me in, I needed clothes and you clothed me, I was sick and you looked after me, I was in prison and you came to visit me.' (Matthew 25:34-36)

PRAYER:

Father, so often I forget to welcome those who are blind, poor, disabled or strangers to me. Embolden my faith! I hear the calling of *Matthew 10:8: Heal the sick, raise the dead, cleanse those who have leprosy, drive out demons. Freely you have received, freely give.* I come to learn how to live out those holy words and muse *Isaiah 55:1: Come, all you who are thirsty, come to the waters; and you who have no money, come, buy and eat! Come, buy wine and milk without money and without cost.* Help me to welcome all without prejudice or restraint. Lord, who sees beauty where the world misses it, let me see it too! I remember *Matthew 25:40: Truly I tell you, whatever you did for one of the least of these brothers and sisters of mine, you did for me.* Reveal to me how I may help 'the least of these' and acknowledge all. Amen.

৩

Day 301
RECEIVING ASSISTANCE

In yoga, there are times when you need help. This could be getting into a pose or learning a modification. Anytime you find yourself reaching for help physically, it can serve as a time to remember to call on the Lord spiritually. What sort of assistance have you received in yoga, as well as, in life? Reflect on who has assisted you recently and how they did it. Commune with Jesus any assistance you may need today.

SCRIPTURE:

LORD my God, I called to you for help, and you healed me. (Psalm 30:2)

PRAYER:

Father, thank you for your assistance and for the supportive people you have placed in my life. I wholeheartedly commune *Jeremiah 17:14: Heal me, O LORD, and I will be healed; save me and I will be saved, for you are the one I praise.* I trust in your redeeming hands. Leaning into you, I recite *1 Samuel 2:2: There is no one holy like the LORD; there is no one besides you; there is no Rock like our God.* Rock and Redeemer, with my foundation in you, teach me how to give and receive assistance here on the mat and in life. Amen.

∽

Day 302
STUDYING ANCIENT TEACHINGS

Like the Bible, yoga is filled with ancient teachings. Both have sacred texts dating back thousands of years yet are alive and useful today for those who take hold of them and apply their truths. How do you maintain a teachable heart? In what ways and in what areas of your life do you feel you are actively learning? Sit still and contemplate *Isaiah 40:20: You have seen many things, but you pay no attention; your ears are open, but you do not listen.* In what ways do you have a hard time being open to new ideas and views? Commune with Jesus.

SCRIPTURE:
Teach me, and I will be silent. And show me if I have erred. (Job 6:24)

PRAYER:
Father, I admit I don't always do a good job listening or focus on learning. Please forgive me and help me to take heed. I am here to inscribe your commands on my heart and to live them out in all my actions. Your *'law is great and glorious' (Isaiah 40:21).* Selah. I remember *James 1:5: If any of you lacks wisdom, he should ask God, who gives generously to all without finding fault, and it will be given to him.* Lord, draw me to your sacred texts and through them, commune the wisdom and knowledge I need to ascend upward on your holy path. Amen.

∽

Day 303
BREATHING EXERCISES — PART 1

Breath of Fire is a cleansing and energizing practice. It is done by first taking a deep breath in through your nose (with your mouth closed), then exhaling quickly and strongly through your nose repetitively. Keep focused on igniting fast, powerful exhales, while letting your inhales come naturally when needed. Finding a rhythm with the breath, continue this exercise for about 30 seconds. After trying breath of fire, reflect on how the Lord energizes you with breath. When your energy is low, what do you do? What serves to reenergize you? Commune with the Lord about your energy and breath.

SCRIPTURE:

I open my mouth and pant, longing for your commands. (Psalm 119:131)

PRAYER:

Lord, my mouth pants for you. Forgive me for the times I turned to external stimulants for energy, for I know that you have deposited more energy than I can ever imagine inside me through your Spirit. I am here to tap into this ever-present holy truth through controlled breathing, and I commune *Psalm 119:43: Never take your word of truth from my mouth, for I have put my hope in your laws.* Amen.

෧෮

Day 304
BREATHING EXERCISES — PART 2

Nadi Shodhana, Alternative Nostril Breathing is thought to help balance the sympathetic/parasympathetic nervous systems and the right/left hemispheres of the brain. To do it, start seated and bring the index and middle fingers of your right hand up to the middle of your forehead while your ring and pinkie fingers shut the left nostril. Inhale slowly through the right nostril, then shut the right nostril with your thumb and exhale out the left. Next, inhale through your left nostril, then shut it and exhale through your right one. Keep reversing for three, five, or seven sets and end by exhaling on the left. Note, most of the time one nostril dominates over the other, and about every 90 minutes, the dominance switches from one side to the other. Alternative nostril breathing evens the breath through both nostrils creating a centering and unifying sensation. Reflect on your nostril breathing and think about all the ways that 'two becoming one' takes on meaning in your life.

SCRIPTURE:
For this reason a man will leave his father and mother and be united to his wife, and the two will become one flesh. (Ephesians 5:31)

PRAYER:
Lord, you are the vine that holds all things together; in you *'we live and move and have our being.' (Acts 17:28)* I breathe in and out in your presence. I thank you for all the wondrous ways you make two become one in life. As I practice alternative nostril breathing, uniting the hemispheres of my mind, I do so to unite my spirit to your Spirit. Guide me in this divine union. Amen.

༄

Day 305
AWARE AND AWAKE — PART 1

Yoga has much to do with harnessing your energy in the present moment and experiencing its fullness. Reminders to listen to your body and recognize when to back off and when to further move into a posture are key to practicing safely and strongly. Cues like 'option to drop your inside knee down or reach your top leg up' in the side plank pose, remind you to check in with your body and see what's needed in that moment. Reflect on the following verses:

> *He is not the God of the dead, but of the living, for to him all are alive.* (Luke 20:38)
> *But if Christ is in you, then even though your body is subject to death because of sin, the Spirit gives life because of righteousness.* (Romans 8:10)

That is why we labor and strive, because we have put our hope in the living God, who is the Savior of all people, and especially of those who believe. (1 Timothy 4:10)

SCRIPTURE:

You did not give me a kiss, but this woman, from the time I entered, has not stopped kissing my feet. You did not put oil on my head, but she has poured perfume on my feet. Therefore, I tell you, her many sins have been forgiven—as her great love has shown. But whoever has been forgiven little loves little. (Luke 7:45-47)

PRAYER:

Lord, thank you for indwelling my being; my hope is in you. I remember *John 12:3: Then Mary took about a pint of pure nard, an expensive perfume; she poured it on Jesus' feet and wiped his feet with her hair. And the house was filled with the fragrance of the perfume.* What grand intimacy! Musing on these words, I fall to my knees and imagine my hair and tears caressing your feet, Jesus. Like Mary, let this practice express my love for you in a vibrant and unbridled way. Thank you for calling, keeping and illuminating me. Here to anoint and be anointed, I say Amen.

❧

Day 306
AWARE AND AWAKE — PART 2

Yoga classes often cause you to become aware of your body and awakened in your spirit in a heightened way. Reminders to check your foot's position or to check in with your intention help foster this sense of awareness and alertness. Reflect on *Mark 13:33: Be on guard! Be alert! You do not know when that time will come.* How do you stay present—aware of your body, breath, thoughts in your mind and impulses of your heart? How do you stay attuned to the Lord's presence in your midst? How alert are you to those around you? Share your responses with Jesus.

SCRIPTURE:

Look, I come like a thief! Blessed is the one who stays awake and remains clothed, so as not to go naked and be shamefully exposed. (Revelation 16:15)

PRAYER:

Father, please forgive me for the ways I have been unaware of your presence and the needs of those around me. I come to foster attentiveness to your Spirit through mindful breathing and movement. I remember *1 Peter 4:7: The end of all things is near. Therefore be alert and of sober mind so that you may pray,* and proclaim *Psalm 57:8: Awake, my soul! Awake, harp and lyre! I will awaken the dawn.* Amen.

෩

Day 307
REPETITION — PART 1

Often directives are repeated to insure that they are heard, understood and re-membered. You might hear directives such as lift your belly up and in, activate your core, and engage your abdominal lock all within a short time period even though they essentially are saying the same thing. How do you handle repeti-tion and how do you learn through it? Remember how the Lord spoke to Peter through a vision about no food being unclean. *Acts 10:10: This happened three times, and then it was all pulled up to heaven again.* The Lord used repetition to make the point. How has the Lord used repetition to teach you a lesson? Commune with Jesus.

SCRIPTURE:

But as soon as they were at rest, they again did what was evil in your sight. Then you aban-doned them to the hand of their enemies so that they ruled over them. And when they cried out to you again, you heard from heaven, and in your compassion you delivered them time after time. (Nehemiah 9:28)

PRAYER:

Gracious and compassionate God, slow to anger and abounding in love, like the Israelites in Nehemiah, time and time again I need to repent. Each time I do, you extend your holy love and forgiveness to me. Thank you, Lord. As you did with Peter in Acts 10:10, drive home any points I need to learn. I remember *Luke 17:4: Even if they sin against you seven times in a day and seven times come back to you saying 'I repent,' you must forgive them.* Let me use repetition to bless. I take heart in *Proverbs 24:16: For though the righteous fall seven times, they rise again.* Please continue to help me rise when I fall, Sovereign King. Amen.

∾

Day 308
REPETITION — PART 2

Many forms of yoga practice the same moves in the same order during every class session. Repetition in your practice offers you the opportunity to deepen, fine-tune and gain confidence in the asanas. Likewise, repetition of prayers and scripture verses can also be a blessing. Fresh revelations may appear in the midst of repetition. Think about the motions your repeat on the mat and the messages you repeat to yourself through your day. How does repetition play a role in your practice and faith walk? Commune with Jesus about the prayers and actions that are most meaningful for you to repeat.

SCRIPTURE:
God has delivered me from going down to the pit, and I shall live to enjoy the light of life.' "God does all these things to a person— twice, even three times—to turn them back from the pit, that the light of life may shine on them. (Job 33:28-30)

PRAYER:
Lord, thank you for delivering me from the pit and letting your light shine on me. Thank you for repeating your message of grace and love through the gospel and for all the ways you teach and strengthen me through repetition. I remember *John 21:15-17: Jesus said to Simon Peter, "Simon son of John, do you love me more than these?"'Yes, Lord,"he said,"you know that I love you." Jesus said,"Feed my lambs."Again Jesus said,"Simon son of John, do you love me?" He answered,"Yes, Lord, you know that I love you." Jesus said,"Take care of my sheep."The third time he said to him,"Simon son of John, do you love me?" Peter was hurt because Jesus asked him the third time,"Do you love me?" He said,"Lord, you know all things; you know that I love you." Jesus said,"Feed my sheep."* Jesus, I love you, I love you, I love you. Deeply desiring to feed your sheep, I say Amen.

∾

Day 309
DEMONSTRATING PERSEVERANCE

There may be times when you are asked to hold a yoga posture longer than you think you can hold it. Reflect on *1 Peter 5:10: And the God of all grace, who called you to his eternal glory in Christ, after you have suffered a little while, will himself restore you and make you strong, firm and steadfast.* How does this apply to your practice? How might this relate to what you are encountering in life? Commune with Jesus.

SCRIPTURE:

But be very careful to keep the commandment and the law that Moses the servant of the LORD gave you: to love the LORD your God, to walk in obedience to him, to keep his commands, to hold fast to him and to serve him with all your heart and with all your soul. (Joshua 22:5)

PRAYER:

Lord, thank you for restoring me and making me strong, firm and steadfast even when I do not think I have it in me. I am here to hold fast to your commands and hear *1 Corinthians 16:13: Be on your guard; stand firm in the faith; be courageous; be strong.* Standing ready and willing to take on any Goliath of a position, I know you will be with me. Your rod and staff comfort and protect me, great Deliverer, my God. Amen.

❧

Day 310
EMBRACING WISDOM

Yoga is thought to cultivate wisdom. The word wisdom in Hebrew is the feminine word *Hochmah* or *Hokmah*; in Greek it is the feminine word *Sophia*. Why might these old languages describe wisdom as feminine? What have you learned from women in the Bible? What have you learned from the women in your life? Commune with the Lord about wisdom.

SCRIPTURE:

Do not forsake wisdom, and she will protect you; love her, and she will watch over you. The beginning of wisdom is this: Get wisdom. Though it cost all you have, get understanding. Cherish her, and she will exalt you; embrace her, and she will honor you. (Proverbs 4:6-8)

PRAYER:

Great I AM, I come to grow in wisdom and understanding, musing *1 Corinthians 13:9: For we know in part and we prophesy in part* and *1 Corinthians 13:12: Now I know in part; then I shall know fully, even as I am fully known.* Thank you, Lord, for fully knowing me—every hair on my head, thought in my mind and meditation of my heart. I hear *Proverbs 19:8: The one who gets wisdom loves life; the one who cherishes understanding will soon prosper* and *Proverbs 16:16: How much better to get wisdom than gold, to get insight rather than silver!* Teach me in Hokmah; lead me in Sophia. Resting in *Proverbs 2:3-5: If you call for insight and cry aloud for understanding...then you will understand the fear of the Lord and find the knowledge of God,* I say Amen.

৩৯

Day 311
PRACTICING BAREFOOTED

Yoga is done barefooted. The Lord's ground is holy. Experiencing God's land with your feet can be grounding and connecting. Reflect on the daily activities you do barefooted. Gently message your feet and think about what environments you consider sacred? How do you discover holiness in the various spaces you enter? Connect with Jesus about sacred ground.

SCRIPTURE:

Then the Lord said to him, 'Take off your sandals; the place where you are standing is holy ground.' (Acts 7:33)

PRAYER:

Lord, here on holy ground, I remove shoes and remember *Exodus 3:5: "Do not come any closer,"* God said. *"Take off your sandals, for the place where you are standing is holy ground."* In utmost reverence to your presence here and everywhere, I say Amen.

ᖇᖇ

Day 312
CLOTHING CHOICES

Yoga can be done in a wide array of clothing choices. Many companies make comfortable, flexible, breathable yoga clothing. They can be a great help in your movement yet might also be a distraction. Read *Isaiah 32:11:Tremble, you compla-cent women; shudder, you daughters who feel secure! Strip off your fine clothes and wrap yourselves in rags.* How does this verse speak to you? What type of clothing do you buy? Where and when do you shop? How do you let the Lord cloth you? Share your responses with Jesus.

SCRIPTURE:
Therefore, as God's chosen people, holy and dearly loved, clothe yourselves with compassion, kindness, humility, gentleness and patience. (Colossians 3:12)

PRAYER:
Lord, teach me about the type of clothing you desire me to wear. Please help me to put on compassion, kindness, humility, gentleness, patience and love above all else. As your child, teach me how to take inventory of my heart and spirit, and clothe myself with these things. Let me strip away any attachment to 'fine clothes' that can wear out and moths may destroy. Forgive me for any ways I have sinned in the way I dress; draw me back into your light. Lord, to be chosen and dearly loved by you, it amazes me. Thank you for clothing me with the same intimacy and care you gave to Adam and Eve in the garden. I realize that my internal clothing mat-ters much more than any external outfit I wear. With reverence, I listen to *1 Peter 5:5: All of you, clothe yourselves with humility toward one another, because, "God opposes the proud but shows favor to the humble."* This is my desire, Father. Amen.

ᖇᖇ

Day 313
THE WEARING-OUT FACTOR OF CLOTHES AND EQUIPMENT

Like all things, yoga clothes and equipment will eventually wear out from much use. Reflect on the new and old items you really value and how you channel your energy into the maintenance and protection of these things. Where is your treasure? How do your actions and reactions reflect it? Commune with Jesus.

SCRIPTURE:

Do not store up for yourselves treasures on earth, where moths and vermin destroy, and where thieves break in and steal. But store up for yourselves treasures in heaven, where moths and vermin do not destroy, and where thieves do not break in and steal. For where your treasure is, there your heart will be also. (Matthew 6:19-21)

PRAYER:

Father, please forgive me for all the times I have focused on earthly things. I come to redirect my energy and to refocus on your truth, love and light. Thank you for refreshing my soul. I remember the parable of the hidden treasure, *Matthew 13:44: The kingdom of heaven is like treasure hidden in a field. When a man found it, he hid it again, and then in his joy went and sold all he had and bought that field.* Lord, help me to let go of any 'things' I am holding on to and to release them into your hands. Let me focus on you, the real treasure! Centered in body, heart, and spirit on your presence within, I say Amen.

❦

Day 314
WITNESSING — PART 1

Yoga classes sometimes have demonstrations to teach you how a pose is done properly. Reflect on the demonstrations you have seen on the mat, both intentional ones by the teacher and unintentional ones you have noted from watching other students. What demonstrations in life stand out, and which have been most helpful? What about demonstrations of God's love? Read *Acts 5:32: We are witnesses of these things, and so is the Holy Spirit, whom God has given to those who obey him*. How do you feel you are a witness? Share your response with Jesus.

SCRIPTURE:

But God demonstrates his own love for us in this: While we were still sinners, Christ died for us. (Romans 5:8)

PRAYER:

Father, thank you for Christ's mighty demonstration love and for all the witnesses of light you have placed in my life. Thank you for making me a witness. I hear *Isaiah 43:12: "I have revealed and saved and proclaimed—I, and not some foreign god among you. You are my witnesses," declares the LORD, "that I am God."* Help me move my body in a special, holy, sacred way that acknowledges and affirms your presence. Focused on taking demonstrations seriously and being a witness of Your love and light, I say Amen.

ॐ

Day 315
VOLUNTEERING

Yoga classes may ask for a volunteer at times. This could mean demonstrating a move or getting something such a block or strap to help someone do their pose. How eager are you to volunteer when one is requested? In what activities or roles are you comfortable volunteering, and conversely, which roles make you uncomfortable? How do you act eagerly to serve the Lord? Commune with Jesus about volunteering.

SCRIPTURE:

Then I heard the voice of the Lord saying, "Whom shall I send? And who will go for us?" And I said, "Here am I. Send me!" (Isaiah 6:8)

PRAYER:

Lord, thank you for calling me to follow you, love you and love others. Please forgive me for the times I have neglected to volunteer for tasks you have desired of me. I come eager to serve, reciting *Psalm 40:7: Then I said, "Here I am, I have come—it is written about me in the scroll."* Father, guide me with your Word to do your will and to walk in your way, for I am ever, only and all for you. Amen.

༄

Day 316
UNCOVERING HIDDEN MEANING

Some parts of yoga may seem obscure. For example, you may place your hands in a seal but do not necessarily feel anything particular happen, or you may be unable to fully describe the benefits you do experience. Likewise with faith, there may be aspects you cannot fully articulate with words. Read *John 14:9: Jesus answered, "Don't you know me, Philip, even after I have been among you such a long time?"* Commune with Jesus about how you can relate to this verse.

SCRIPTURE:
The disciples did not understand any of this. Its meaning was hidden from them, and they did not know what he was talking about. (Luke 18:34)

PRAYER:
Sovereign Lord, I come humbly to you, for there is so much you taught that I have failed to hear, failed to understand and failed to live in my daily life. Please forgive me. I commune the words the apostles spoke in *Luke 17:5: Increase our faith!* Yes, Lord, grow my faith. With deepest desire to keep on your straight and narrow path of Life, I say Amen.

༄

Day 317
A TIME — PART 1

In yoga there is a time to inhale and a time to exhale. There is a time to lift up and a time to bow down. There is a time to engage and a time to soften. A class frequently begins with you cultivating a sense of openness and readiness in the child's pose. Next, various series of active poses are done. Lastly, ends by having you surrender in the corpse pose, then roll to one side as a mark of rebirth. This class cycle is much like nature—the sun rises and sets, the moon waxes and wanes, the tides rise and fall. Yoga offers a time to explore these natural harmonies. Stop and draw your attention to the rhythms of your days. Reflect on your daily patterns from when you pray to when you practice yoga. How can you become more attuned with life's innate harmonies and the Lord's divine timing? Commune with Jesus.

SCRIPTURE:

There is a time for everything, and a season for every activity under the heavens: a time to be born and a time to die, a time to plant and a time to uproot, a time to kill and a time to heal, a time to tear down and a time to build. (Ecclesiastes 3:1-3)

PRAYER:

Lord, thank you for the rhythms of my life from my heartbeat to my breath. You tenderly care for me in each moment. I hear *Ecclesiastes 3:11: He has made everything beautiful in its time. He has also set eternity in the human heart; yet no one can fathom what God has done from beginning to end.* O Lord, your mysteries are far beyond my comprehension. Thank you for placing eternity in my heart. With the focus of moving to the beat of your love, I say Amen.

෧෨

Day 318
A TIME — PART 2

From the people in the practice space to the pace and postures of the class, each practice is unique. There is a time to do a headstand and a time to refrain. There is a time for a scripture passage on grace and a time for one on perseverance. How do you experience each practice as unique and accept the variation that comes on the mat? How do you embrace variety in life? Commune with Jesus about what sort of a 'time' you are experiencing now.

SCRIPTURE:

A time to weep and a time to laugh, a time to mourn and a time to dance, a time to scatter stones and a time to gather them, a time to embrace and a time to refrain from embracing, a time to search and a time to give up, a time to keep and a time to throw away, a time to tear and a time to mend, a time to be silent and a time to speak, a time to love and a time to hate, a time for war and a time for peace. (Ecclesiastes 3:4-8)

PRAYER:

Father, thank you for providing different emotions and experiences through which I can learn and grow. I recognize and have come to appreciate the uniqueness that each time on the mat offers me and remember *Matthew 9:15: Jesus answered, "How can the guests of the bridegroom mourn while he is with them? The time will come when the bridegroom will be taken from them; then they will fast."* Lord, help me discern what emotions and actions are appropriate for each time and space. Inviting you to set the tone for this practice, I say Amen.

෯

Day 319
EXPERIENCING YOGA BLISS

Yoga bliss is a common expression used to describe the feeling often experienced after practicing. Have you experienced this joyful, rejuvenating, purifying sensation? Reflect on the activities that seem to refresh your spirits and people who seem to give you energy. Also note any ones that feel draining to you. Pause and commune with Jesus.

SCRIPTURE:

And on that day they offered great sacrifices, rejoicing because God had given them great joy. The women and children also rejoiced. The sound of rejoicing in Jerusalem could be heard far away. (Nehemiah 12:43)

PRAYER:

Lord, thank you for refreshing my spirits and bringing me newfound joy in your light and love every time I come onto the mat. Your presence heals, cleanses and anoints me. Delighting in this blessing, I proclaim *Psalm 21:1: How great is his joy in the victories you give!* Hear my heart as I commune *Psalm 28:7: The LORD is my strength and my shield; my heart trusts in him, and he helps me. My heart leaps for joy, and with my song I praise him.* Amen.

༄

Day 320
ASKING QUESTIONS

Yoga teachers will often ask reflective questions for you to ponder during a class. What questions have caused you to stop and think recently? Sit up straight, close your eyes and picture Jesus with you. Hear this question directed to you: "What do you want me to do for you?" Respond to Jesus.

SCRIPTURE:

"What do you want me to do for you?" Jesus asked him. The blind man said, "Rabbi, I want to see." "Go," said Jesus, "your faith has healed you." Immediately he received his sight and followed Jesus along the road. (Mark 10:51-52)

PRAYER:

Father, thank you for healing touches. I recall the story of Jesus healing the ten lepers in *Luke 17:15-17: One of them, when he saw he was healed, came back, praising God in a loud voice. He threw himself at Jesus' feet and thanked him—and he was a Samaritan. Jesus asked, "Were not all ten cleansed? Where are the other nine?"* Lord, may I be like the Samaritan and use this practice to thank you for all the wondrous ways you have restored me from headaches to heartbreaks. Illumine me in my innermost being here on the mat. Amen.

༄

Day 321
SPECIFIC TYPES OF YOGA

A few include Ashtanga, Bikram, Iyengar, Kundalini and Yin. What types of yoga have you tried? What have you learned from them? How have they provided you an opportunity to connect with others and share the Lord's love and light?

Commune with Jesus about how open are you to explore and understand other practices.

SCRIPTURE:
For everything God created is good, and nothing is to be rejected if it is received with thanksgiving, because it is consecrated by the word of God and prayer. (1 Timothy 4:4-5)

PRAYER:
Lord, I receive this opportunity to practice with you in thanksgiving. Let your presence shine forth in this experience and all others. It is my intention to *'find out what pleases you' (Ephesians 5:10)*. Help me to keep an open heart and know what places to visit and explore so that I may discover your goodness in all. I remember *Acts 17:23: For as I walked around and looked carefully at your objects of worship, I even found an altar with this inscription: TO AN UNKNOWN GOD. So you are ignorant of the very thing you worship—and this is what I am going to proclaim to you.* Likewise, before I speak, help me to look around carefully and gain insight about others perspectives in the space. Surrendered in love, I say Amen.

༄

Day 322
ASHTANGA YOGA

The well known yogi K. Pattabhi Jois is recognized for the development of Ashtanga yoga. Ashtanga translates as eight-limbed, referring to the limbs outlined by Patañjali in the Yoga Sutras. This type of yoga focuses on strength, flexibility, balance and stamina and is often thought of as 'power yoga'. Practices are comprised of a progressive series of postures and have you focus on your breath. Pondering these elements of your practice, reflect on how you have progressed in terms of strength and flexibility through your time on the mat. Consider how you have progressed in terms of balance and stamina both physically and spiritually. Commune with Jesus.

SCRIPTURE:

Be diligent in these matters; give yourself wholly to them, so that everyone may see your progress. (1 Timothy 4:15)

PRAYER:

Lord, I come to diligently treat my body, mind and spirit as your temple. I remember *1 Timothy 4:8: For physical training is of some value, but godliness has value for all things, holding promise for both the present life and the life to come.* Lord, let this practice be a practice of godliness. I love you, and I desire for my thoughts, words and actions to powerfully reflect it. Amen.

∽

Day 323
BIKRAM YOGA

Bikram Choudhury developed Bikram yoga. Bikram is recognized as an intense routine of twenty-six postures that begins and ends with breath work. The room is set to a temperature of over 100 degrees Fahrenheit to stimulate a lot of sweat. The combination of heat with these particular postures is thought to detoxify the body. Reflect on what activities and actions seem purifying to you, and in what ways you may need to feel cleansed now. Commune with Jesus about anything that seems toxic in your life.

SCRIPTURE:

I will cleanse them. They will be my people, and I will be their God. (Ezekiel 37:23)
Cleanse me with hyssop, and I will be clean; wash me, and I will be whiter than snow. (Psalm 51:7)

PRAYER:

Lord, I thank you for your cleansing touch. Please remove anything from my life that is toxic. I remember *Zechariah 3:19: This third I will bring into the fire; I will refine them like silver and test them like gold. They will call on my name and I will answer them; I will say, 'They are my people,' and they will say, 'The*

LORD is our God.' Let the external and internal heat in my yoga practice remind me of your purifying presence. With gratitude for your holy, refining fire, I say Amen.

❧

Day 324
CHAIR YOGA

Chair yoga is simply yoga done from a chair and is often a great starting place for people who are overweight, elderly or recovering from injuries. It may also be a good practice for a long plane ride or for taking a break while seated in an office chair. From a seated position in a chair, reach your arms up and back, twisting your core and elongating your spine as you gaze back. Take a few deep breaths and then reverse directions. While doing so, think about how you may be seated in your ways, not alert and responsive to what is happening in you and/or around you. Commune with Jesus about how to be engaged and active from a stationary position.

SCRIPTURE:

Wake up, sleeper, rise from the dead, and Christ will shine on you. (Ephesians 5:14)

PRAYER:

Lord, please forgive me for the ways I have been a sleeper. Wake me up in your light. Wake me up to your calling for love, mercy and justice. Shine on me, in me and through me. Let me explore ways to be refreshed in body, word and spirit from a chair. Help me not to sit stagnantly but to stretch vibrantly and to grow in each position and place. I hear *Isaiah 50:4: The Sovereign LORD has given me a well-instructed tongue, to know the word that sustains the weary. He wakens me morning by morning, wakens my ear to listen like one being instructed.* Lord, whether on a chair or on the mat, may I actively respond to your voice. Amen.

❧

Day 325
HOLY YOGA

Holy Yoga is type of yoga that focuses on connecting people with Christ. Holy Yoga was founded in 2003 by Brooke Boon in Phoenix, Arizona, and is now an international ministry. Reflect on the activities and experiences that draw you to God. Ponder why you may be situated where you are today and what the Lord may have planned. Reflect on *Matthew 1:18-21: This is how the birth of Jesus the Messiah came about: His mother Mary was pledged to be married to Joseph, but before they came together, she was found to be pregnant through the Holy Spirit. Because Joseph her husband was faithful to the law, and yet did not want to expose her to public disgrace, he had in mind to divorce her quietly. But after he had considered this, an angel of the Lord appeared to him in a dream and said, "Joseph son of David, do not be afraid to take Mary home as your wife, because what is conceived in her is from the Holy Spirit. She will give birth to a son, and you are to give him the name Jesus, because he will save his people from their sins."* The Father chose Jesus' parents for specific reasons, and He chose your parents for specific reasons, too. Reflect on the lessons you have learned from those around you and the experiences that have particularly shaped you—giving you a heighten sense of direction and an infusion of faith.

SCRIPTURE:

From one man he made all the nations, that they should inhabit the whole earth; and he marked out their appointed times in history and the boundaries of their lands. God did this so that they would seek him and perhaps reach out for him and find him, though he is not far from any one of us. (Acts 17:26-28)

PRAYER:

Lord, thank you for placing me in specific environments to hear messages you've designed for me and for all the relationships that have helped me grow closer to you. I come to this space to listen for what you may reveal today. I hear *Luke 2:19: But Mary treasured up all these things and pondered them in her heart.* Likewise, I ponder and treasure the blessings you have brought and the lessons you have taught. I am ready and willing to listen and obey any insights or messages you may share with me here. Amen.

Day 326
HOT YOGA

Hot Yoga is often defined as yoga practiced in environments set at (or naturally in) 90 degrees (or higher) Fahrenheit. Stimulating large amounts of sweat, the heat purifies the body and enhances your range of flexibility. People either find it enjoyable or uncomfortable. How do you respond to heat in yoga classes, as well as, in life? Reflect on physical, emotional, mental and spiritual heat. Commune with Jesus.

SCRIPTURE:
This is what the LORD says to me:"I will remain quiet and will look on from my dwelling place, like shimmering heat in the sunshine, like a cloud of dew in the heat of harvest." (Isaiah 18:4)

PRAYER:
Father, thank you for heating, cooling, cleansing and caring for me. I remember *Hosea 13:5: I cared for you in the wilderness, in the land of burning heat.* O Lord, you protect me in the heat and save me from harm. Refine me. I hear *Daniel 11:35: Some of the wise will stumble, so that they may be refined,* and *Daniel 12:10: Many will be purified, made spotless and refined.* Thank you, Lord. I listen to *Psalm 12:6: And the words of the LORD are flawless, like silver purified in a crucible, like gold refined seven times.* Wondrous Truth! Jesus, baptizer *'with the Holy Spirit and with fire' (Luke 3:16),* let your holy fire ablaze in, through and around me. Amen.

◌

Day 327
IYENGAR YOGA

Iyengar yoga is a style developed by B.K.S. Iyengar that emphasizes correct posture and precise alignment. This style commonly uses props and is often done for therapeutic purposes. In what ways do you keep attention to detail in your practice and in your life? How are you growing in the godly qualities listed in today's scripture 2 Peter 1:5-8? Commune with Jesus.

SCRIPTURE:

For this very reason, make every effort to add to your faith goodness; and to goodness, knowledge; and to knowledge, self-control; and to self-control, perseverance; and to perseverance, godliness; and to godliness, mutual affection; and to mutual affection, love. For if you possess these qualities in increasing measure, they will keep you from being ineffective and unproductive in your knowledge of our Lord Jesus Christ. But whoever does not have them is nearsighted and blind, forgetting that they have been cleansed from their past sins. (2 Peter 1:5-8)

PRAYER:

Lord, thank you for cleansing me of my sins. Please help me never to forget this truth and to be intentional with everything I do in life. I hear *2 Peter 1:10: Therefore, my brothers and sisters, make every effort to confirm your calling and election. For if you do these things, you will never stumble.* Father, may I further see and understand your divine purpose for me as I move on the mat. I desire to pay attention to every detail and correctly align myself in Spirit so that your holy energy will flow through me. I attune to *1 Timothy 4:16: Watch your life and doctrine closely. Persevere in them, because if you do, you will save both yourself and your hearers.* At watch, I say Amen.

૦∾૦

Day 328
KIDS YOGA

Children can be blessed through the practice of yoga just as adults can. Kids often do not over-think how to do poses such as the crow pose; they simply try the pose and see what happens. This sort of willingness and openness to explore is refreshing and hope-filled. How has a child rejuvenated your spirits? Likewise, how has Scripture helped you have a spirit of endurance and encouragement with children? Reflecting on your childhood, what activities did you try out as a kid, and who encourage you with them? Where in your life now could you use a spirit of encouragement and fresh hope? Commune with Jesus about encouragement and the hearts of children.

SCRIPTURE:

For everything that was written in the past was written to teach us, so that through the endurance taught in the Scriptures and the encouragement they provide we might have hope. (Romans 15:4)

PRAYER:

Father, thank you for providing me with stamina and patience. I come to the mat with childlike eagerness. Let your words take root and shape me from the inside out as I practice. I remember Paul's letter in *Romans 15:5-6: May the God who gives endurance and encouragement give you the same attitude of mind toward each other that Christ Jesus had, so that with one mind and one voice you may glorify the God and Father of our Lord Jesus Christ.* Thank you for your indwelling Spirit that provides the daily strength I need to interact with those around me. Guide me in sharing this spirit of endurance and encouragement with your children—young and old alike. Let this practice be an embracing family experience. Amen.

৩৩

Day 329
KUNDALINI YOGA

Kundalini yoga, developed by Yogi Bhajan focuses on the activation of the kundalini energy that is thought to be stored at the base of the spine. Many breathing techniques are used in this type of yoga. Pondering kundalini energy, reflect on how you feel the Lord's energy working in you. Read *John 7:37-38: Let anyone who is thirsty come to me and drink. Whoever believes in me, as Scripture has said, rivers of living water will flow from within them.* Where do these rivers start and where do they end? How can you tap into this presence within you? Commune with Jesus.

SCRIPTURE:

To this end I strenuously contend with all the energy Christ so powerfully works in me. (Colossians 1:29)

PRAYER:

Lord, thank you for filling my being with your living energy. I come to further tap into it, hearing *Philippians 2:12 (MSG): Be energetic in your life of salvation, reverent and sensitive before God. That energy is God's energy, an energy deep within you, God himself willing and working at what will give him the most pleasure.* What a tremendous blessing! Lord, teach me to fully activate that energy—your energy within me. Amen.

৩৩

Day 330
LAUGHTER YOGA

Laughter yoga sprung up in 1995 when Dr. Madan Kataria, a physician from Mumbai, India started teaching laughter exercises to a small group in a park. Laughter yoga combines unconditional laughter with yogic breathing (pranayama) and postures. It is thought to release positive energy and support feelings of being healthy and happy. Have you ever giggled in a class? Releasing pent-up frustration through laughter can feel cathartic. Think of the last time you really laughed. Noting it, sit still and laugh for one minute. Commune with Jesus about how you feel.

SCRIPTURE:

Hannah prayed: I'm bursting with God-news! I'm walking on air. I'm laughing at my rivals. I'm dancing my salvation. (1 Samuel 2:1 MSG)

PRAYER:

Father, thank you for the gift of laughter. I come to position my body, heart and spirit in a way that is ready to walk on air and burst joyfully with good news like Hannah. I hear *Psalm 35:9 (MSG): But let me run loose and free, celebrating God's great work, Every bone in my body laughing, singing, "God, there's no one like you. You put the down-and-out on their feet and protect the unprotected from bullies!"* Let me move in a way that expresses this sort of boundless radiance and confidence in you. I remember *Psalm 14:7 (MSG): Is there anyone around to save Israel? Yes. God is around; God turns life around. Turned-around Jacob skips rope, turned-around Israel sings laughter.* Thank you for replacing my doubt with hope, my sadness with joy and my darkness with light. Help me to do likewise. Amen.

༄

Day 331
OUTDOOR YOGA

No special place is needed for yoga. All that is needed is a willing heart. How do you connect with God in nature? Think of how the beauty of nature captivates you—whether it's the stars, sky, fish, seas, mountains, valleys, flowers or trees. Have you practiced in nature? If so, what was your experience? Spend a minute outside before your practice and take note of the expansiveness surrounding you.

SCRIPTURE:
The God who made the world and everything in it is the Lord of heaven and earth and does not live in temples built by human hands. And he is not served by human hands, as if he needed anything. Rather, he himself gives everyone life and breath and everything else. (Acts 17:24-25)

PRAYER:
Lord, Psalm 8 is my prayer.
LORD, our Lord,
how majestic is your name in all the earth!
You have set your glory
in the heavens.
Through the praise of children and infants
you have established a stronghold against your enemies,
to silence the foe and the avenger.
When I consider your heavens,
the work of your fingers,
the moon and the stars,
which you have set in place,
what is mankind that you are mindful of them,
human beings that you care for them?

You have made them a little lower than the angels
  and crowned them with glory and honor.
You made them rulers over the works of your hands;
  you put everything under their feet:
  all flocks and herds,
  and the animals of the wild,
the birds in the sky,
  and the fish in the sea,
  all that swim the paths of the seas.
LORD, our Lord,
  how majestic is your name in all the earth!
Amen.

ᗡᗡ

Day 332
PARTNER YOGA

Partner yoga involves doing yoga moves with another person. An example of a partner move is doing the warrior 2 pose back-to-back with someone. Have you tried yoga with a partner, and if so, what was your experience? What are some of the challenges and blessings you are currently encountering in your relationships? Reflect on how you've been joining with others and read *Acts 1:14: They all joined together constantly in prayer, along with the women and Mary the mother of Jesus, and with his brothers.* Commune with Jesus.

SCRIPTURE:
For where two or three gather in my name, there am I with them (Matthew 18:20)

PRAYER:
Lord, thank you for the community you have blessed me with here on the mat and in life. Let each gathering be a time that is centered on you. I recite *Ephesians 4:16: From him the whole body, joined and held together by every*

supporting ligament, grows and builds itself up in love, as each part does its work. Help me to feel this sort of connectedness. Acknowledging *Ephesians 2:21: In him the whole building is joined together and rises to become a holy temple in the Lord*, I say Amen.

∽

Day 333
PRENATAL YOGA

Many women practice yoga throughout their pregnancies. Pregnancy can be a time when you experience the Lord's presence in a wondrous way. Whether or not pregnancy (yours or that of someone close to you) is having any an effect on your life now, pause and reflect on how pregnancy is symbolic of growing from the inside out. In what ways are you experiencing the fullness of the Lord's love in your life? In what areas of your life could love expand? Commune with Jesus.

SCRIPTURE:
And I pray that you, being rooted and established in love, may have power, together with all the Lord's holy people, to grasp how wide and long and high and deep is the love of Christ, and to know this love that surpasses knowledge—that you may be filled to the measure of all the fullness of God. (Ephesians 3:17-19)

PRAYER:
Lord, I come to grow in your holy light from the inside out. I recite *Philippians 1:9-10: And this is my prayer: that your love may abound more and more in knowledge and depth of insight, so that you may be able to discern what is best and may be pure and blameless for the day of Christ.* Breath by breath, posture by posture, may the seed of your Spirit grow in me, and may I bear fruit that will last. As I come into the full expression of poses here on the mat, let my spirit likewise reflect a full expression of love. Amen.

∽

Day 334
YOGA WITH WEIGHTS

Many yoga studios offer classes that include holding light weights while doing some of the postures. This adds a layer of strength and endurance training into your practice. How do you add strengthening exercises to your weekly routine, whether by including weights in your yoga practice or resistance tubing in a group fitness class? Likewise, how do you physically strengthen your heart through cardio exercise such as biking, running or swimming? Finally, how do you aim to strengthen your mind and spirit in a godly fashion? Commune with Jesus about sculpting and strengthening from the inside out.

SCRIPTURE:
Afterward, the prophet came to the king of Israel and said, "Strengthen your position and see what must be done, because next spring the king of Aram will attack you again." (1 Kings 20:22)

PRAYER:
Lord, I am here to become stronger in you—physically, emotionally and spiritually. Please sculpt me in each position and enable me to see what must be done. May I kindle a spirit of commitment to cardio and strength training for I know they play a role in treating my body as your temple. I take heart in *Exodus 15:13: In your unfailing love you will lead the people you have redeemed. In your strength you will guide them to your holy dwelling.* Lord, to you the glory, Amen.

ᑫᓚ

Day 335
YOGALATES

Yogalates is a combination of yoga and Pilates. Pilates has a great focus on strengthening and toning your deep core muscles, and as with yoga, the movement is very intentional. Your core is your digestive and cleansing center. Yogalates can provide a beautiful opportunity to let God cleanse you internally and strengthen the core of your being. How have you felt the Lord wash away iniquity and purify you? Reflect on feelings you have experienced in your gut, from a sense of intuition to adrenaline butterflies, and commune with Jesus.

SCRIPTURE:
Wash away all my iniquity and cleanse me of my sin. (Psalm 51:2)

PRAYER:
Lord, thank you for being *'a gracious and compassionate God, slow to anger, abounding in love and faithfulness', 'who forgives all my sins and heals all my diseases' (Psalm 86:15; Psalm 103:3).* I come to engage with you from the innermost places of my essence. Please strengthen me from the inside out using any practices or postures you deem important to transform my body, mind and heart into vessels pleasing to you. Amen.

杧Ω

Day 336
YIN YOGA

Yin yoga is a style of yoga that holds poses for several minutes. The deep stretching of yin yoga supports the connective tissues around the joints. It is intended to open the energy channels of the body to prepare it for meditation. Yin is considered the stable, still, hidden aspect of things, whereas, yang is considered the changing, active and revealing aspect. Yin is associated with feminine energy and the moon, whereas, yang is associated with masculine energy and the sun. A yin approach is often taken in a restorative class. Conversely, an advanced power class is more yang in nature. How do you find balance between active power-focused classes and gentle restorative ones? Can you find the joy and beauty in both types of experiences and classes (yin and yang)? Which one comes natural to you? Reflecting further on yin, what about the Lord may be perceived as feminine? The Hebrew word for Spirit is *Ruach* or *Rauh*, which is feminine, and the Aramaic word for the Lord's divine presence is *Shekinah*, which is feminine. Note that Aramaic is thought to be the everyday language that Jesus spoke. Connect with Jesus about yin and yang energy and essence.

SCRIPTURE:

The day is yours, and yours also the night; you established the sun and moon. (Psalm 74:16)

PRAYER:

Lord, thank you for day and night, sun and moon, yin and yang, and for your unchanging nature and active compassion. Your true nature is beyond my comprehension. I muse *Genesis 1:26: Then God said, Let us make mankind in our image, in our likeness and the Message version of this verse 'God spoke: Let us make human beings in our image, make them reflecting our nature'*. What an indescribable gift—men and women both made in your image. Shekinah, I rejoice in *Isaiah 66:13: As a mother comforts her child, so will I comfort you; and you will be comforted over Jerusalem.* Amen.

৩৩

Day 337
FRESH AIR, WIND AND SPIRIT

Yoga stimulates the senses and helps you become attuned to your breath. As shared in Day 21, the Greek word for Spirit is *pnuema*. Pnuema also translates to wind or breath. Pondering the relationship between these elements, meditate on the following verses:

> *Right before light was spoke into being 'Spirit of God was hovering over the waters'* (Genesis 1:2)
> *The Holy Spirit will come upon you.* (Luke 1:35)
> *But you will receive power when the Holy Spirit comes on you.* (Acts 1:8)

SCRIPTURE:

As you do not know the path of the wind, or how the body is formed in a mother's womb, so you cannot understand the work of God, the Maker of all things. (Ecclesiastes 11:5)

PRAYER:

Lord, thank you for placing your Holy Spirit in me even though I have yet to realize its full power. I come to intimately experience a connectedness to your

Spirit as I breathe in and out and hear *Ezekiel 37:6: I will put breath in you, and you will come to life. Then you will know that I am the LORD.* Acknowledging you in upmost love, I breathe Amen.

༄

Day 338
MIRRORS

Many yoga spaces have mirrors for you to examine your form and make any necessary changes in the poses. When you look at yourself in a mirror, what effect does it have on you? If you have a mirror nearby, take a minute and slowly examine your face, then scan your whole body. Commune with Jesus about anything that became present to through this activity.

SCRIPTURE:

Do not merely listen to the word, and so deceive yourselves. Do what it says. Anyone who listens to the word but does not do what it says is like someone who looks at his face in a mirror and, after looking at himself, goes away and immediately forgets what he looks like. (James 1:22-24)

PRAYER:

Lord, here I am, your child. Thank you for my face and each body part specially arranged, fashioned and formed by you. I come to remember to put your Word into motion with my entire being and hear *Jeremiah 24:7: I will give them a heart to know me, that I am the LORD. They will be my people, and I will be their God, for they will return to me with all their heart.* Thank you, Lord; I give you my whole heart. I recognize *1 Corinthians 13:12: For now we see only a reflection as in a mirror; then we shall see face to face.* Even though I do not see myself clearly when I look in the mirror, you do! In gratitude for you seeing and knowing me fully, I say Amen.

༄

Day 339
BANNERS

Most yoga rooms have blank walls, with no banners, signs or logos to distract you. Visualize the space you normally practice in or scan the room if you are currently in it. Are there any banners? How can you experience the Lord as your banner? Read the following passage slowly then close your eyes and visualize it. *Song of Solomon 2:4: Let him lead me to the banquet hall, and let his banner over me be love.*

SCRIPTURE:
Moses built an altar and called it The LORD is my Banner. (Exodus 17:15)

PRAYER:
Lord, you are my banner, and your banner over me is love. Thank you! I delight in *Isaiah 49:22: This is what the Sovereign LORD says: See, I will beckon to the nations, I will lift up my banner to the peoples,* and am energized by *Isaiah 62:10 (MSG): Pass through, pass through the gates! Prepare the way for the people. Build up, build up the highway! Remove the stones. Raise a banner for the nations.* Raising up a banner of love, I say Amen.

⤳

Day 340
DARKNESS

Yoga spaces are often dimly lit, especially during the final relaxation pose. What effect does this have on you? What effect does darkness have on your sleeping patterns, and how is darkness good? How has the Lord called to you into darkness and made you into a light? Meditate on *1 Peter 2:9: But you are a chosen people, a royal priesthood, a holy nation, God's special possession, that you may declare the praises of him who called you out of darkness into his wonderful light.*

SCRIPTURE:
To govern the day and the night, and to separate light from darkness. And God saw that it was good. (Genesis 1:18)

PRAYER:

Lord, I thank you for separating light and darkness and for the blessing of nights as well as days. Thank you for speaking to me in dimly environments such as the yoga room and for shedding your Spirit's light on me. I remember *Mark 1:35: Very early in the morning, while it was still dark, Jesus got up, left the house and went off to a solitary place, where he prayed.* Lord, in still, quiet, dark places you silently commune with me. With gratitude for your inner light, I say Amen.

∽

Day 341
CANDLES

Candles are often set out in yoga classes. In fact, some classes are even called candlelight classes. If you have taken a candlelight yoga class, what effect did the candles have on you? If possible, set a candle in front of you. Meditate on *Psalm 118:27: The LORD is God, and he has made his light shine on us.*

SCRIPTURE:

Do not gloat over me, my enemy! Though I have fallen, I will rise. Though I sit in darkness, the LORD will be my light. (Micah 7:8)

PRAYER:

Lord, thank you for being my light and for the calming, centering presence of candles. Seeing these little lights as small symbolic reminders your great light, I muse *2 Corinthians 4:6: For God, who said, "Let light shine out of darkness," made his light shine in our hearts to give us the light of the knowledge of God's glory displayed in the face of Christ.* Dear Lord, please let your light radiate and reside in my heart. As David said in *2 Samuel 22:29: You are my lamp, O Lord*, so do I. Amen.

∽

Day 342
BURNING INCENSE

Incense is sometimes burnt at the beginning or end of a class to create a pleasing aroma. Ponder aromas and the various scents that enliven you and calm you. Read *2 Corinthians 2:14-16: But thanks be to God, who always leads us as captives in Christ's triumphal procession and uses us to spread the aroma of the knowledge of him everywhere. For we are to God the pleasing aroma of Christ among those who are being saved and those who are perishing. To the one we are an aroma that brings death; to the other, an aroma that brings life. And who is equal to such a task?* Think of the smells of the people in your life—those close to you and those you have recently encountered. What can you note about them and what might your smell be? Commune with Jesus.

SCRIPTURE:

In this way present the food offering every day for seven days as an aroma pleasing to the LORD. (Numbers 28:24)

PRAYER:

Lord, I desire to spread your fragrance wherever I go and to be a pleasing aroma for you. I hear *Ephesians 5:1-2: Follow God's example, therefore, as dearly loved children and walk in the way of love, just as Christ loved us and gave himself up for us as a fragrant offering and sacrifice to God.* Lord, may I infuse any space I enter with the aroma of love. Surrendered, I permeate Alleluia. Amen.

Ꮿ

Day 343
MAKING ROOM

Yoga spaces are often small, and you may be asked to move your mat over to make room for another student. Reflect on how you make room for others in yoga and how do so in life—from spending quality time with a spouse to listening to someone share their perspective that differs from yours. Next, consider how you make room for the Lord in the midst of these environments and relationships.

SCRIPTURE:

Make room for us in your hearts. (2 Corinthians 7:2)

PRAYER:

Lord, I come to be entirely filled with your presence and understand that it starts with making room in my heart. Clear my heart of all clutter and distractions that prevent me from this holy fullness. I deeply desire to love others as you love them; help me make room for this sort of love. I remember *Colossians 4:5: Be wise in the way you act toward outsiders; make the most of every opportunity.* Guide me in making room in my schedule and heart for interactions with 'outsiders'. I hear *John 14:2: My Father's house has many rooms; if that were not so, would I have told you that I am going there to prepare a place for you?* Jesus, thank you for making room for me in your heart. Let me do likewise, intentionally blessing those who lay down a mat beside me to practice and those beside in life. Amen.

౿

Day 344
VARYING LEVELS

There are people with all sorts of various skills, talents and abilities in yoga classes. Some are more flexible, others have a better sense of balance and others have great endurance. This is a beautiful thing—each body is wonderfully unique! Reflect on *1 Corinthians 12:27: Now you are the body of Christ, and each one of you is a part of it.* How can you feel truly connected to those around you on the mat and in your life? Do you have a spirit of appreciation for their gifts, even the ones that differ from your gifts? Commune with the Lord about your talents and the talents of those around you.

SCRIPTURE:

And God has placed in the church first of all apostles, second prophets, third teachers, then miracles, then gifts of healing, of helping, of guidance, and of different kinds of tongues. Are all apostles? Are all prophets? Are all teachers? Do all work miracles? Do all have gifts of healing? Do all speak in tongues? Do all interpret? (1 Corinthians 12:28-30)

PRAYER:

Lord, I thank you for the gifts and talents you have given me, as well as, the ones you've given to those around me. Help me grow in a sense of unity—recognizing and appreciating the diversity of blessings you so graciously give. Let me feel a spirit of answerability to your calling to use my skills and abilities. I remember the rebuilding of the city walls in *Nehemiah 3:28: Each in front of his own house.* They each contributed and did their part. Guide me in doing mine. Amen.

෨ঌ

Day 345
EMBRACING ALL AGES

One of the blessings of yoga is that you can do it at any age. Infants do some postures without even knowing they are doing yoga, and some moves are accessible for the elderly. This is part of the beauty of yoga. What changes have you noticed in your body as you age? How have you been able to embrace these changes? How you can grow, strengthen and contribute at this stage of your life? Share your responses with Jesus.

SCRIPTURE:

Very truly I tell you, when you were younger you dressed yourself and went where you wanted; but when you are old you will stretch out your hands, and someone else will dress you and lead you where you do not want to go. (John 21:18)

PRAYER:

Lord, as I stretch for you, refine my body as you see fit. No matter my physical age, I am still your child. Father, I remember *1 Timothy 4:12: Don't let anyone look down on you because you are young, but set an example for the believers in speech, in conduct, in love, in faith and in purity.* Whether I am younger or older, new to yoga or experienced—I know you have a plan for me and heed *Genesis 18:10-12: The LORD said, "I will surely return to you about this time next year, and Sarah your wife will have a son." Now Sarah was listening at the entrance to the tent, which was behind him. Abraham and Sarah were already very old, and Sarah was past the age of childbearing. So Sarah laughed to herself as she thought, "After I am worn out and my lord is old, will I now have this pleasure?"* With reverence and trust, I take your plan for me seriously. Focused on setting an example in speech, conduct, love, faith and purity on and off the mat, I say Amen.

⤳

Day 346
FELLOWSHIP — PART 1

People often form a sense of community when they gather to practice yoga. Have you felt this sense of community with those who practice beside you? Reflect on how you experience a spirit of connectedness in each area and activity of your life. How does the Lord bless, strengthen, and at times, cleanse your relationships with others? Commune with Jesus about your sense of connectedness.

SCRIPTURE:
Christ loved the church and gave himself up for her to make her holy, cleansing her by the washing with water through the word, and to present her to himself as a radiant church, without stain or wrinkle or any other blemish, but holy and blameless. (Ephesians 5:25-27)

PRAYER:
Lord, thank you for the blessing of fellowship. Thank you for making me to be a church, a temple of Spirit, and light to those who enter the doors of my life. I muse *Ecclesiastes 4:12: Though one may be overpowered, two can defend themselves. A cord of three strands is not quickly broken.* Lord, may your Spirit be the third strand of all my relationships. Committed to be a radiant dwelling for you, I say Amen.

⤳

Day 347
FELLOWSHIP — PART 2

A yoga kula is a group that comes together with a common set of beliefs and a desire to grow, develop and learn. It is a community; you are there to inspire, support and talk with others who practice alongside you. Who have you gotten to know as a result of your practice and how have you accepted and formed a sense unity with them? Also reflect on how do you do this in life. Commune with Jesus.

SCRIPTURE:

May the God who gives endurance and encouragement give you the same attitude of mind toward each other that Christ Jesus had, so that with one mind and one voice you may glorify the God and Father of our Lord Jesus Christ. Accept one another, then, just as Christ accepted you, in order to bring praise to God. (Romans 15:5-7)

PRAYER:

Lord, thank you for accepting me and uniting me with others in love and light. Please forgive me for the ways I've been unaccepting. Help me foster a spirit of receptiveness here on the mat. I hear *Romans 12:3-5: For by the grace given me I say to every one of you: Do not think of yourself more highly than you ought, but rather think of yourself with sober judgment, in accordance with the faith God has distributed to each of you. For just as each of us has one body with many members, and these members do not all have the same function, so in Christ we, though many, form one body, and each member belongs to all the others.* Lord, may a sense of oneness in you be formed in this space and in my life. Amen.

༺༻

Day 348
FELLOWSHIP — PART 3

Most yoga studios give a reward when you refer a friend, such as five dollars off your next class. The reward might even be greater than what a studio can offer through your time together. Perhaps your friend joins you and connects with Jesus in a new and profound way! Who have you invited to yoga and with whom have you recently exchanged faith stories? How do you invite others to experience the things you find significant in life? Note how you were introduced to yoga as well as faith in Jesus. What invitations are present now? Pause and reflect.

SCRIPTURE:

And if I go and prepare a place for you, I will come back and take you to be with me that you also may be where I am. (John 14:3)

PRAYER:

Lord, thank you for preparing a place for me and welcoming me in love, light and grace. Help me to do likewise on the mat. May my faith bless the hearts of others. Desiring to move reverentially along your holy path, I say Amen.

∽

Day 349
PRACTICING ALONE

Yoga is often practiced solo. A wondrous spiritual connection can happen when you practice yoga alone. Especially when you're feeling depleted and/or lonely, invite the Lord into that solitary space. Hagar felt hopeless, neglected, abused and discarded, and it was in that place of emptiness and abandonment that God met her. When have you felt lonely or abandoned? Have you felt the Lord meet you in that space? Hagar is the only female in the Bible to give God a name. Can you relate to the Lord as the 'God who sees me'?

SCRIPTURE:

She gave this name to the LORD who spoke to her:"You are the God who sees me," for she said,"I have now seen the One who sees me." (Genesis 16:13)

PRAYER:

Lord, thank you for being the God who sees me. I remember *Luke 5:16: But Jesus often withdrew to lonely places and prayed*, and *Luke 22:41: He withdrew about a stone's throw beyond them, knelt down and prayed.* Father, help me to be like Jesus—retreating often to quietly commune with you. I take heart in *John 14:18: I will not leave you as orphans; I will come to you.* Jesus, I feel you come to me when I need you most. I feel you call, love, keep and anoint me. I know my practice is never alone, for your Spirit is with me. Father, I am drawn to this mat to abide in you. Please wrap me in your unfailing love. Amen.

◌⌇⌇

Day 350
YOGA RETREATS

Yoga retreats provide the opportunity to get away from your day-to-day routine and silently commune in spirit and truth. How has the Lord brought you to a barren place to draw you closer to Him? Where have you gone to spend time alone with the Lord? How does the Lord speak tenderly to you when you retreat? Take a mini retreat by spending the next few moments communing with Jesus.

SCRIPTURE:

Therefore I am now going to allure her; I will lead her into the wilderness and speak tenderly to her. (Hosea 2:14)

PRAYER:

Father, I retreat from my daily activities and tasks to simply attune to your voice. Drawing to you, I hear *Luke 4:42: Jesus went out to a solitary place*, and *Mark 6:32: So they went away by themselves in a boat to a solitary place.* The mat is my solitary place to be fully present to you and refreshed in Spirit. Thank you for this retreat and for each retreat you so graciously give to me big and small alike. Amen.

◌⌇⌇

Day 351
QUIET SPACE — PART 1

Many studios have a no talking rule in the yoga space before class begins. This is put in place so that you can focus on preparing your body, mind and spirit for the practice without any external distractions. Observe your yoga space and note any external sounds that are present, as well as, any internal sounds (a.k.a. a dialogue you are having with yourself). Aim to shift your focus away from anything distracting and read *Isaiah 55:8-9: "For my thoughts are not your thoughts, neither are your ways my ways," declares the LORD. "As the heavens are higher than the earth, so are my ways higher than your ways and my thoughts than your thoughts."* Reflect on how do you prepare your body, mind and heart for a practice, as well as, how you do so for family time or an important meeting. Commune with Jesus.

SCRIPTURE:
Be still, and know that I am God. (Psalm 46:10)

PRAYER:
Father, prepare my body, mind and heart for this time together. I hear *Psalm 103:11: For as high as the heavens are above the earth, so great is his love for those who fear him.* What a glorious truth. In reverence, I muse *Psalm 110:1: The Lord says to my lord: Sit at my right hand until I make your enemies a footstool for your feet.* Resting in you, Lord, I say Amen.

༄

Day 352
QUIET SPACE — PART 2

There is no need to say any words while practicing yoga. The only thing needed to be heard is your breath. Instructors are often taught to use the fewest possible words to safely cue the asanas. Quietness helps you be fully present in the space. Cues may be given to return your focus to your intention and/or breath. Think about how you quiet your mind of distracting thoughts. How you sit a quiet place, literally and spiritually, and attune to the Spirit? Meditate on *Ecclesiastes 5:2: Do not be quick with your mouth, do not be hasty in your heart to utter anything before God. God is in heaven and you are on earth, so let your words be few.*

SCRIPTURE:
Come with me by yourselves to a quiet place. (Mark 6:31)

PRAYER:

Lord, I come to this quiet place to turn my attention to you—not to speak but to listen. Let my to-do list, emotions and events of the day cease to consume my thoughts. Permeate my mind, heart and entire being with your holy light. Visualizing *Acts 12:17: Peter motioned with his hand for them to be quiet,* I listen when the instructor cues quietness. Let these moments remind me to be fully present to your Spirit. Forgive me for the words I have uttered in haste, without first reflecting on your holiness. I remember *Proverbs 4:20-23: My son, pay attention to what I say; turn your ear to my words. Do not let them out of your sight, keep them within your heart; for they are life to those who find them and health to one's whole body. Above all else, guard your heart, for everything you do flows from it.* Lord, guard my heart in your Word here on the mat. I acknowledge *Deuteronomy 32:47: They are not just idle words for you—they are your life.* Your Word is Life. Let it bring healing to my body, and let my words be few. As St. Francis of Assisi put it, when we pray to God we must be seeking nothing—nothing. So with nothing to say or seek, I listen for your voice. Please speak tenderly to me, Father. Amen.

෨෧

Day 353
MUSIC — PART 1

Many yoga classes use music. How aware are you of the music when you practice? How does it enrich your experience and draw you into a spirit of praise? What songs touch your heart? What songs teach you about love and grace? Spend a minute reciting the lyrics of a favorite song in your mind and heart and invite the Spirit to speak to you through it. As the vibration of the music gently ends, be intimate with the silence that emerges.

SCRIPTURE:

Let the message of Christ dwell among you richly as you teach and admonish one another with all wisdom through psalms, hymns, and songs from the Spirit, singing to God with gratitude in your hearts. (Colossians 3:16)

PRAYER:

Father, let the spiritual songs played here in this space bring praise and honor to you. I desire to feel the lyrics and rhythms in my heart and to learn from them as I move on the mat. I remember *Acts 24:25-26: About midnight Paul and Silas were praying and singing hymns to God, and the other prisoners were listening to them. Suddenly there was such a violent earthquake that the foundations of the prison were shaken. At once all the prison doors flew open, and everyone's chains came loose.* Lord, there is holy power in songs that honor you—power to break shackles, bring justice and shower mercy on those who love you. Empower and teach me through songs here on the mat and in life. Amen.

෨෮

Day 354
MUSIC — PART 2

In yoga there are times when the teacher may sing a few stanzas of a prayer or poem or invite all present in the space to sing. Think about how you may have lifted up a prayer, blessing or song from the mat. On what occasions does the Lord put a song in your mouth? Meditate on *Psalm 40:3 He put a new song in my mouth, a hymn of praise to our God.*

SCRIPTURE:

The Lord your God is with you. He is mighty to save. He will take great delight, he will quiet you with his love, he will rejoice over you with singing. (Zephaniah 3:17)

PRAYER:

Father, your majestic nature is like an all-powerful song that tenders and rejuvenates my spirit. Thank you for placing a new song on my lips when I need it and for giving me a voice to express adoration to you. I hear *Psalm 147:1: Praise the Lord. How good it is to sings praise to our God, how pleasant and fitting to praise him.* As I move my body and lips on the mat, may I do so in a pleasing way that unites my spirit with Your Spirit. Let my soul sing Hallelujah and Amen.

෨෮

Day 355
GREETINGS

A warm, sincere greeting is generally thought to be an important element of a practice experience. How are you greeted when you attend a class? Conversely, how do you greet others at yoga, as well as, in your work environment, at home and while running errands? Commune with Jesus.

SCRIPTURE:

The angel went to her and said, "Greetings, you who are highly favored! The Lord is with you." (Luke 1:28)

PRAYER:

Lord, please teach me to greet others with the same love, care and grace with which your Spirit greets me. Father, forgive me for the times I have forgotten to share a warm greeting. I remember how Paul's letters were filled with such heart-felt greetings. *Romans 16:16: Greet one another with a holy kiss. All the churches of Christ send greetings,* and *1 Corinthians 16:20: All the brothers and sisters here send you greetings. Greet one another with a holy kiss.* Additionally, my heart is touched by the very personal greeting expressed in *Colossians 4:12: Epaphras, who is one of you and a servant of Christ Jesus, sends greetings. He is always wrestling in prayer for you, that you may stand firm in all the will of God, mature and fully assured.* Let me extend these sorts of wholehearted greetings as I prayerfully move on and off the mat. Amen.

ᘒ

Day 356
INTRODUCTIONS

Yoga is filled with introductions—from new poses to new people. In some yoga classes, the instructor will have you turn and introduce yourself to your neighbor before the class begins. Reflect on the introductions that have touched you in the yoga space, as well as, any that seem to standout on your faith journey. In life, what introductions have been significant? Commune with Jesus.

SCRIPTURE:

...(for the law made nothing perfect), and a better hope is introduced, by which we draw near to God. (Hebrews 7:19)

PRAYER:

Lord, I treasure this time with you and am excited about what you may introduce to me here—holy words, new poses and/or new people. I remember Abigail, a God-fearing woman, who, when she heard what her husband had done, acted quickly and prepared for an introduction to David. Abigail got gifts ready and went off to meet him, and as written in *1 Samuel 25:23: When Abigail saw David, she quickly got off her donkey and bowed down before David with her face to the ground.* That powerful introduction saved her life! I also remember Abraham's servant meeting Rebekah, and how she lovingly responded to the stranger in *Genesis 24:18: "Drink, my lord," she said, and quickly lowered the jar to her hands and gave him a drink.* Lord, she fed his camels, too, and got a wonderful marriage proposal out of the introduction. Father, like Abigail and Rebekah, may I be attentive and caring in introductions. Thank you for each encounter and the blessings it brings. Amen.

∽

Day 357
NAMES

There are many pose names in yoga. It can be challenging to remember and embody the precise alignment and nuances of them. Likewise, people's names can seem challenging to remember, as well as, particular details learned about them. How is your memory with names, and with what sort of seriousness do you treat them? Reflect on your name, its meaning and how it feels to hear it. Now close your eyes and picture the Lord calling you by name.

SCRIPTURE:

Jesus looked at him and said, "You are Simon son of John. You will be called Cephas" (which, when translated, is Peter). (John 1:42)

PRAYER:

Lord, thank you for calling me by name. I remember *Genesis 17:5, 15: No longer will you be called Abram; your name will be Abraham, for I have made you a father of many nations. God also said to Abraham, "As for Sarai your wife, you are no longer to call her Sarai; her name will be Sarah* and *Genesis 32:28: Then the man said, "Your name will no longer be Jacob, but Israel, because you have struggled with God and with humans and have overcome."* Father, I also remember *Genesis 35:10: God said to him, "Your name is Jacob, but you will no longer be called Jacob; your name will be Israel." So he named him Israel.* What a beautiful thing—you empower and bless us through names. Help me to do likewise. Amen.

⚬〜⚬

Day 358
DECLARING PRAISE — PART 1

Recognizing and acknowledging your teacher and those around you can be a wondrous way to demonstrate the Lord's love. How do you see your practice as a spiritual act? Likewise, how do you view other routine activities as spiritual acts? Can you find intimacy with the Lord while cleaning dishes, writing bills, taking out the trash, and visiting neighbors? Commune with Jesus about what may be praiseworthy in the little moments that occur on the mat and in your life.

SCRIPTURE:

Stand up and praise the LORD your God, who is from everlasting to everlasting. Blessed be your glorious name, and may it be exalted above all blessing and praise. (Nehemiah 5:9)

PRAYER:

Father, let everything I do be an act of praise to you and a blessing to others. Help me to find and acknowledge all that is praiseworthy and good. I recite *Exodus 15:2: The LORD is my strength and my defense; he has become my salvation. He is my God, and I will praise him, my father's God, and I will exalt him.* Yes, Lord, I desire to exalt you in all my actions, words and ways. Forgive me the times I have neglected to do so. I declare *Deuteronomy 32:3: I will proclaim the name of the LORD. Oh, praise the greatness of our God!* Let this practice ignite a relentless passion to see the praiseworthy acts happening around me. Amen.

༄

Day 359
DECLARING PRAISE — PART 2

Yoga teachers may recognize and draw attention to a student's form—saying something like, "beautiful form, Sarah," or "great warrior 1, Tom." It feels good to be noticed and appreciated. Beyond acknowledging good form, teachers often appreciate students' efforts by saying things such as "good adjustment," "way to keep with it," "I can tell you have been working on your practice," and so on. There is something to be learned through each one of these experiences and the absence of such experiences. Interestingly, in Leah's marriage to Jacob, as described in Genesis, she felt unloved by Jacob, and after giving birth to her first three sons, her focus was on obtaining his love. After the birth of her fourth son she said, "Praise the Lord." Like Leah, in what ways do you find yourself striving for the approval of others? How do you handle a lack of acknowledgment and conversely, how do you keep praise from becoming a source of pride? How do shift your focus from the approval of others to God's approval? Commune with Jesus about recognition.

SCRIPTURE:
She conceived again, and when she gave birth to a son she said, "This time I will praise the LORD." So she named him Judah. (Genesis 29:35)

PRAYER:
Lord, I come to praise you. Please forgive me for the ways I find myself seeking the approval of others, for yours is all that matters. Refresh my perspective here on the mat. I remember *John 6:27: Do not work for food that spoils, but for food that endures to eternal life.* Working to bear fruit that

will last, I join Paul in communing *Galatians 1:10: Am I now trying to win the approval of human beings, or of God? Or am I trying to please people? If I were still trying to please people, I would not be a servant of Christ.* Whether or not I receive recognition for my works on the mat or in life, may I recognize and acknowledge the efforts of others. Father, who notes all my works, I join Leah, declaring, "Praise the Lord!" Amen.

ᢙ

Day 360
DECLARING PRAISE — PART 3

In the yoga space, as in life, encouraging words often give you a lift when you really need it. Identify a few people who encourage you and in what ways they do so. Also note, who you encourage and how you do it. Read *Romans 1:12: That is, that you and I may be mutually encouraged by each other's faith.* What does this look like in your life? Commune with Jesus.

SCRIPTURE:
When he arrived and saw what the grace of God had done, he was glad and encouraged them all to remain true to the Lord with all their hearts. (Acts 11:23)

PRAYER:
Lord, thank you for being a constant source of encouragement for me and for surrounding me with others who refresh my spirit in your Word. Please help me to do likewise. I recognize *Romans 15:4: For everything that was written in the past was written to teach us, so that through the endurance taught in the Scriptures and the encouragement they provide we might have hope.* Yes, your scriptures bring hope. I hear the words Paul shared with the church of Corinth in *2 Corinthians 7:4: I have spoken to you with great frankness; I take great pride in you. I am greatly encouraged; in all our troubles my joy knows no bounds.* With honesty and conviction, may I express these words of Paul to those around me. Encouraged brotherly and sisterly love, I say Amen.

ᢙ

Day 361
NEWS

Sometimes news is delivered in a class. Announcements can range from details about an upcoming event to a classmate's birthday. What news or announcement has caused you to pause, reflect and/or consider something new recently? Read *Psalm 112:7: They will have no fear of bad news; their hearts are steadfast, trusting in the LORD*. Commune with Jesus about this verse and any current news in your life.

SCRIPTURE:

When the news reached Pharaoh's palace that Joseph's brothers had come, Pharaoh and all his officials were pleased. (Genesis 45:16)

PRAYER:

Lord, thank you for being present with me through all the news I encounter on the mat and in life. Through good report and bad report, you carry me. I here to focus on and rejoice in the good news of your unfailing love. In gratitude for all the good news that has come my way, I proclaim *Romans 10:15 How beautiful are the feet of them who bring good news!* Amen.

❧

Day 362
DEEP CONVERSATIONS

Sometimes before or after a class there is an opportunity to have a deep conversation with another person. Likewise, your practice provides a wonderful opportunity for you to intimately commune with the Lord. What types of conversations have arisen for you in the yoga space? Who do you feel deeply connected to in life and what conversations have seemed to profoundly touch you? Share your responses with Jesus.

SCRIPTURE:

Six days later, three of them saw that glory. Jesus took Peter and the brothers, James and John, and led them up a high mountain. His appearance changed from the inside out, right before their eyes. Sunlight poured from his face. His clothes were filled with light. Then they realized that Moses and Elijah were also there in deep conversation with him. (Matthew 17:1-3)

PRAYER:

Lord, I come to commune with you. As I deepen into postures here on the mat, teach me how to deepen my relationships with the Spirit-filled people you have placed in my life. I remember Joseph being united with his brothers in *Genesis 45:15: And he kissed all his brothers and wept over them. Afterward his brothers talked with him.* Like Joseph, may I intimately commune with those you desire for me to be in relationship with, even if we have had a difficult past, or the current circumstances do not seem ideal. Guide me in openhearted and meaningful conversations here in the mat and in my life. Amen.

༄

Day 363
RECITING

There may be recitations of sacred words in yoga classes. Interestingly, the English word meditate comes from the Latin word that means to rehearse. Think about what scriptural words give you peace and encouragement as you rehearse them, and what verses or prayers you have memorized. Share the holy words that intimately touch you with Jesus.

SCRIPTURE:

Because He turned His ear to me, I will call on Him as long as I live. (Psalm 116:2)

PRAYER:

Lord, I am here to center my body, mind and spirit on you. Let the verses I hold deepest in my heart melodiously pulse through my entire being as I move on the mat. I recite *Psalm 45:1: My heart is stirred by a noble theme as I recite my verses for the king; my tongue is the pen of a skillful writer.* Breathing and experiencing the blessing of your presence, I say Amen.

༄

Day 364
INVOCATIONS AND INTENTIONS

An invocation is often done in a yoga class. It may be communed by saying something like *Lokah Samastah Sukhino Bhavantu.* This saying can be translated as *may all beings everywhere be happy and free.* Invocations aim to connect those in the room with a higher purpose. Essentially they offer a way to help you focus on what is true, noble, right, pure, lovely, and admirable. Take a moment to create an invocation for your practice.

SCRIPTURE:

Finally, brothers and sisters, whatever is true, whatever is noble, whatever is right, whatever is pure, whatever is lovely, whatever is admirable—if anything is excellent or praiseworthy—think about such things. (Philippians 4:8)

PRAYER:

Righteous Father, I come to meditate on the things that are true, noble, right, pure, lovely, admirable, excellent and praiseworthy. Focus me on the wonderful things you have so lavishly given to me. With upmost gratitude for your presence, love and light, I say Amen.

৩০

Day 365
THE MANTRA OM

Om is a common word associated with yoga. It is thought of as a beginning and uniting sound representing 'ultimate reality'. It is often drawn out into four parts A-U-M, and the 'vibrational silence beyond'. Interestingly, shal*om* is a Hebrew word, which is generally thought to mean peace. For example, Prince of Peace in Isaiah 9:6 is Sar Shalom in Hebrew. However, the meaning of shalom extends beyond peace. It signifies completeness, wholeness, health, fullness, harmony, welfare, safety, soundness, prosperity and perfectness. What sounds resonate the Lord's presence to you? What words do you speak over others as blessings? Commune with Jesus about words that may carry sacred energy.

SCRIPTURE:

Then said Jesus to them again, Peace be unto you: as my Father hath sent me, even so send I you. (John 20:21KJV) *Note, the Hebrew translation of the word Peace in this verse is Shalom.

PRAYER:

Lord, I hear *1 Samuel 25:6 (KJV): Thus shall ye say to him that liveth in prosperity, Peace be both to you, and peace be to thine house, and peace be unto all that thou hast.* In spirit and truth, may I commune this blessing. Help me to understand the sacredness of your words. 'Shalom' is my mantra for this practice, Father. Please let its vibrational essence radiate from me. With wholehearted love, I resonate Amen.